THE WORLDS OF GERRY AND SYLVIA ANDERSON

THE WORLDS OF GERRY AND SYLVIA ANDERSON

THE STORY BEHIND INTERNATIONAL RESCUE

IAN FRYER

FONTHILL

Fonthill Media Language Policy

Fonthill Media publishes in the international English language market. One language edition is published worldwide. As there are minor differences in spelling and presentation, especially with regard to American English and British English, a policy is necessary to define which form of English to use. The Fonthill Policy is to use the form of English native to the author. Ian Fryer was born in Blackpool and educated in Leeds; therefore British English has been adopted in this publication.

Fonthill Media Limited
Fonthill Media LLC
www.fonthillmedia.com
office@fonthillmedia.com

First published in the United Kingdom and the United States of America 2016

British Library Cataloguing in Publication Data:
A catalogue record for this book is available from the British Library

Typeset in 10.5pt on 13pt Sabon
Printed and bound by CPI Group (UK) Ltd, Croydon, CR0 4YY

Foreword

Where there's a will, there's a way—a saying that's hung around for millennia—but seldom more graphically shown than in the life and creative world of Gerry Anderson, as tracked and beautifully expressed by Ian Fryer in this book. It was certainly a humble beginning that Gerry emerged from with very little offer of help. They were tough times for Gerry and his older brother Lionel, the only one he could really talk to, but they forged in Gerry a will and iron-clad determination that wherever fate would lead him, he would handle it with all he had and do his very best to make it a success.

Then, with the start of commercial television maybe his luck was on the turn. He found a job as a sound editor, which was something he'd always had a keen interest in and which would stay with him for the remainder of his career. Sounds and voices interested him, and he had the perception to hear and even judge what possibly lay behind them, rather than what was being conveyed by speech.

I drew a lucky card on this one—Gerry happened to tune in on a BBC/TV series titled *Compact*, which was produced in the hopes of giving *Coronation Street* a run for its money—then, as now, it was never out of first place in the ratings. I was brought in as a rather aggressive American editor, Russell Corrigan, to add a little fizz to the show and to also help tumble 'The Street' from the top of the 'most viewed' listings. It did work for a few months, but then, inevitably, the ratings returned to their usual formation and *Coronation Street* was ruling the roost once again and *Compact* bowed out. But Gerry had spotted enough to reckon that the voice of Corrigan would fit the character of Scott Tracy the way he wanted it. I was sorry that *Compact* did not work out, but just what was I stepping into now? I decided that Gerry's instincts added up to a lot more than my personal speculations. That's the effect the man had on you, and somehow I knew I'd never regret the move.

In the meantime, Gerry would receive a boost from an unexpected source, not quite yet, but it would come and when it did it would be dramatic. Lew Grade, a silent mentor, but a firm believer in Gerry, had somehow arranged a showing of *Thunderbirds* on American television; the public loved it, and demanded the series be shown in its entirety—it was. *Thunderbirds* was flying high.

The deeper Ian Fryer dug into the outer fabric of the Anderson phenomena the more reasons he found for its unstoppable rise to success. All departments in an Anderson production were run by seasoned professionals, masters of their trade who really knew what they were doing and loved doing it. They in turn would pass on their 'know-how' to the fledgling newcomers on the way up. Nobody got in the way of anyone else—mutual respect was part of each work place. It was an immaculate process that produced only the best.

As a final note, we need 'Chroniclers'—people should know how certain events come to pass. Because of the age we live in, and with technology playing such a large part in it, we are able to see and marvel at legions of the 'finished product'—we're surrounded by them. Most of us have seen and been entertained by the showings of Gerry Anderson's many productions (they have acquired a worldwide audience—they're very accessible), but how did they get there? That could be interesting.

Ian Fryer's extremely knowledgeable and fascinating book will take you all the way from the opening page and tell you all you want to know. I'm glad you stepped in out of the rain Ian, to give us this never-before-published salute to one of the major figures in British screen entertainment.

Shane Rimmer
Potters Bar
June 2015

Acknowledgements

Thanks must go to all manner of people for all manner of reasons related to the writing and research of this book. Firstly to Jay Slater, my publisher, for trusting me with the project in the first place. Mike Jones was a great help with picture research, and is my companion in the ongoing adventure that is *FAB Magazine*. Everyone at Fanderson, Gerry Anderson's Official Appreciation Society, has been an inspiration to me over the years, with their constant enthusiasm and the many, many hours put in out of the sheer love of a group of television series made some fifty years ago. Take a bow Nick Williams, John Wilkinson, Jay Mullins, Melanie McHale, Stuart Drummond, Derek Eaton, Stephen Brown, Lynn Simpson, and finally Jacqueline Dear, who is also my partner and so has had to put up with me being constantly busy, exhausted, and occasionally grouchy for months on end—sorry.

Thanks also to Protyre, the tyre fitting company that now uses Les Bowie's old factory unit on Bath Road, Slough, in which AP Films shot *Four Feather Falls, Supercar,* and *Fireball XL5*. If you're in the area, buy some tyres from them.

Also thanks must go to Chris Bentley and Andrew Pixley, the best two writers in the business, from whom I've tried to learn by example; to Shane Rimmer, no mean writer himself, and his wife Sheila, who have been endlessly helpful and encouraging; and to Andrew Staton, who gets me to do things when I can't really be bothered, a vital skill for a writer working to a deadline. Finally to my mum, Lona Fryer, who I hope I've made just a little bit proud.

Contents

Foreword		5
Acknowledgements		7
A Note on Sources		11
List of Abbreviations		13
Introduction		17
1	Early Days	21
2	The Gold Rush	25
3	*The Adventures of Twizzle*	28
4	Les Bowie	32
5	*Torchy the Battery Boy*	34
6	*Four Feather Falls*	38
7	*Space Patrol*	45
8	*Supercar*	50
9	Lew Grade	65
10	*Fireball XL5*	68
11	Derek Meddings	78
12	*Stingray*	81
13	*Thunderbirds*	91
14	*Thunderbirds* at the Movies	109

15   Other Worlds: British '60s SF Beyond the Andersons   115

16   *Captain Scarlet and the Mysterons*   117

17   *Joe 90*   129

18   *Doppelgänger*   138

19   *The Secret Service*   143

20   *UFO*   153

21   The Collapse of the UK Film Industry   168

22   *The Protectors*   172

23   *The Investigator*   184

24   *Space: 1999*   190

25   *Space: 1999* Year Two   205

26   Rebirth: Gerry Anderson Post-*Space: 1999*   215

Bibliography   223

A Note on Sources

When writing a book on the subject of the series created by Gerry and Sylvia Anderson, one should not attempt doing so without the help of certain books—fortunately, I have had many of them at my elbow (almost constantly) for several months.

On the early lives of Gerry and Sylvia Anderson there are two main sources—the biographies of the two people concerned. The official biography of Gerry Anderson, *What Made Thunderbirds Go* by Simon Archer and Marcus Hearn, is a model of how such a book should be written and was a great help—you really need to own a copy. Also particularly valuable is Sylvia Anderson's *My Fab Years!*, which tells the story of the AP Films/Century 21 productions from the often neglected point of view of Sylvia Anderson.

Nicholas Parsons' book *My Life in Comedy: With Just Touch of Hesitation, Repetition and Deviation* is a fascinating piece of work covering his entire career, including his work with AP Films. The remarkable Mr Parsons also granted me an interview for FAB a couple of years ago, and time has certainly not dimmed his capacious memory. Derek Meddings' career is covered by two excellent books: *21st Century Visions*, by Derek Meddings and Sam Mitchell, and *Special Effects Superman: the Art and Effects of Derek Meddings*, the latter being especially good on his post-Anderson work. Meddings' co-designer Mike Trim's work is covered in fascinating detail in *The Future was Fab: The Art of Mike Trim* by Anthony Taylor with Mike Trim. *The Hollywood Professionals Vol. 2* contains an excellent chapter on the career of Lewis Milestone, written by Kingsley Canham.

Several books by Chris Bentley have been incredibly useful in the research and writing of this book. *The Complete Gerry Anderson: The Authorised Episode Guide* might just be the single most useful book ever written, and my copy is just about falling to pieces. Also extremely useful were Chris's *The Complete Book of Thunderbirds*, *The Complete Book of Captain Scarlet and the Mysterons*, and *The Complete Book of Gerry Anderson's UFO*.

The Birth of the Movies by D. J. Wenden gave me some valuable material on the early days of British filmmaking and the career of George Pearson. Several editions of *Film Review*, F. Maurice Speed's annually published guide to the film scene in Britain, were extremely helpful, providing, in particular, an interesting insight into the production of filmed television in the UK before the formation of ITV (thanks also to the charity shops that still keep them). Valuable material on the early days of ITV was found in Brian Henry's *British Television Advertising: The First 30 Years*. Much information about the British special effects industry and the career of Les Bowie I have gleaned from the superb website Matte Shot, which you can find at nzpetesmatteshot.blogspot.co.uk/

Also online and of great help was The Complete Gerry Anderson Comic History at www.technodelic.pwp.blueyonder.co.uk and the amazing Space: 1999 Catacombs site at catacombs.space1999.net/

The Great British Picture Show by George Perry was extremely valuable in covering the ups and downs of the British film industry and the Gainsborough studios years. Also invaluable was Alexander Walker's *Hollywood England: The British Film Industry in the Sixties*. Details of the lower budget end of British filmmaking I found in Steve Chibnall and Brian McFarlane's *The British 'B' Film*, a truly amazing piece of writing and research.

Also a great help were back-issues of *FAB*, the magazine of *Fanderson: The Official Gerry Anderson Appreciation Society*, currently edited by myself and Mike Jones. Further information about Fanderson, which has kept the flame of Gerry Anderson alive for well over thirty years, can be found at www.fanderson.org.uk

List of Abbreviations

ABC: Associated British Company, the ITV franchise holder for the English midlands and north from 1956 to 1968. Also American Broadcasting Company, one of the traditional 'Big Three' US television networks since it began broadcasting in 1943.

ABPC: Associated British Picture Corporation, the British film company that owned Elstree Studios, operating from 1927 until 1969, when it was taken over by EMI. ABPC also owned the ITV franchise holder ABC.

AP Films: Also known as APF, this stood for Anderson Provis Films after the original two main figures in the company—Gerry Anderson and Arthur Provis.

AP: See AP Films.

A-R: Associated-Rediffusion, the ITV franchise-holder for London and the Home Counties between 1954 (first broadcasting from September 1955) and July 1968. For its last four years, it appeared under the name Rediffusion London.

ATV: Associated Television, the ITV franchise holder for the English midlands on weekdays and London on the weekend from 1955 to 1968. From 1968 to the end of 1981, ATV broadcast to the midlands seven days a week. Lew Grade was ATV's managing director for most of the company's life.

BBFC: British Board of Film Censors, responsible for classifying for age and censoring films for British cinema release. Known as British Board of Film Classification since 1985.

CBC: Canadian Broadcasting Company, the publically owned national broadcaster of Canada.

CBS: Columbia Broadcasting System, one of America's traditional 'Big Three' national television networks. CBS has broadcast since 1941.

CGI: Computer Generated Imagery, the process by which many on-screen effects for motion pictures are created, including the 2004 Thunderbirds movie and the 2015 Thunderbirds Are Go television series.

D&AD: Design and Art Direction was formed in 1962. Formerly known as British D&AD, it is an educational charity that exists to promote excellence in design and inform, educate, and inspire those working in the creative industries.

DN Productions: Production company owned by Nicholas Parsons from the 1950s to make advertising and documentary films. The initials were taken from Denise Bryer and Nicholas Parsons, who were at the time married.

EMI: Electric and Musical Industries, the recording company and industrial combine that bought ABPC in 1969, making it the owner of Elstree Studios and the largest force in British filmmaking.

EP: Extended Play, generally referring to a 7-inch vinyl record, with narrower grooves and sound compressions, enabling them to hold up to seven and a half minutes per side instead of the usual four minutes—but still be played by a standard 45 rpm phonograph.

FCC: The Federal Communications Commission, the government organisation that has regulated interstate communications via radio and all forms of television in the United States since 1934.

GHW: GHW productions was set up by J. Arthur Rank in 1937 to finance and produce films with a religious message. When they ceased making films, its Gate Studios were used as a post-production facility by other production companies, including AP Films, which used the studios for dialogue recording on some of its productions. The 'W' is thought to stand for director Norman Walker, the leading figure in the company.

HTV: Harlech Television, commonly known as HTV, holder of the ITV television broadcasting franchise for Wales and the west of England from July 1967 (broadcasting from May 1968) until its licence ended at the end of 2013.

ITC: Incorporated Television Company, the television production and international distribution company formed and run by Lew Grade. ITC bought AP Films in the early 1960s.

ITV:	Independent Television, Britain's first commercial television network, formed as a result of the Television Act 1954. Funded by advertising, ITV represented the first challenge to the BBC's broadcasting monopoly and helped television achieve mass popularity in Britain.
LAMDA:	London Academy of Music and Dramatic Art.
MGM:	Metro-Goldwyn-Mayer, the Hollywood studio that owned MGM-British Borehamwood Studios, then closed it down in late 1969, midway through production on UFO.
NBC:	National Broadcasting Company, one of American television's 'Big Three' networks that has been broadcasting since 1940. NBC bought AP Films' 1962 series Fireball XL5, the first British TV series to be broadcast coast-to-coast on US television.
NFFC:	National Film Finance Corporation—Britain's government-mandated film funding agency, which operated from 1949 until Margaret Thatcher's government wound it up in 1985.
PP Films:	The film company set up by Arthur Provis after he resigned from the board of AP Films. The meaning of the letters 'PP' is unknown.
RADA:	Royal Academy of Dramatic Art.
RAI:	Originally Radio Audizioni Italiane, Italy's national public broadcaster has been known as RAI since 1954.
RPM:	Revolutions Per Minute—the speed at which vinyl records play. In the case of Century 21 mini albums, 33⅓ RPM.
SF:	Science Fiction.

Introduction

Slough, Berkshire, England, July 2015. Despite the fast-approaching summer solstice, the skies have finally begun to deliver the rain they have been promising all day. The steel grey of the skies matches the steel walls of the identical modern buildings as I travel down Edinburgh Avenue on the Slough Trading Estate. Turning off onto Stirling Road, the buildings begin to change in character and eventually we reach a row of single-storey units of a distinctive early to mid-1960s design, far smaller than the newer buildings around the corner. Moss grows on the corrugated metal peaks of the roofs of these older units.

Finding a parking space, I stop the car and get out to be greeted by the distinctive smell of chocolate and syrup from the Mars confectionery factory on nearby Dundee Road. I am outside 696/697 Stirling Road, the home of Sovrin Plastics Limited and a Volkswagen car spares specialist. The building was scheduled to be demolished in a months' time, though it subsequently received a temporary stay of execution.

The reason I am standing in the rain outside a doomed factory unit is that, fifty years earlier, some of the most popular programmes on the world's television screens were produced here at what was then AP Film Studios. One of the smallest film studios in Britain was, appropriately, producing SF adventure series in miniature, which thrilled family audiences the world over. These included *Stingray*, *Captain Scarlet and the Mysterons*, and, of course, the company's biggest success of all, *Thunderbirds*.

Here we all are, well into the twenty-first century that the series predicted. One thing that nobody could have predicted was that *Thunderbirds* would never fade away, returning every few years to be rediscovered by a new audience. Somehow, the series' very '60s take on modernism has become timeless, the selfless altruism of its heroes ever more attractive. *Thunderbirds* has transcended its era and changing fashions to reach the status of a true classic.

Gerry Anderson is the nearest thing British filmmaking has ever had to a Walt Disney figure—someone whose very name suggests a certain type of entertainment completely different to anything else that might be out there. To this day, it is common shorthand to call the series his company made in a magical period from 1959, when they made their first independent production *Four Feather Falls*, to early 1977, when *Space: 1999* completed production, Gerry Anderson series. When AP Films renamed itself, each series was even branded in this way—'A Gerry Anderson Century 21 Production'.

Gerry Anderson never liked to claim that he was the sole artistic voice on his productions, often likening himself to the captain of a ship. The television series and films produced by the AP Films/Century 21 crew were the result of a unique group of talents coming together in unique circumstances. A core group of hard-working technicians and artists fell into making puppet films virtually by accident; this was at first through sheer desperation to keep the company afloat, developing into an absolute determination to make the best puppet films the world had ever seen. In the process, the company changed the British film industry and in many ways ensured its survival in the difficult days of the late '70s and early '80s.

With the phenomenon of Britain as a fashionable place in and of itself long dead, large-scale American productions such as the *Star Wars* films and *Alien* were drawn to the UK, at least in part because of the existence of a nucleus of effects and model technicians unrivalled in the film world. Although he was struggling at this point to mount his own productions, this was Gerry Anderson's legacy to the British film industry that he loved and spent virtually his entire working life in.

This book is not just about the work of Gerry Anderson, but also about Sylvia Anderson, Reg Hill, John Read, and Arthur Provis, the original partners in AP Films. It is also about Barry Gray, who provided the thrilling music for the series, Derek Meddings, Brian Johnson, and the rest of the huge team of model makers and special effects technicians that helped make the series so spectacular. It is about design geniuses such as Bob Bell, Keith Wilson, and Mike Trim, and about Tony Barwick, who wrote an incredible number of superb scripts. It is about so many people—a huge cast and crew of extremely talented people who all came together to produce a unique group of series and films.

The achievement of the Anderson series has for too long been categorised as a purely technical triumph; a beautiful-looking series, with scripts that are in the popular memory either ignored or derided. This is not a helpful or especially interesting way of looking at a series of programmes, which have held generations of viewers transfixed. Let's extend to these millions of people the basic courtesy of assuming that they were reacting to something they found interesting, rather than just mindlessly watching a series of clever launch sequences and well-designed models—people can be funny like that.

The puppet and live-action programmes and films made by the Anderson team say things about the times in which they were made, sometimes purposely and sometimes accidentally, only detectable with the benefit of hindsight. When the company was finally given the opportunity to make live-action productions after years of trying, the impulse was to make adult dramas such as *Doppelgänger* and *UFO*. When handed the largest budget in television history for *Space: 1999*, the series that emerged was often beautiful, poetic, and questioning about humanity's place in the universe.

The Anderson series rarely took the easy route. Having happened upon a winning formula, the impulse was only to see how it could be expanded upon and improved. While *Thunderbirds* represented the high watermark of Supermarionation's popularity, nobody knew it at the time. In the words of screenwriter William Goldman, in his book *Adventures in the Screen Trade*, 'nobody knows anything'. Any of the series that followed *Thunderbirds* could have been an even bigger hit. A search for perfection in miniature eventually came as close to achieving the status of art as anything could within commercial television. It is high time the AP Films and Century 21 productions were treated seriously as drama, and one of the purposes of this book is to fill that gap.

Another thing this book attempts to do is place the Anderson productions within the context of the times in which they were made. When Gerry Anderson gave up the life of a jobbing sound editor to attempt to become a director, this was not some weird, quixotic impulse—there were real opportunities out there to be grasped at the dawn of commercial television in Britain. His career and the history of AP Films, Century 21, Group Three, and the other Anderson production companies did not happen in a bubble. They happened within the context of an increasingly derelict British film industry and the boom and bust of a filmed television sector, led by probably the only person working in British television more export-minded than Gerry Anderson—Sir (later Lord) Lew Grade.

Let's take that journey together from the editing suite at Gainsborough Pictures, via papier mache marionettes held aloft with carpet thread, to triumphs such as *Thunderbirds*, *UFO*, and *Space: 1999*, to a film historian getting wet outside a plastics factory. The future was fantastic.

Ian Fryer
Bradford
June 2015

1

Early Days

Gerry Anderson got his start in the film business in 1945, when he wrote to the Colonial Film Unit as part of his ongoing campaign to gain a foothold in the industry. Working in almost every part of the government propaganda unit, Gerry had the great good fortune to find himself in the orbit of George Pearson, who had been a pioneer of British filmmaking in the days of silent movies. In 1914 he directed *A Study in Scarlet*, the first film to feature Sherlock Holmes on-screen, while in 1929 he directed a British film with British actors in Hollywood.

His career had declined to the extent that he was working on cheap 'quota quickies' in the 1930s—low-budget films designed to fulfil the legal quota of British-produced films required to be shown in UK cinemas under the terms of the Cinematograph Films Act 1927. The CFU was formed in 1939 as a part of the war effort, most of its films being aimed at audiences in British controlled parts of Africa. After the war it was largely concerned with making instructional films for the same areas, as well as short features explaining aspects of life in Britain to potential immigrants needed to fill a severe shortage of workers. As late as the 1940s, the CFU were still producing silent films, as many of the venues in which the films would be screened were in remote rural areas with no sound facilities. The ability to tell a story visually was all-important.

Aged seventy by the time Gerry joined the Colonial Film Unit, Pearson taught Gerry the techniques of film editing, and how to fix in the cutting room the mistakes a director might have made. By extension, this taught Gerry some of the fundamentals of film directing. Pearson remained active and highly thought of within the film industry, working until the age of eighty-one; he was awarded the OBE in 1951.

Gerry's time at the CFU was to be quite brief. During the following year he heard of an opening for a second assistant editor at Gainsborough Films, and grabbed the chance with both hands. Little did he know then, but times were changing at Gainsborough, which was one of the top film producers in England at the time.

The company had been formed in 1924 by producer Michael Balcon and director Graham Cutts. Based at the time at Islington Studios, Gainsborough had given the young Alfred Hitchcock his first chance in the film industry, both as a cameraman and a director. In 1928 the company became part of the large Gaumont-British Picture Corporation, with Balcon in charge of production for the whole combine. At the time, Gaumont made more expensive and prestigious films, while Gainsborough were known for productions smaller in both budget and status.

Balcon left in 1936, having returned from a long working trip to America to find the company in financial crisis, as the British film industry in general reaped the harvest of a period of profligate spending. At the same time, flour manufacturer and movie mogul J. Arthur Rank took a major interest in Gaumont-British. Gainsborough drew strength from the new ownership, and became the dominant producer of films for the home market, with popular and frugally-made fare such as the Will Hay comedies.

Gainsborough's most famous period was between 1942 and 1946, when they inaugurated a hugely successful series of costume melodramas, starting with *The Man in Grey* (1943), which made a star of James Mason. These, and a group of contemporary-set films using the same basic themes, tapped into the huge female market, the men being largely away fighting the war. From 1946, Rank took more direct control of Gainsborough, alienating those who had made the company such a success. At around the same time that Gerry Anderson joined the company, he installed producer Sydney Box to take charge of production.

Despite having produced the massively successful melodrama *The Seventh Veil* in 1945, Box's background and instructs were in documentary realism, and this was the direction in which he took Gainsborough. The box office results were poor and, despite occasional major successes such as *Miranda* (1948), Rank lost patience and closed the studios in 1950.

Gerry worked on films from the back end of Gainsborough's period of mass popularity, helping to edit the company's 1945 smash-hit *The Wicked Lady* for the sensibilities of American audiences. He was more directly involved in *Caravan* (1946) and the Technicolor-shot *Jassy*, the last of the Gainsborough costume films, released in August 1947. In both cases he worked under editor Charles Knott.

By the time *Jassy* was released, Gerry found his career interrupted by two years of compulsory national service, which he spent in the RAF. Although this is generally considered to be a nuisance and delay in his progress (no doubt as it was by Gerry himself), Gerry Anderson maintained a lifelong interest in aviation. This was in part due to his idolising of his older brother Lionel, who was a crew member on de Havilland Mosquito bombers and was killed in action in 1944. Series such as *Supercar* were notable for including realistic-sounding technical dialogue between pilot Mike Mercury and his team. The former RAF Radio Telephone operator always produced series with correct radio procedure, which eventually led to the famous FAB call-sign.

In 1948, Gerry returned to Gainsborough (companies had a legal requirement to keep a position open for their workers on return from national service). As previously noted, the company was in the process of being wound down thanks to disappointing returns from Sydney Box's era in change of production. Now a dubbing editor and working from Gainsborough's new base at Pinewood, where he would return in 1973 with *Space: 1999*, he worked on the popular costume mystery *So Long at the Fair*, which received its first UK screening on 31 May 1950.

Time had run out for Gainsborough though; their Lime Grove Studios had been sold off to the BBC, who would utilise the facilities for many years. With no prospect for regular employment within the Rank filmmaking empire, Gerry found himself, out of necessity, becoming a freelance sound editor. His first work in this capacity was on *The Clouded Yellow*, produced by Betty E. Box, the sister of Sydney Box, his old boss as Gainsborough. A hard and fastidious worker, Gerry soon gained a good reputation and found work on other productions.

Worthy of note in this period is *Devil Girl from Mars*, Gerald Anderson's (as he was billed during his editing career on those films, which actually credited his contribution) first SF project. Released in May 1954, this was a production by the brothers Edward J. and Harry Lee Danziger. It was directed by David MacDonald, who had been director on the Gainsborough production *Snowbound*—the very film Gerry had been working on when he was called up for his national service.

Since then, MacDonald's career had noticeably declined, mainly due to his having directed two much-derided flops for Gainsborough in a row, both released in 1949: *The Bad Lord Byron* and *Christopher Columbus*. Although their films and television series have gained a patina of nostalgia over the years, the Danzigers made popular entertainment as cheaply as possible, and it was an axiom within the business that to be working for the Danzigers was a sign that your career was in trouble.

Nevertheless, there were bills to pay and Gerry needed to work, completing the editing in a speedy six weeks. *Devil Girl from Mars* is actually quite striking visually, despite revealing its theatrical origins by taking place mainly indoors on the set of a hotel bar. Patricia Laffan's mini-skirted patent leather outfit has helped the film maintain a cult following over the years, as has one of the most ridiculous robot props in movie history. Particularly notable are the creative sound effects Gerry employs, a feature that would also be prominent in the early productions of AP Films as low production values would be partially disguised by making the stories sound convincing.

In the case of *Devil Girl from Mars*, titular bad girl Nyah arrives in a spaceship—director of special effects Jack Whitehead actually does good work on the film—which is accompanied by extremely loud sound effects that really help give a sense of its great size and power. The simple, but effective, visual effects of Nyah's ray gun vaporising its targets are also highly effective. The absurd robot, which looks like nothing so much as a man tottering about enveloped in a giant cardboard box, is made more believable by the sonar-like sound effect Gerry adds to the soundtrack during its appearances. While the six weeks Gerry spent working on *Devil Girl from Mars* clearly did nothing to advance his career, it does demonstrate what a fine craftsman he'd become.

The increasing internationalisation of the film business had Gerry working on productions based abroad, such as *Never Take No for an Answer*, shot in Italy in 1952, *South of Algiers* (1953), made on location in Tunisia and Algeria, and *They Who Dare*. This was a large-scale production partially made on the island of Cyprus featuring Britain's brightest new star, Dirk Bogarde, who had also featured in two other films Gerry worked on *So Long at the Fair* (1950) and *Appointment in London* (1953—released in the USA two years later as *Raiders in the Sky*).

They Who Dare, released in the UK in February 1954, saw Gerry becoming friendly with the film's director, Lewis Milestone. An old Hollywood pro, who had been directing since 1925 and won a Best Picture Oscar in 1930 for *All Quiet on the Western Front*, Milestone had a terrifying reputation, but was coming to the end of his career as a 'name' film director. His next big film project, the 1959 Korean War drama *Pork Chop Hill*, was on the insistence of its star, Gregory Peck, who was a big fan of *All Quiet of the Western Front*. His name was attached to two other major films, *Ocean's Eleven* (1960) and *Mutiny on the Bounty* (1962), on which he was basically directing the traffic on films controlled by the on-screen talent, rather than the writers or director.

The main thrust of Milestone's subsequent career was on television, directing episodes of series including *Have Gun, Will Travel* (1957–63) and *The Richard Boone Show* (1963–64) before his retirement in 1964. Gerry Anderson often mentioned Lewis Milestone as influential on his decision to make his own productions. By the mid-1950s, the opportunities for entrepreneurial new British filmmaking talent were in commercial television.

2

The Gold Rush

After completing his final cinema production in 1955, the crime thriller *A Prize of Gold* for American director Mark Robson, Gerry Anderson set about expanding his professional horizons. His resolve to strike out on his own as a director, despite having never directed, and eventually form his own production company, was not as quixotic a decision as it might seem. Although famous old film studios such as Lime Grove and Teddington were closing down, they were quickly reopening for television production. There were real opportunities out there for those intrepid enough to take them.

Television first became a popular national medium in Britain with the coronation of Queen Elizabeth II on 2 June 1953. Ownership of a television set was very far from being universal, but, if not everyone had a television, most people knew someone well enough to view theirs. Thus, whole streets would crowd round a tiny screen to view the BBC's ground-breaking coverage of the big occasion. An estimated 20.4 million people watched at least half an hour of the ceremony on the 2.7 million sets in use at the time.

The BBC had begun its television service, the first in the world, in 1937, which initially only reached London and the south-east of England. The service was suspended immediately on the declaration of war in September 1939, and not resumed until 7 June 1946, after which it slowly expanded to other parts of Britain. The BBC's television service generally failed to connect with the wider public, its broadcasts aimed solidly at upper-middle class audiences and tastes.

The Television Act of 1954 paved the way for the introduction of commercial television (as television with advertising was known in Britain at the time), despite strong parliamentary opposition, which is, to modern eyes, truly from another era. Lord Esher, for example, foretold of a descent into 'a planned and premeditated orgy of vulgarity'. His views were far from uncommon among the political classes. The bill had been introduced to parliament late in the life of the Conservative government, which had won the 1951 election. A new election was due to take place no later than 1956, and the Labour opposition was clear that if they were elected to government they would scrap the whole idea of commercial television.

This introduced enormous pressure to have the bill passed and the government were forced to use their parliamentary guillotine to curtail the second reading stage, extended due to the level of determined opposition to the bill. The final stages of passing the act were rushed through in ten days and the act received its Royal Assent on 30 July 1954.

It was to be over a year before a new broadcast network, Independent Television (or ITV), was ready to go on air. However, a thriving sector making filmed programming for commercial television had developed in Britain, as enterprising filmmakers began to use Britain as a base for making filmed productions for the international television market—this largely meant the US, where television was growing at an astonishing rate and was hungry for material to air. The available supply of old movies was quickly used up and producers flocked to the UK to take advantage of the pool of high-quality crews, technical facilities, and English-speaking acting talent available at a much lower cost than their Hollywood equivalents.

Douglas Fairbanks Jr, son of Hollywood royalty and a great Anglophile (he was awarded an honorary KBE in 1949), was one of the earliest to use British production facilities for this purpose, buying Elstree Studios from British National Films in 1953. He set into production the twenty-five-minute anthology series *Douglas Fairbanks, Jr. Presents*, which was a great success that ran for 155 episodes. It first screened between 1953 and 1957, and was either hosted by or starred Fairbanks himself.

Soon other American-based stars, who were no longer shining so brightly in their cinematic careers, were making their way to the UK to star in television productions such as *The Errol Flynn Theatre* and *Colonel March of Scotland Yard*—both of which debuted in 1956. Many American writers and directors were attracted to Britain by the promise of paid work, at a time when the major studios were contracting in size and the McCarthy blacklist had prevented many with perceived left-wing sympathies from gaining employment.

The already mentioned Danziger Brothers, who originally moved into film production in 1949 after having previously dubbed foreign-language films into English at their sound studio, relocated to England in 1952. Between then and their leaving the film business in 1962, they made over 140 second-feature films and half a dozen television series.

In 1955 Gerry Anderson joined the television gold rush. He applied for a job as a director with Polytechnic Films, who were about to enter production with Pete Collins on a series entitled *You've Never Seen This*. Suddenly, jobbing sound editor Gerald Anderson was pitched head-first into the life of a director, travelling Europe filming novelty variety acts and people with unique abilities. The series only lasted only a few episodes on the fledgling Associated-Rediffusion channel before disappearing.

Although *You've Never Seen This* was soon lost to history, Gerry Anderson now had a track record as a director and a new ally in the form of Arthur Provis, the cameraman who accompanied Gerry on his travels through Europe. The Polytechnic Films team also included Reg Hill and John Read, and with the company facing near-certain bankruptcy, Anderson, Provis, Hill, and Read left to form Pentagon Films. One of many tiny companies aiming to produce adverts and documentaries, Pentagon gained a few advertising commissions, and soon found themselves in need of a part-time secretary.

Sylvia Anderson, at this point known as Sylvia Thamm, had a mixture of showmanship and art in her blood, with a boxing promoter father and a mother who was a trained dressmaker with an artistic personality. Her own artistic traits were developed through piano and singing lessons and an interest in school amateur dramatics. Sylvia was also academically gifted, and studied Economics and Sociology at the London School of Economics.

On graduating she was determined to forge a career in show business, and looked for work in the film business with no success until she answered an advert for a part-time secretary. The Pentagon Films partners were keen and ambitious, but not well organised, and Sylvia Thamm soon became a vital part of the team. Pentagon came and went as their money ran out, despite filming a few adverts.

Anderson and Provis were keen to keep their core of talented artists and technicians together, so formed a new company—AP Films.

3

The Adventures of Twizzle

'Have you heard of a Twizzle toy? You haven't? Well that's because there's only one of them.'

Created and produced by Roberta Leigh
Music by Leslie Clair, arranged and conducted by Barry Gray, with lyrics by
    Roberta Leigh
A Banty Books Production made by AP Films
52 × fifteen-minute episodes
First broadcast Wednesday 13 November 1957 (Associated-Rediffusion)

Twizzle, a boy doll with legs that 'Twizzle' to extend to great length, escapes from the toy shop in order to prevent his being purchased by a naughty girl. Out in the world be meets and has adventures with other toys and animals.

The story of puppet series on post-war British television actually begins on the radio in 1950, with the introduction of a dedicated children's strand, *Listen with Mother*. Broadcast every weekday on the BBC Home Service at 1.45 p.m. for fifteen minutes, the series soon became a national institution, with pre-school children all over Britain settling down for a diet of stories and nursery rhymes. The success of *Listen with Mother*, which at its peak had over a million listeners, had BBC executives planning to adapt the concept for its television service, which at that point had a monopoly of television broadcasting in the UK.

The task was put in the hands of *Listen with Mother*'s producer, Freda Lingstrom, though it only coalesced gradually. In 1950 Lingstrom created *Andy Pandy*, which was performed live until 1952 when the BBC Film Unit made twenty-six fifteen-minute episodes on film that were repeated every year until 1970, when thirteen replacement episodes were made in colour. In December 1952, *Flower Pot Men* debuted, presenting the adventures of Bill and Ben and their flowery friend Weed. By 1953, a third series was introduced, *Rag, Tag and Bobtail*, allowing the by-now three days per week strand to be given the umbrella title *Watch with Mother*. The final puppet series in *Watch with Mother* was *The Woodentops*, which began in 1955 along with *Picture Book*, a series with an onscreen presenter that encouraged children to be creative.

Each of the series was created or co-created by Freda Lingstrom, and their style of production and storytelling betrays her background in radio. Each episode of *Rag Tag, and Bobtail* was shot in a single take using glove puppets on a simple woodland set. The simple visuals are secondary to the narration, which explains absolutely everything that happens on-screen. Similarly, *Andy Pandy* used a narrator and very long takes for the adventures of the puppet boy and his teddy bear and doll friends. *The Woodentops* allows the visuals to carry more of the action, presenting tales of a middle-class, rural nuclear family, complete with patronisingly-named cleaning lady Mrs Scrubbit.

This is the *Watch with Mother* series, which bears the most similarities with the early Anderson puppet shows and is slightly more sophisticated than the others in the group. The puppets themselves are designed to look like wooden figures, which was a clever way of making budgetary restrictions and a lack of realism an integral part of *The Woodentops* format.

Only two years after the *Watch with Mother* line-up was finalised it is hard to imagine that some of its series were not starting to look a little dated, and watching them before screening the only surviving episode of *The Adventures of Twizzle* is very instructive in gauging the kind of impact the series must have had when it debuted in November 1957.

The most immediately apparent differences are in the production of the series. *Watch with Mother*'s '50s line-up was, at heart, television made by radio people. *The Adventures of Twizzle* was television made by filmmakers, and the contrast presented by the sole-surviving story of the series, the pilot episode 'Twizzle and Footso', is startling.

The episode begins with an orchestrated theme tune, as opposed to the simple piano and vocals of the *Watch with Mother* shows, and even some animation of the text in the opening credits. The story opens with a well-designed street set by Reg Hill seen at night (involving a more intricate lighting set up than daytime lighting). The camera performs an interesting dolly and pan movement, which is followed by a dissolve to the inside of the toy-shop in which Twizzle lives. In short, there is more use of the visual grammar of film in the first forty seconds of *The Adventures of Twizzle* than in the entirety of the '50s line-up of *Watch with Mother*.

The puppets themselves, although somewhat crude-looking compared to what would come later, have moving jaws, giving them at least a semblance of lip-synching. This is vital to the storytelling of the series, as the dialogue is coming from the characters themselves, rather than a narrator with a Received Pronunciation accent the likes of which was never heard in large parts of Britain. Not that Twizzle does not have one of those in the person of Nancy Nevinson, but she is a hairsbreadth more natural sounding to modern ears and does not dominate the narrative in the manner of *Watch with Mother*.

The world Roberta Leigh creates for *The Adventures of Twizzle* is fascinating; far darker and more complex than anything children would have encountered in *The Woodentops*. Twizzle, a boy doll with special legs that can 'twizzle' longer, lives in a shop with a kindly old shopkeeper and his toy friends. All is well until a horrible little girl, Sally Cross, browbeats the shopkeeper into selling her Twizzle for less than he is worth or else she will 'cry and scream and stamp'.

Sally is due to come back the next day with the money, so that night Twizzle decided to run away. As one of the other toys explains, the alternative is grim: 'It's better to run away on your own than to belong to a naughty child. She'll pull off your arms and legs in no time at all.'

Free from the threat of dismemberment by Sally, Twizzle finds the open road lonely and arduous: 'The world is a big and lonely place, and there's no one to talk to except myself.' Seeking shelter in a barn, Twizzle meets Footso, a cat who has run away from home because the children there laugh at his big paws.

Roberta Leigh's series format contains far more of the spirit of the Brothers Grimm than it does the playtime world seen in BBC's alternative. Instead of an idealised nuclear family and a mission to teach youngsters about the world, *The Adventures of Twizzle* (which could be argued to be aimed at a slightly older audience) is about lonely runaways bonding. While Twizzle escapes the prospect of domestic abuse from his naughty girl owner, Footso is mocked for how he looks and must leave home to find acceptance. Together these two outsiders are stronger and they prepare to embark on adventures.

The episodes were directed by Gerry Anderson at space rented at Islet Park, an Edwardian mansion situated on the banks on the Thames at Maidenhead. This was not the most suitable of studio facilities, being prone to flooding in wet weather. It was all the company could afford, however, as the budget for the series was a mere £450 per episode, one of the main reasons why AP Films had secured the contract to make the series. The company was desperate for work, having received a few advertising commissions, a field they had dipped into during the days of Pentagon Films when they made a commercial for Kellogg's Sugar Ricicles featuring a marionette of Enid Blyton's character *Noddy*. Several of the partners of AP Films had been forced to take outside work while the company looked for work, including Gerry Anderson's direction of two episodes of *Martin Kane, Private Investigator* for Harry Alan Towers. Here he would meet a young actor called David Graham for the first time, the two forming an instant bond.

The *Twizzle* episodes were shot quickly, to a schedule of one completed episode every two days. The shooting often carried on into the night, as the production team had to work around the availability of Derek Meddings, who was working with Reg Hill on the sets after being employed during the day on film and advertising projects for special effects producer Les Bowie.

The Adventures of Twizzle was instantly successful when it was broadcast by Associated-Rediffusion from November. The series was even exported, being screened on Australia's ABC television network, which always welcomed British series. Roberta Leigh was more than happy with the results, and pitched a new series idea to A-R—*Torchy the Battery Boy*.

4

Les Bowie

The father of the British tradition of high-quality camera and miniature effects was actually Canadian. Les Bowie was discovered for film work in the most unusual of circumstances; while in the same prisoner of war camp as a producer for Rank Films, his skills as a painter were put to use helping to put on entertainment shows for the inmates, and more clandestine uses such as producing false travel papers for potential escapees.

Thus, in 1946, he was employed at Rank, at this point Britain's largest film producer, as a scenic artist, painting backdrops for outdoor scenes being filmed in the studio. He also learned the art of matte painting under the tutorage of the legendary 'Pop' Day. Matte painting is the painting of part of a scene that could not otherwise be achieved on a reasonable budget, usually on a sheet of glass placed in front of the camera, with the live action taking place in the rest of the scene not covered by the paint. At its best, this method produced entirely undetectable results, but at the time it was extremely time consuming—a good matte painting would take several months to complete. Bowie's artistic training allowed him to revolutionise the process—to demonstrate, he produced his first painting using the new method in a day.

This resulted in him quickly being appointed head of Pinewood's matte department. While there, he worked with Albert Whitlock, who went on to become the most in-demand matte artist working in American cinema, his work including Alfred Hitchcock's films, the 1974 epic *Earthquake* and the original *Star Trek* series.

In 1950, Bowie went freelance along with Vic Margutti to form forming Bowie-Margutti Films. When Margutti left the partnership to return to work at Pinewood, Bowie formed his own production unit as part of Anglo-Scottish Films, and later his own independent effects house, Bowie Films. Through these companies Bowie provided mattes, miniatures, and mechanical effects for British films both large and small for the next thirty years, at his peak of productivity employing seventy-five people. His contribution often uncredited, Bowie's pioneering effects work featured many SF productions such as Hammer's *The Quatermass Xperiment* (1955) and *Quatermass 2* (1957). He is especially well-known for his work on Hammer productions, working on most of the studio's horror films until their final horror picture *To the Devil, A Daughter* in 1976.

Although for most of his career Les Bowie worked on lower budgeted films, towards the end of his life he was employed on expensive American productions using British studio facilities, such as *Star Wars* (1977) and *Superman: The Movie* (1978), for which he was part of the effects team that won a Special Achievement Award for Visual Effects. Tragically, Les Bowie died in January 1979, his final credit being for John Badham's remake of *Dracula*, released later the same year, in which Frank Langella recreated his Broadway stage success. The Academy Award was collected by the rest of the effects team, Colin Chilvers, Denys Coop, Roy Field, Derek Meddings, and Zoran Perisic.

Les Bowie and Gerry Anderson were acquainted, and AP Films acquired from Bowie the Ipswich Road studios on the Slough Trading Estate, which they used for the filming of *Four Feather Falls*, *Supercar*, and *Fireball XL5*. Vital members of the AP Films/Century 21 crew also got their start with Bowie, who, as he himself was too busy with other work to help with *The Adventures of Twizzle*, recommended Derek Meddings to them. Meddings moonlighted from his 'day job' with Anglo-Scottish Films, where he took over Bowie's old production team when Les went to work on Disney's *Swiss Family Robinson* in 1960. Starting out on *Supercar* as Derek Meddings effects assistant (once Meddings finally joined AP Films full time) was Brian Johncock (later Johnson), who also came from Anglo-Scottish and went on to be in charge of the model effects for *Space: 1999* before winning Academy Awards as part of the effects teams on *Alien* (1979) and *The Empire Strikes Back* (1980).

5

Torchy the Battery Boy

'High up in the sky there's a big twinkling star.
It's Topsy Turvy Land, where you can do whatever you want.'

Created and produced by Roberta Leigh
Music and lyrics by Roberta Leigh, arranged by Barry Gray
A Pelham Films Production made by APF, Maidenhead
26 × fifteen-minute episodes
First broadcast Thursday 2 February 1960 (Associated-Rediffusion)

Torchy, a battery-powered living doll with a magic torch on his hat, travels to Topsy Turvy land in a space rocket made by his creator, Mr Bumbledrop. There live toys running away from cruel children who didn't look after them properly.

With *Torchy the Battery Boy*, AP Films were allowed a larger production budget and set their sights on making the new series look more visually complex and impressive than the previous one—a pattern that would be repeated many times over the following years. With more intricate sets to create, art director Reg Hill was given an assistant in the form of Bob Bell. Bob had previously been a matte painter, but on *Torchy the Battery Boy* a different set of artistic talents were needed; he helped make miniature props and sets, which were now in three dimensions as opposed to the flat-painted backgrounds normally used for *The Adventures of Twizzle*.

Bob was to become one of the mainstays of AP Films/Century 21 Studios, remaining on its staff for the rest of the studio's existence and staying with the Andersons for their live-action detective series *The Protectors*. When

Reg Hill moved on to become one of the producers of the Supermarionation series, Bob was promoted to art director. After *The Protectors*, Bob had a considerable career in television and film art direction. He was art director on the first season of Albert Fennell, Brian Clemens, and Laurie Johnson's 1976 series *The New Avengers*, working with production designer Syd Cain. The pair left this series to perform the same roles on producer Euan Lloyd's large-scale action film *The Wild Geese*, which was released in 1978.

Notable other productions he worked on include ITC's 1980 *portmanteau* horror series *The Hammer House of Horror* and the following year's movie version of the Thames Television sitcom *George and Mildred*, made by largely the same company and working with the same production designer, Carolyn Scott. Bob worked with Syd Cain again on *Lion of the Desert* in 1981.

Unlike *The Adventures of Twizzle*, *Torchy the Battery Boy* affords us the luxury of a full series of twenty-six AP Films-produced episodes available to view. Although there were many variations due to individual circumstances, it was the general pattern in television production to produce television series in multiples of thirteen, as this equals a quarter of a calendar year. Thus, twenty-six episodes screened weekly, as opposed to the more modern practice of screening children's series daily, would last a broadcaster six months.

In terms of Roberta Leigh's writing, many of the same themes, which can be seen in the single remaining episode of *Twizzle*, are picked up and developed in *Torchy the Battery Boy*. The series is wildly imaginative and enthusiastic in both the production and writing departments, but retains an undercurrent of loneliness and misery.

The starting point for the series is Mr Bumbledrop, an elderly Irishman who lives in a small house with a large garden along with Pom-Pom, his French Poodle. Mr Bumbledrop is happy because the local children play in his garden on the see-saw and swings, which provides him with some company. A naughty girl, Bossy Boots, spoils this idyllic scene by encouraging the other children to behave badly. She has them tie their toys to some kites Mr Bumbledrop has provided, but a strong wind blows them all away, along with Pom-Pom, who was holding on to one of the kites. Bossy Boots stops the children playing in the garden until he gets all their toys back.

Mr Bumbledrop is close to tears at how lonely he will be, which provides an interesting development, by modern standards, for a children's series. Many children's television series today exclude adults from their narratives, much less the elderly, and it would be regarded as strong stuff indeed to confront the very real issue of loneliness among older people. Mr Bumbledrop is too old to search for the missing toys, but he has a touch of Geppetto about him and sets about making his own surrogate son to look for them. By including a battery in his body and a torch bulb in his hat, the boy doll can walk and talk like a real boy. His torch light turns out to be magic, and if Torchy makes an appropriate rhyme the beam can find anything. The magic beam finds the toys on a twinkling star in the heavens. Overjoyed at this success, Mr Bumbledrop then makes a rocket so Torchy can travel up to the star.

Unfortunately for Mr Bumbledrop, when Torchy lands on the star it turns out to be Topsy Turvy Land, a haven for abused toys that were owned and abused by naughty children. Here the toys walk and talk and do whatever they want, and have no intention of ever coming back to Earth to return to their previous life of misery. Bossy Boots has abused her doll Flopsy so much (pulling her stuffing out, among other things) that even when given the power of speech and movement on Topsy Turvy Land she remains brain damaged, and has to invent her own piggle-poggle words for the ones she cannot remember. Similarly, Pom-Pom the dog does not want to come back, even when Torchy tells her how lonely Mr Bumbledrop is, as here she can talk and eat chocolate and bones all day long.

The result is that not only has poor Mr Bumbledrop lost the company of the local children and his beloved dog, but he does not even have the regular companionship of Torchy—his surrogate son. Torchy decided to live on the twinkling star, coming back to earth for weekly visits in order to have his battery changed.

Roberta Leigh makes no attempt to sugar-coat the state of childhood. Most of the children we see are irredeemably naughty, and even ones who are not naughty when we first meet them decide later on that it is more fun to be bad. When first we meet Bogey, he is being bullied by Bossy Boots (in episode one), but when we revisit his character (now named Bad Boy Bogey, and given a splendidly goonish voice by Kenneth Connor—similar to Peter Sellers' Bluebottle) in episode fifteen, he is far naughtier than even Bossy Boots. Even a corrective trip to Topsy Turvy Land has only a temporary effect on his behaviour; his mother, Mrs Meany-Mouth reports in episode seventeen that Bogey is being unexpectedly good, but by episode twenty four ('Bogey and the Statues') he's worse than ever, breaking statues in the park and tying Torchy up with string so that he'll play with him.

By this point in the production of *Torchy the Battery Boy*, AP Films were planning their next production, which would be made without Roberta Leigh. This would have obvious financial implications, as the company had made *The Adventures of Twizzle* and *Torchy the Battery Boy* for a fee from Roberta Leigh. Leigh had made the agreement with Associated-Rediffusion to provide the series and as producer was making a profit from AP Films work. If AP Films could generate their own property to make for the ITV network, then all the money would come to them.

Consequently, *Four Feather Falls* was born, while Roberta Leigh continued making puppet series of her own, with some degree of success. *Torchy the Battery Boy* was successful enough for a second batch of episodes to be ordered by Associated-Rediffusion. As before, Leigh acted as producer and wrote all the scripts, while Vivian Milroy, who would go on to direct *Coronation Street*, directed the episodes for Associated British Pathé. The same voice artists were retained and the puppets and sets made by AP Films continued to be used, but the episodes looked somewhat different, largely due to Milroy's directorial style being different to that of Gerry Anderson.

As became clear with *Four Feather Falls*, the Anderson style was different on many levels to that of Roberta Leigh, though it is interesting to note the similarities in what was to follow. *Four Feather Falls* retained the basic arrangement of puppets in a fifteen-minute format, with a song in every episode. Both Anderson, who was emerging as the main driving force among the AP Films partnership, and Leigh shared a refusal to talk down to their young audience. *Four Feather Falls* was to be to have strong action-adventure elements along with comedy, songs, and a degree of magic. Where Anderson and his team differed from Leigh was that the fairy-tale settings were left behind in favour of far more realistic settings. Magic was retained as a part of the format, in the form of Tex's magic feathers, but kept in the background as a sort of junior version of the Magical Realism literary tradition.

The Adventures of Twizzle and *Torchy and Battery Boy* present communities whose members have rejected their previous homes for various reasons. *Four Feather Falls* is about characters living in a healthy, functioning society. Even the main villains, Pedro and Fernando, generally lack the edge that Bossy Boots and Bogey (who often seem genuinely unpleasant) have in *Torchy*. *Twizzle* and *Torchy* as series have an air of sadness and loneliness, which is completely absent in *Four Feather Falls*, a place that is sunny—both literally and figuratively.

6

Four Feather Falls

'*The four feathers on this hat are magic.*
They enable Tex Tucker's dog and horse to speak and his guns to fire without him
even touching them.'

Created by Gerry Anderson and Barry Gray, produced by AP Films
Music and lyrics composed, arranged, and conducted by Barry Gray, songs
    sung by Michael Holliday
Made by APF, in association with Granada TV Network
39 × fifteen-minute episodes
First Broadcast Thursday 25 September 1960 (ITV Network)

Sheriff Tex Tucker protects the town of Four Feather Falls with the aid of
magical feathers in his hat, which allow his guns to fire without him touching
them, and both his dog and horse to speak.

Puppet films were keeping AP Films afloat, and Gerry was determined to
make the best puppet films he could in the hope that someone would give him
a break into live action. *Torchy the Battery Boy* was a visible step forwards
from AP's previous collaboration with Roberta Leigh, *The Adventures of
Twizzle*, but he was sure that more was possible. At this point in time, it might
seem like an odd move for Gerry Anderson and Arthur Provis to move from
making the comparatively traditional children's fairy-tale material of *The
Adventures of Twizzle* and *Torchy the Battery Boy* to the Wild West.
    The idea came originally from Barry Gray, with the pilot script written
by Mary Cathcart Borer. In 1959, the television Western was at its peak of
popularity, with long-running hits such as *Bonanza* and *Gunsmoke* (retitled

Gun Law in the UK) running in peak time. America was also producing live-action Westerns for the children's market, such as *The Lone Ranger* and *Champion the Wonder Horse*, which generations of children were to grow up watching. The decision to make the first AP Films solo production a Western was no stab in the dark; it was a clever way of reducing the risk to their enterprise. Even at this early stage of his career as a producer, Gerry was consciously moving away from making material purely for children and aiming at something acceptable to the whole family.

Hiring popular singer Michael Holliday to perform five songs, one of which was to be performed in all but seven episodes of the series, also helped set down a marker for the planned direction of the series. Holliday was a very popular British performer in the pre-beat boom '50s, who had the ability to sing in a manner quite remarkably like Bing Crosby. Unlike the explicitly child-centred songs featured in *Torchy*, Barry Gray wrote for Holliday a suite of songs that were pleasant, pacy Western-tinged ballads, which parents were likely to enjoy. They were later to be released as an EP record, extending the cross-promotional activities of *Four Feather Falls* still further.

Although planned from the outset as a production independent of Roberta Leigh, the AP Films partners (Anderson and Provis) disagreed about the future direction of the company. Anderson was for expansion, but had to turn down the offer of buying the Islet Park mansion they were using as studio facilities. Provis was for the company making a second series of *Torchy* with Leigh, alongside *Four Feather Falls* to spread the financial risk. A split became inevitable and Provis resigned from the company after photographing the first eleven episodes of *Four Feather Falls*. The remaining directors, Gerry Anderson, John Read (who took over from Provis as director of photography), and Reg Hill, recruited the future Mrs Anderson (Sylvia Thamm) to join the board.

The completed pilot of *Four Feather Falls* urgently needed a backer, having been self-financed by AP Films. Anglo-Amalgamated co-owner Stuart Levy expressed an interest, but his business partner Nat Cohen blocked this. The pair did recommend the pilot to Manchester-based ITV contractor Granada Television, and to Gerry's enormous relief Granada agreed to finance a thirty-nine-episode series. Cohen and Levy must have liked something they saw in the AP Films setup, as early in the following year they hired the company to produce a cinema support feature, which was to become *Crossroads to Crime*. Islet Park was unsuited to the task of hosting the larger scale of production represented by *Four Feather Falls*, so AP acquired space (four times larger) at Ipswich Road, on the Slough Trading Estate, from special effects producer Les Bowie—the employer of Derek Meddings.

This space was quickly transformed into shooting stages, production offices, and workshops, allowing the production line that made the next thirty-eight episodes to crank into life. Similar to the previous two series, *Four Feather Falls* began with a single writer producing the scripts—Phil Wrestler took on this role after Mary Cathcart Borer wrote the first two episodes. Abraham

Philip Wrestler had been a film editor since the 1940s, and had worked on ITC's 1957 co-production with the American ABC network *O.S.S.* His screen writing career began with *Four Feather Falls* and ended with the 1962 B-movie *Crosstrap*, starring Laurence Payne. Wrestler wrote the next twenty-six fifteen-minute episodes, managing with some aplomb the not-inconsiderable task of coming up with viable plots that could be told in that timeframe while also fitting in a musical number.

From episode twenty-nine ('The Ma Jones Story') most episodes were written by Jill Allgood. Two stories—'Safe as Houses' and 'Fancy Shooting'— were written by Martin Woodhouse, who obviously impressed the producers as, in conjunction with his brother Hugh Woodhouse, he wrote all but one episode of *Supercar*'s first production block. Woodhouse was quite a polymath, having been a medical doctor, engineer, pilot, and computer expert, as well as a scriptwriter and author. His most notable screen work outside the Anderson fold was on *The Avengers*, writing five episodes for the Patrick Macnee and Honor Blackman partnership and one for the 1965 Diana Rigg series.

The increasing size of AP Films saw Gerry Anderson gradually step back from the role of directing the episodes after number thirteen; the episode 'Trapped' was the first of the company's productions to be directed by someone other than Anderson himself, in this case David Elliott. The pair alternated episodes from this point until 'Horse Thieves', which saw Alan Pattillo's debut as director. Pattillo had previously been a sound editor, latterly for Irving Allen and Albert R. Broccoli's Warwick Films before joining AP Films as a director, proving also a talented writer and script editor. Anderson would rarely direct after this, taking on the pilot episodes of *Supercar*, *Fireball XL5*, and *UFO*, setting the style of the shows before handing over the reins to others.

The series made its intentions clear right from the opening scenes, with a dramatic crash of lightning followed by the camera tracking down an eerie Western street, seemingly only populated by a few horses until we see the our hero, Tex Tucker, whose guns lift and fire of their own accord. The accent was on drama and spectacle, and fascinatingly the scene would be virtually repeated eight years later for the opening sequence of *Captain Scarlet and the Mysterons*. By the time the series ended, with the Alan Pattillo-directed 'Ride 'em Cowboy', the producers were able to mount a full rodeo with some extremely well-done trick-riding scenes. Although much happier with what his company had produced than he had been with the previous Roberta Leigh formats, *Four Feather Falls* was still not what Gerry Anderson wanted to be making, and an offer to make a B-movie for Anglo-Amalgamated seemed to be a heaven-sent opportunity for AP Films to break into new markets.

Directed by Gerry Anderson from a script by Alun Falconer, the resulting production, 'Crossroads to Crime', was decently produced and acted, and made an effort to introduce some action and location shooting into the mix. Fifty-five years since the film was developed, there is a patina of nostalgia that makes pleasant viewing, but on its release in November 1960, the film did not generate a great deal of success. No further offers of productions came from Anglo-Amalgamated and AP Films' financial situation quickly became desperate.

Nicholas Parsons was the epitome of the smooth Englishman; he was discovered by the Canadian theatre impresario Carol Levis doing impressions and working in small repertory theatres in Glasgow while working during the day on the Clydebank shipyards. He achieved fame in the '50s and early '60s as the posh-sounding comic stooge to the nationally popular working-class comedian Arthur Haynes, the pair splitting in 1962 allegedly because Parsons was getting too much attention. This high profile made him an unexpectedly famous addition to the *Four Feather Falls* voice cast when he asked his then-wife Denise Bryer to have Gerry Anderson consider him for the voice of Tex Tucker.

Known today mainly for his comedy roles in the *Carry On* movies and in the BBC's 1982–92 sitcom *'Allo 'Allo!*, Kenneth Connor was best known as a radio performer in the late 1950s. His vocal dexterity meant he was called upon as a 'spare' member of *The Goon Show*, filling in when one of the regular cast was indisposed. In 1958, the year before *Four Feather Falls* was produced, Connor appeared in *Carry On Sergeant*, the first in the long-running series. He remained a busy vocal performer, and while providing voices for *Four Feather Falls'* characters he was also recording the second series of *Torchy the Battery Boy*, which was being made by Associated British Pathé.

Denise Bryer was one of the original Anderson voice artists, having provided the voice of the title character in *The Adventures of Twizzle*. This was not the first puppet voice she had provided though, having been the voice of Noddy for the television series *The Adventures of Noddy*. This led to Bryer voicing the part for a television commercial for Kellogg's Sugar Ricicles made by Gerry Anderson and Arthur Provis' Pentagon Films. She returned to AP Films for *Four Feather Falls*, giving voice to characters including Martha Jones and Little Jake. At the time she was married to actor Nicholas Parsons, who offered his services to the production as the voice of Sheriff Tex Tucker. Although she had a long period away from the Anderson firm, she remained a popular voice artist with projects including *Hector's House* (1968). In 1982, she provided voices for *Star Fleet*, a British revamp of the Japanese puppet SF show *X-Bomber*. This included a memorable voice for the main villain, Commander Makara, which formed the basis of Bryer's voice for Zelda in the following year's Gerry Anderson production *Terrahawks*.

David Graham—the larynx behind hundreds of different voices for series as diverse as *Four Feather Falls*, *Doctor Who*, and *Peppa Pig*—began his professional association with Gerry Anderson in the summer of 1957, with the television series *Martin Kane, Private Investigator*. Gerry was hired at very short notice to direct an episode of this low-budget crime drama, and bonded with David Graham over their shared fear of heights when presented with a script with a climax involving climbing to a great height. Gerry remembered the young actor when he was casting for voices in *Four Feather Falls*, which was the beginning of an association that lasted through *Supercar, Fireball XL5, Stingray, Thunderbirds*, and *The Secret Service*. David was also one of the original Dalek voice artists, and through a long career has remained busy as both an actor and voice artist.

Named by one wit, *The Man Who Would be Bing* (the title of Ken Crossland's 2004 biography of the singer), Michael Holliday was remarkable in that his voice suggested not so much a hint of Bing Crosby as a complete demonic possession by the golfing old crooner. The Liverpool-born singer was originally christened Norman Alexander Milne on 26 November 1924, and his relaxed style and smooth, Crosby-esque crooning turned him into a major British star. While *Four Feather Falls* was in production, Holliday scored his last big UK hit with 'Starry Eyed', which reached number one in November 1959, and he was still regarded as a hot recording act by the time the series debuted in February 1960. The laid-back image hid a darker, more complex reality. Holliday was deeply insecure, suffering terribly from stage fright. Gerry Anderson discovered during the *Four Feather Falls* song recording sessions that Holliday could not even bear anyone being in his eye-line while singing in the studio, convinced that he pulled faces while singing. Holliday's fragile mental state was worsened by a dip in his professional fortunes when the rise of The Beatles and other beat groups wiped out the market for ballad singers. He suffered a mental breakdown in 1961, and committed suicide on 26 November 1963, aged only thirty-eight.

Four Feather Falls deserves remembering for its refusal to talk down to its audience—the Roberta Leigh series operated similarly in their refusal to idolise the state of childhood, but they were operating in what was basically a fairy-tale environment. With *Four Feather Falls* AP Films were telling far more realistic stories in a setting that would have been highly familiar to the whole family—the American West. In 1959, when the series began production, Westerns were an absolutely integral part of the media landscape.

In America, this was the peak year of television Western production, with no less than twenty-six series airing in prime time. This reflected the perception of the Western as an adult genre, but its roots in television was as a source of children's programming a decade earlier. Movie serials and second features were no longer being produced, the backbone of which were low-budget Westerns popular with children at Saturday matinees. Instead, these were sold to television, forgotten movie heroes such as *Hopalong Cassidy*'s William Boyd unexpectedly finding themselves heroes to a new generation of children. Other rediscovered stars included singing cowboys Roy Rogers and Gene Autry, a fact not lost on the makers of *Four Feather Falls*.

As these children's Westerns fell away, the adult Western rose, led by long-running hits *Gunsmoke* and *Bonanza*, which both debuted in 1955. This dominance was reflected in the British television schedules. Examining the schedules for the week *Four Feather Falls* was first broadcast on 25 February 1960, BBC Television, at this point in time the lone national broadcaster, showed five Westerns. If you were watching the more commercially-minded ITV (which was split into nine regions, each with different schedules) there were no less than seventeen Western series available to watch, depending on which region you lived in.

Two series even managed the ultimate ITV accolade of being screened across the network at the same time—*Wagon Train* and *Maverick*. These were joined by *Four Feather Falls*, the first AP Films series to be fully networked—and also the last for many years. As already mentioned, the singing cowboy stars Roy Rogers and Gene Autry were now well-known to young television audiences, and this enabled AP Films to easily tailor their Western series to the same basic format as *Twizzle* and *Torchy*—fifteen-minute episodes, each containing a song. The ante, however, was upped considerably by the hiring of Michael Holliday to provide the singing voice of Sheriff Tex Tucker, which represented something of a coup for the series.

In general, the *Four Feather Falls* puppets are noticeably better looking than their counterparts in *Torchy the Battery Boy*. Freed from the influence of Roberta Leigh, and able to draw upon Western character types, the AP Films sculptors rose to the challenge, gleefully creating perhaps the most extreme caricatures in the history of the Anderson shows. Grandpa Twink, to pick one example, has a huge head compared to his body.

Tex Tucker himself is an interesting meeting of puppet design and voice artist. He was by far the most realistically designed character, being the nearest thing to a realistic puppet seen in an Anderson series until *Captain Scarlet and the Mysterons*. This befitted Tex's status as *Four Feather Falls*' straight man and source of moral authority. Tex's almond-shaped eyes suggest Roy Rogers, while the scripts and Parsons' vocal delivery give the character a tougher edge than was present in Rogers' on-screen persona. A facially caricatured Tex Tucker might have overbalanced the series in a comedic direction, when a large part of the show's appeal actually comes from its action-adventure elements. It is interesting to note that for AP Films' first independent production, action and excitement and a more realistic setting was added to the existing mix of magic, comedy, and songs.

Granada had seemed happy enough with the series, accepting the episodes in Manchester without much comment and in return sending cheques back to Slough. Gerry even found himself in the privileged position of being the producer of a nationally networked series, making its debut on Thursday 25 February 1960 at 5.00 p.m.; opposite a BBC children's programme entitled *Playbox*, an old, established BBC show that had been running since 1955. The final contracted episode of *Four Feather Falls* was duly delivered to Granada and was broadcast at the end of the series' initial run on 27 October 1960. The series appeared to have been successful within the limits of a fifteen-minute children's series, and has been the subject of much spin-off merchandise.

Gerry was eager to discuss ideas with Granada for a follow up and had prepared a sales brochure for their next project while *Four Feather Falls* was still in production. The northern ITV contractor made no contact with the company following the delivery of the final episode. After some phone conversations, Gerry was informed over lunch with a director of Granada that the company would not be ordering a follow-up series. AP Films had achieved so much on meagre resources, but now all seemed lost.

Oddly, the first AP Films series to be herded from the range and sent to Boot Hill was *Four Feather Falls*, which was last screened (by the station that had originally commissioned it—Granada) at 5.05 p.m. on Friday 26 July 1968. *The Adventures of Twizzle* and *Torchy the Battery Boy* still received occasional screenings for another five years. Both had their final screening on Southern Television in 1973 on 10 April and 8 January respectively, ending an era of children's broadcasting.

Space Patrol

On leaving AP Films, Arthur Provis threw himself into finding opportunities for work, forming a long-lasting working relationship with none other than Roberta Leigh. Leigh's ambitions as a television producer were undimmed, and the first fruit of this new partnership was *Sara and Hoppity*, a decidedly odd puppet series for younger children about a young girl whose naughty toy doll gets her into trouble when nobody else can see. Based on a series of books written by Leigh, *Sara and Hoppity* was billed as A Wonderama Production, but it was made by PP Films for Associated-Rediffusion.

The business side of this arrangement is quite interesting, and displays Leigh's high degree of business acumen. Wonderama seems to have been Roberta Leigh's business vehicle in which the copyright of her creations was held, while PP Films (as much as can be assumed fifty years after the date) was a film production company created by Arthur Provis and Bill Palmer, the art director on *Sara and Hoppity*. After this series was completed, Leigh then purchased an existing production company, National Interest Picture Productions, which was first established in 1925 as Publicity Pictures. This company produced animated advertising films and short subjects designed to fill out cinema screening bills.

During the Second World War, Publicity Pictures made training films for the British Armed Forces, after which they changed their name to National Interest Picture Productions and continued in the same vein, as well as making industrial information films—hiring Reg Hill as a model maker and animator. Hill stayed with the company for some twelve years before he began working with Gerry Anderson. Once Roberta Leigh bought the company in 1962 it still made military training and industrial films, with such titles as *Worms in Sheep*, *RAF D/F Emergency Organisation*, and *Liver Fluke Disease*.

Owning both the production company and the copyright holder was a clever move, also adopted by Harry Salzman and Albert R. Broccoli for their James Bond films. These were made by Eon Productions, but for copyright purposes were made for Danjaq S.A., a company registered in a country where the tax laws were somewhat more lax than those of the United Kingdom. The first National Interest/Wonderama production, which began shooting in 1962, was *Space Patrol*. Unlike *Sara and Hoppity*, which was a logical continuation of Leigh's earlier creations *The Adventures of Twizzle* and *Torchy the Battery Boy*, made for a slightly older audience, *Space Patrol* took AP Films' increasingly adventure-filled scientific creations head-on.

Thirty-nine half-hour episodes of *Space Patrol* were produced for Associated British's ITV contractor, ABC Television. The format of the series was ostensibly very similar to *Fireball XL5*, but in reality the two series were produced in such an unusual and different manner that the two shows could not be more different. The smaller ambitions of Leigh and Provis allowed them to make a series more diverse, and in some ways more interesting than *Fireball XL5*; *Space Patrol* was freed from having to tailor its appeal quite so much to the perceived needs of the American market.

While the crew of *Fireball XL5* worked for the World Space Patrol, the titular organisation *Space Patrol* was far more inclusive, including personnel from Venus and Mars. This more inclusive atmosphere extends to the human crew members, the regular characters Professor Haggerty and his daughter were both Irish. The series characters work as an ensemble, so we have an American-accented captain of the spaceship Galasphere 347, Larry Dart, but he does not dominate the proceedings in any way. Just as important to the narratives are his fellow crew members Husky, who is from Mars, and Slim, who is a Venusian. *Space Patrol* is run by Colonel Rayburn, who is from Earth, but relies heavily on his Venusian secretary, Marla.

The universe of *Space Patrol*, set in the year 2100, sees Earth working in partnership with Mars and Venus, and we see Colonel Rayburn often interacting with officials and presidents of these planets. This throws up an interesting contradiction in the series; although in 1962 it was widely accepted that the other planets in our solar system are uninhabited, *Space Patrol* gives them cultures and civilisations. Despite this, in many ways the series has a higher degree of scientific accuracy than *Fireball XL5*—the production actually hired a space consultant, Colin Ronan.

While Fireball is basically a conventional rocket, the Galasphere craft is shaped like a child's spinning top, making no concessions to conventional aerodynamics, which would be meaningless during travel in outer space. *Space Patrol* also accepts that even travel between the planets in our own solar system would take a long time (although apparently Mercury is three days travel from Earth, which is pretty good going). Thus, after the Galasphere takes off, its crew enter a suspended animation chamber for the length of the journey, while the ship is run by robot control.

Some of the design work on *Space Patrol* is also exemplary. While the Fireball characters simply took oxygen pills before going on a space walk or exploring a planet without breathable air, Larry Dart and his crew have well-designed space suits—it should be said they also have hover jet bikes, which are suspiciously similar to those seen in *Fireball XL5*, as is Colonel Rayburn's rotating desk. The futuristic city that comprises Space Patrol headquarters is a far more complex structure than Space City, with an interconnected transport tube system that we see operating. The building from which we see Galasphere 347 take-off and land from is a particularly lovely design, the top section of the structure coming up to meet the craft as it lands.

The puppets are designed to be rather more realistic than the ones AP Films were using, correctly proportioned despite having a moving mouth mechanism. This puts them more in line with the puppet designs for *Sara and Hoppity* than those of *Torchy the Battery Boy*. Sometimes this works very well, but more often *Space Patrol* serves to highlight why some of the design choices made over in Slough were actually very astute. Many of the puppets lack expression, which put a great burden on the voice artists to carry the emotional weight of the dialogue. Two factors worked against this: firstly, the Martian and Venusian accents used by Husky, Slim, and other characters were deliberately unemotional in tone; secondly, the voice cast were recording up to eight episodes per day, which were hardly ideal conditions for deeply considered line readings.

Often the series is simply unable to hide the cheapness of its production— every now and again Roberta Leigh, the writer, will make demands that Roberta Leigh, the producer, is simply unable to meet. The climax of the episode 'The Water Bomb' sees missiles strike the Martian moon of Phobos, the results being simply absurd; as the production had no budget for pyrotechnics, we simply see two large holes punched into the surface of the moon.

The most cursory glance at any episode of *Space Patrol* reveals that the series was produced on a shoestring budget, but the series nonetheless retains a real fascination. The soundtracks, as with any such series, were recorded first, in the converted attic of Roberta Leigh's Hampstead home by voice actors Dick Vosburgh, Libby Morris, Ysanne Churchman, Ronnie Stevens, and Murray Kash.

The episodes themselves were filmed on 35-mm film in converted churches, firstly in Stoke Newington, then in Harlesden. The series seems to have been shot in batches of thirteen by director Frank Goulding and his crew. Every scene (per batch of episodes being produced) that required a particular set was shot together, this was done in order to save the time and cost of erecting the different sets as needed. The episodes were edited by Len Walter, previously a colleague of David Lane in the *Ghost Squad* cutting rooms, who later was employed by Century 21 Productions as supervising editor on *Thunderbirds* and *Captain Scarlet and the Mysterons*, among other of the company's productions.

Possibly the most interesting credit on *Space Patrol* is that of electronics by F. C. Judd. One might be forgiven for thinking this meant Frederick Charles Judd was responsible for the lights on the control panels or some such technical details. In fact, Judd was responsible for the show's score, which was so unusual and ground-breaking that it is possible it was not regarded as music at all. Instead it might be seen as an electronic soundscape adding atmosphere to the soundtrack. Today we are more used to deliberately repetitive electronic music, but Judd's contribution still sounds bold and cutting edge.

He produced the score using tape manipulation, tape loops, and tone generators using *musique concrète* techniques, which Judd helped to popularise, writing the earliest-known book on the subject in 1961. Taken from a theoretical basis invented by Pierre Schaeffer in the 1940s, briefly put, *musique concrète* involves taking sounds made using recording from sources including non-musical sources and the human voice. The process of recording and editing the sounds into their final form is equally as important as the production of the actual sounds themselves, an idea taken from film making.

On *Space Patrol*, the resulting compositions are sometimes brilliantly atmospheric, shots of Space Patrol headquarters being accompanied by harsh, rhythmic industrial noises, which sound like a precursor to the *musique concrète*-inspired industrial music scene, which sprang up in the 1980s. This is preceded by a shot of Galasphere 347 flying past the camera and towards a planet, the repeating five-note audio pattern the ship makes as it passes is the nearest thing *Space Patrol* has to a theme tune. It is certainly the series' audio signature—an instantly recognisable signal to anyone within earshot that the programme has begun. Unfortunately, in scenes requiring a build-up of tension, F. C. Judd's score is not at all helpful, highlighting just how much Barry Gray's music brought to the Supermarionation shows.

The sound of the Galasphere is a lovely, comforting noise, which fits perfectly with the craft looking like a child's toy. Actually, much of the content of *Space Patrol* really is lovely, and then butts up against the show's harder-edged aspects—Roberta Leigh's scripts tend not to add too much sugar coating. Sample dialogue: 'There's been an explosion in the Launching Room. Everyone was killed!' Despite its very low budget, but perhaps aided by the sheer quirkiness of its execution, *Space Patrol* was quite successful, though on nothing like the scale of the Anderson-produced puppet series. Nevertheless it was screened in various ITV regions until 1970, and was the subject of comic adaptations in television and later in children's comic *The Beezer*. It was even exported, with some success, to the US, Australia, and Malta.

Space Patrol proved to be the high water mark of Leigh and Provis's production partnership, their subsequent productions, such as *Send for Dithers* and *Wonder Boy and Tiger*, receiving only limited distribution. A colour pilot film for a follow-up series to *Space Patrol*, entitled 'Paul Starr', was made in 1964, the title character's voice provided by Ed Bishop. Colour photography showed that Leigh and Provis could not muster the production values to compete with the Anderson productions and the idea, perhaps mercifully, went no further. They came close to getting a live-action series off the ground, a pilot film of *The Solarnauts* being produced in 1967 on 35-mm film for ABC Television Productions, apparently with finance from American International. It is actually pretty good when seen today, but the idea never went beyond the pilot film stage, partially due to ABC ceasing to exist as an entity within the ITV structure soon afterwards, the company becoming the dominant partner in Thames Television.

Arthur Provis continued in the film industry working on industrial and advertising films, while Roberta Leigh, tiring of the struggle to get her productions on the air, returned to her previous calling as a writer of romantic fiction—with great success.

Supercar

'*Satisfactory. Most Satisfactory.*'

Produced by Gerry Anderson
Music composed, arranged, and conducted by Barry Gray
Created by Gerry Anderson and Reg Hill
ITC (Incorporated Television Company Limited)
Copyright 1960 AP Films Limited
Filmed by APF at AP Film Studios, Slough in association with ATV, Associated
    Television Ltd
An ITC Worldwide distribution
39 × twenty-five-minute episodes
First broadcast Saturday 29 January 1961

In the Nevada desert a laboratory team develops Supercar, a top secret vehicle, which can fly to the edge of space and travel under the sea. The team use Supercar to help people in need, but must protect its secrets from the criminal Masterspy.

A reunion with Nicholas Parsons, the now-retired sheriff of Four Feather Falls, kept the wolf from APF's door. While the AP Films board were contemplating a bleak future for the company, Parsons was busy drumming up trade for his own production company—DN Productions. He approached Ken Fox, uncle of the actors James and Edward Fox and managing director of the coaching holiday film *Blue Cars Holidays*.

Speaking to *FAB Magazine* in 2012, Nicholas Parsons explained how his unusual approach worked:

I said, 'I've got three ideas for you, but I'm an actor, I don't have them on paper. I'll demonstrate them for you.' One of them was this way-out [idea] using gibberish, another was like a foreign film with subtitles.

I did the demonstration and he said, 'Well there's only one for me' and that was the gibberish one, so I was contracted. He said, 'Listen, what we want are these three commercials and we need a documentary and we're also going to do an Advertising Magazine. We've only got this amount of money,' I think it was £3,250. I wanted to get my production company set up so I accepted it, but I thought, 'How am I going to do this on a shoestring budget?'

The answer Nicholas came up with was to return to a company he had dealt with before, one he knew could produce high-quality results on the smallest of budgets—AP Films.

I spoke to Gerry Anderson. I said, 'Gerry, I've got to do these three commercials and an advertising film as well, and the thing is there's hardly any money in it'. I told him what was involved and Gerry was wonderful.

He said, 'I'll tell you what I'll do Nicholas, I'll split the fee with you. We'll use my studio and my technicians'. The money was peanuts in relation to what we were trying to do, but Gerry said afterwards it was a saviour. He was trying to keep the studio going while he tried to sell *Supercar* and he said, 'In a way you saved me, because I'd got this modest amount of money which helped keep the studio going.'

Nicholas Parsons devised three commercials, co-starring his wife Denise Bryer (who had been, of course, a voice artist for *The Adventures of Twizzle* and *Four Feather Falls*). Two were designed to appear like foreign films, with the characters speaking in French- and German-sounding gibberish. The third, in which Parsons and Bryer appear as Martians looking down on Earthling Blue Cars holidays makers with their space-telescope, was highly popular, winning top prize in the 1961 Television Mail advertising awards.

The audience of advertising professionals at the awards ceremony were aghast; not only had this set of newcomers won the top award, but they had gone against an unwritten rule of the industry—the advertiser had dealt directly with the filmmakers without going through an advertising agency.

No further offers of commercials came the way of AP Films or Parsons and Bryer, as Parsons explains:

We hadn't come from the advertising world and they were pretty miffed that we had won the award. Neither of us received an enquiry again to do commercials. But that's show business!

In the meantime, there was the business of the longer, fifteen-minute travel film Nicholas Parsons and AP Films had to make for Blue Cars holidays. This was by far the biggest film project DN Productions had taken on, and the making of the film proved an arduous task for director Parsons:

> It was a travel film, which we filmed abroad. It was made by Gerry's technicians— John Read shot it. We went abroad first with a full unit and we had the most ghastly weather. We first went to Switzerland and our transport was Blue Cars buses, because that's what we were advertising. We were going across the border to Italy but we didn't have the right permits. We were turned back at the border and we came home. I remember when I got back my wife said, 'We're bankrupt'— we'd spent all the money!
>
> I got in touch with Gerry and I said, 'We've got a little bit in the can, but not much'.
>
> He said, 'I think we'd better send a crew back and we'll try to mount it again'. Gerry taught me a valuable lesson, because I wasn't an experienced film maker. He said, 'You've got to get more coverage', and I hadn't realised that. You can't have the whole thing being mountains and rivers; you've got to have a cutaway to this and a cutaway to that. You need to do lots of little clips which you can cut in and make a film. And so we then went to Spain—it was just me and John Read. So off I went and we filmed endlessly, came home and put together this film, with me talking about all these different places. John filmed it and was the sound recordist. We cut the film together; I sat in with the Editor and had all Gerry's technical backup and his technicians.

As well as the footage shot in Switzerland and Spain, Nicholas called in a favour from his comedy partner in order to film some framing footage for the location film:

> I got my friend Arthur Haynes to take part in it. I wrote this little story where I was showing my home movie films to my friends and the plumber comes in and interrupts and sits down and chat to me. I did a deal with Arthur where he could have a holiday wherever he wanted in return for being in the film. It was shot in Gerry's studio and it was transmitted. I've lost the film now. I don't know where it is, which is a shame.

The finished film was delivered to Blue Cars, who were very happy with it and arranged for it to be screened in the London area. This inadvertently caused a major controversy within British commercial television, as Nicholas Parsons explains:

> What actually happened was that Blue Cars was a subsidiary of Rediffusion. So Ken Fox, the head of Blue Cars, said, 'Let's make an advertising film and we'll put it into the Advertising Magazine slot'. Rediffusion was the company who ran commercial television for the London area, so that was where the Advertising Magazine was seen. Blue Cars said to their parent company, 'You have this slot, let's take the whole fifteen minutes'.

'Alright,' they said, 'why not?'

The ITA (Independent Television Authority) had never intended that an Advertising Magazine go all to one advertiser. The whole concept was that it was for a number of people who could take a thirty second or one minute slot. It was called Jim's Inn and Jim would talk about a product for thirty seconds and the whole premise was built around that. The ITA went bananas because this was never intended. We'd broken the ground rules, this was illegal. We'd unintentionally killed the advertising magazine!

Nicholas Parsons and AP Films association ended on a note of controversy, but Parsons had received a valuable grounding in filmmaking basics. This he used in the '70s when he returned to documentary making, producing a series of half-hour movies for Rank, which went out as supporting features on the company's Odeon cinema chain.

AP Films still struggled for survival. The profit margins on *Crossroads to Crime* and the Blue Cars advertising films were not enough to keep the company afloat. With the order book empty, the AP Films board saw no option but to go into voluntary liquidation. At the last moment, however, Gerry Anderson grasped at one final straw.

He called his friend Frank Sherwin Green, a highly experienced production manager and associate producer who had found odd bits of work for the company during thin times in the past. At this point, Green was busy working on series such as *Tales from Dickens* (1958) for Harry Alan Towers and *Interpol Calling* for ITC/Rank/Wrather Productions (1959). Informing Green (who, almost twenty years later, would be associate producer on the second series of *Space: 1999*) of the severity of the situation and asking if there was any work available, AP Films were suddenly and unexpectedly thrown a more substantial lifeline than they could have dreamed of.

Green knew Connery Chapel, a film and theatre critic, journalist, author, and occasional screenwriter, who had just written two episodes of *Interpol Calling*. It was possible that Chapel could be convinced to introduce Gerry to Lew Grade, the most powerful figure in commercial television. One visit to Ipswich Road later, Chapel was impressed enough to arrange a meeting with Grade.

Events moved quickly at this point, and by the early evening Gerry Anderson was in Lew Grade's office with the sales brochure for AP Film's ambitious new project, *Supercar*. With Grade's trademark mixture of decisiveness, business acumen, and *chutzpah*, he promised an immediate order for twenty-six episodes, provided that the projected budget of £3,000 per episode could be cut in half. After an all-night session at AP Films cutting costs to the bone, the best that could be done was to reduce the budget by a third. In the event this was good enough: *Supercar* was immediately put into production to meet a tight delivery deadline. AP Films lived to fight another day.

Heading the voice cast was thirty-three-year-old Graydon Gould as *Supercar*'s pilot Mike Mercury, the first of many Canadian actors to provide voices for Anderson series. Born in Prince Albert, Saskatchewan, Gould moved to Britain in 1957 and soon began getting parts in low-budget series such as Edward J. and Harry Lee Danziger's *The Vice*. Gould's two episodes starred future *Captain Scarlet and the Mysterons*' voice artists' Donald Gray and Neil McCallum—the former as one-armed detective Mark Saber. Gould's roles got bigger and the productions more prestigious: a steady stream of roles in one-off television productions including *Armchair Theatre* and *ITV Play of the Week* was joined by roles in films including *Floods of Fear* (1958), directed and co-written by Charles Crichton—a highly-rated former Ealing Studios director who would later be one of the regular roster of directors on both series of *Space: 1999*.

While *Supercar* was still on its original broadcast run, Gould starred in another children's SF series, *Pathfinders to Venus*. This eight-episode serial was made by ABC Television and broadcast from 5 March 1961, featuring Gould as Captain Wilson. A few years after *Supercar* he starred in another ITC series, the children's adventure series *The Forest Rangers* (1963–65) as Chief Ranger George Keeley. This was a co-production with Canada's CBC, and was the first Canadian series ever to be shot in colour.

The other members of the voice cast had appeared in previous AP Films productions. David Graham returned from *Four Feather Falls* playing Doctor Beaker in the hesitant, stuttering style he would later adapt for Brains in *Thunderbirds*. Graham would also supply the grunts and shrieks of Mitch the Monkey and the human voice of the recurring character of Jimmy Gibson's brother Bill.

George Murcell was rehired from the cast of *Crossroads to Crime*, his Professor Rudolph Popkiss given a warm, grandfatherly German accent. In the post-war era it was quite common to see German experts in aviation and rocketry, as many were recruited for American civil and military organisations after the liberation of Germany. Murcell also created the voice of *Supercar*'s recurring villain, Masterspy, using a heavy eastern-European accent, which fitted perfectly with the huge, menacing figure represented by the puppet character.

Sylvia Thamm (who had become Sylvia Anderson too late for her change of status to be reflected in the first season credits) was the source of any female voice used in the series and also of the *Supercar* team's boy mascot, Jimmy Gibson. All the voices in the series were supplied by these four, each proving adept at recreating a wide array of accents.

Gerry Anderson took the role of producer for the increasingly busy AP Films operation, but did direct the pilot episode of *Supercar*, known as 'Rescue', although there is no onscreen title. To save money creating an optical for the end credits that would only be used in that episode, David Elliott (one of the regular roster of directors on the series) was given the credit instead.

The rest of the episodes on *Supercar*'s first series were directed by Elliott, Alan Pattillo, and Desmond Saunders, who joined the team of directors from episode twelve; his first assignment was the Woodhouse brothers' script 'Ice-Fall'. The pressured environment of *Supercar*, trying to create miniature miracles on a tiny budget, would hardly have been a new experience for Saunders. Although this was his first directorial work, he had come from the low-budget B-movie production line of the Danziger Brothers' New Elstree studios. Although Desmond Saunders did not return for *Fireball XL5*, he was to be one of the main directors on future Supermarionation series, becoming supervising director by the time of *Captain Scarlet and the Mysterons*.

John Read, naturally, returned as director of photography, with his main camera operator being Leeds-born Julien Lugrin, along with an uncredited Kumar Soni, returning from similar duties on *Four Feather Falls*. Lugrin would remain as camera operator for *Stingray* before being promoted to lighting cameraman for *Thunderbirds* and each subsequent Supermarionation series until *The Secret Service*.

Gordon Davie was editor on *Supercar* for the first eight episodes, after which he alternated episodes with Bill Harris. Davie had been with AP Films ever since *The Adventures of Twizzle* as an uncredited assistant editor, including the company's emergency dubbing work on *Further up the Creek*. He remained with AP as editor on *Fireball XL5* before leaving for a major film project—this was an assistant editor role on Carl Foreman's war movie *The Victors* (1963). Bill Harris would only stay on as editor for *Supercar*'s first series, before being promoted to direct episodes of the show's second series and of AP Films' follow-up, *Fireball XL5*.

Archie Ludski was on board as sound editor on *Supercar*'s early episodes. Born Arnold Adolph Ludski, he was a highly experienced sound editor whom Gerry would have known from his days at Gainsborough. Ludski was joined from episode ten by John Peverill, the pair alternating episodes until episode eighteen, at which point Peverill took over completely, save for a return by Ludski for episode twenty-three. John Peverill stayed with AP Films/Century 21 for the remainder of the company's life.

The *Four Feather Falls* puppetry team of Christine Glanville, Mary Turner, and Roger Woodburn were joined by Eddie Hunter (who remained as a puppet designer, maker, and operator on *Fireball XL5*, as well as being credited for 'Puppet Properties' on *Thunderbirds*' pilot episode 'Trapped in the Sky') and Yvonne Cutler, later to become Yvonne Hunter. A second puppet unit also operated with Cecil 'Buster' Stavordale returning from *Torchy the Battery Boy*, while his wife Madge worked on the puppet wardrobe department.

Music was, naturally, provided by Barry Gray, but now he was working in a completely different style to anything he had previously worked on. *Supercar* was basically a dramatic series, requiring a lot of orchestral suspense and action cues, as opposed to the mixture of Western songs and other music he had provided for *Four Feather Falls*.

However, there was one song that was sung by Mike Sammes—this was the theme tune for the series. Sammes was a vocal session group arranger and singer who worked very extensively (although he was largely uncredited) across a range of media with his vocal harmony group The Mike Sammes Singers. Formed in 1957, this group performed on a huge array of advertising jingles through the '60s and '70s, as well as appearing on many hit records and recording their own albums and singles. The Mike Sammes Singers were employed three times on Anderson productions, providing a re-recorded vocal for the *Supercar* theme music used for the show's second series, plus singing on the themes for *Stingray* and *The Secret Service*.

Barry Gray's *Supercar* score is an interesting one to listen to. His style of composition is still developing, as is the use of music in the series. Music in *Supercar* is used more sparingly than it would be in other series, by which time a method of underlining particularly important or dramatic events with orchestral 'stings' was developed; this was improved over the years and through the different series. Gray's arrangements are in a higher key than he tended to use in later series. One of Barry Gray's great abilities as an arranger was to make a relatively small orchestra sound huge and impressive. One of the main ways in which he did this was by utilising the brass section, giving them low notes to play. In *Supercar* the main sound is of strings and woodwind—the signature Gray sound was yet to be arrived at.

Not all of the music used in *Supercar* was by Gray, though. To pad out the available compositions composed specifically for the series, library music was also used, which was composed by Edwin Astley. As well as composing for music libraries (and, incidentally, the music for *Devil Girl from Mars*, which Gerry Anderson had been sound editor on back in 1953), Astley was one of the main composers of music for ITC's live-action adventure series. As the Anderson series became more numerous, Barry Gray was able to develop a library of his own compositions, which could be used when necessary, thus *Space: 1999* was to feature music dating as far back as *Supercar*.

Who actually thought of the idea that became *Supercar* has been the subject of some disagreement among the published accounts of those concerned. The credits to the series state that the series is 'from an original idea by Gerry Anderson and Reg Hill', and Gerry Anderson's official biography states that the idea for *Supercar* was developed while *Four Feather Falls* was still in production. Sylvia Anderson, however, states in her biography that AP Films had no projects in development when it became clear that Granada were not about to order a new series of *Four Feather Falls*. She claims *Supercar* was based on a series of children's stories she had submitted to Collins publishers.

What is known, though, is that significant contributions to the series format were made by Martin and Hugh Woodhouse. Hugh was a comedy writer who had co-written the films *Nearly a Nasty Accident* (1961), starring Jimmy Edwards and *Torchy the Battery Boy* and *Four Feather Falls'* voice artist Kenneth Connor, and *Dentist on the Job* (1961), again featuring Connor, now paired with popular comedian Bob Monkhouse who would later contribute voices to the film *Thunderbirds Are Go*.

Faced with the mammoth task of writing twenty-two scripts for *Supercar*, Hugh called upon his older brother Martin, who had written two episodes of *Four Feather Falls*. To the basic format of *Supercar*, its creator Professor Popkiss, and pilot Mike Mercury, the Woodhouse's added a character called Dr Horatio Beaker that had been created by Hugh for a series proposal called *Beaker's Bureau*, which was rejected by the BBC. *Supercar* launched Martin Woodhouse as a writer, and he went on to write for series such as *Emergency-Ward 10*, *The Man in Room 17*, *Doctor Finlay's Casebook*, and seven episodes of *The Avengers*.

Supercar proved very successful, both on the ITV network—although unlike *Four Feather Falls*, the episodes were screened at different times across Britain—and in America. Although the series had not been picked up by any of the national television networks, it sold well in syndication and was very widely seen. The first American merchandising for an AP Films series was produced, including a comic published by Gold Key in 1962, which ran for four issues in 1962 and '63.

The series was also seen by British comic fans as, like *Four Feather Falls*, TV Comic licensed the show for a long-running strip that ran from March 1961 until September 1964. It remained one of the most popular strips on the comic for its entire run, and only stopped because publisher Polystyle had its licence to publish its *Supercar* and *Fireball XL5* strips withdrawn as City Magazines wanted them for its upcoming new title *TV Century 21*.

Supercar was first screened in the UK at 5.40 p.m. on Saturday 29 January 1961, a change from the midweek, after-school slots awarded to *The Adventures of Twizzle*, *Torchy the Battery Boy*, and *Four Feather Falls*. The reason behind the weekend screenings of the series, and the next two Supermarionation shows, was to do with ATV's commissioning of the series, internal ITV politics, and access to the valuable London market. From its inception in 1954 until the major change in the network's contracts in 1968, ITV's London service was split between Associated-Rediffusion (rebranded Rediffusion London in 1964) during the week and ATV London at weekends. The managements of the two companies did not get on well, and would often refuse to screen each other's most popular series. In short, if ATV did not grant *Supercar* an advantageous slot while it was broadcasting to London, there would have been a very good chance that it would not be seen at all in Britain's largest commercial television market.

Lew Grade ordered a second batch of thirteen episodes, which featured some personnel and on-screen changes from the first season. Besides the new recording of the theme song, given a noticeable bounce via the new vocal by The Mike Sammes Singers, the episodes came from a new writing team: Gerry and Sylvia Anderson.

The name Supermarionation for the puppet processes being used by AP Films was used in *Supercar*'s sales literature for the first series, but was first credited on-screen for the second series episodes. The name was possibly inspired by Dynamation, one of the names given to Ray Harryhausen's blend of stop-motion animation and live action appearing together on the screen in films such as *Jason and the Argonauts* (1963) and *The First Men in the Moon* (1964).

In the art department, Reg Hill was now billed as art supervisor, while Bob Bell's fast-developing skills were recognised with a promotion to art director. Bill Harris left the editors suite in order to direct episodes, remaining as a director on the following year's *Fireball XL5*. David Elliott stepped back from the director's chair in order to act as production supervisor.

Derek Meddings finally joined the AP Films staff on a permanent basis from Les Bowie's company, *Supercar*'s extensive model work finally proving too much for Meddings' previous activities moonlighting for AP. He also gained an assistant, in the form of Brian Johncock, who also came from Bowie's Anglo-Scottish company. He had worked with Bowie on films such as *Quatermass 2* (1957), and would work with him again in the period between production on *Supercar* and *Fireball XL5* on Hammer's *Kiss of the Vampire* (1963) along with Ian Scoones, who also ended up working for AP Films.

The larger budget and expanding ambitions of the production allowed for the recruitment of extra personnel. John Read remained as director of photography, but gained the services of Ian Struthers as lighting cameraman—these two titles being interchangeable in normal filmmaking parlance. The photographic department also gained a new camera operator; Julien Lugrin now alternated episodes with the highly experienced Geoff Meldrum, who had started out in the industry as a 'focus puller' on 1949's *The Third Man*.

Alan Perry joined the AP team on *Supercar* as a 'clapper loader'—an assistant to the director of photography who loads the raw film stock into the camera and operates the clapperboard. Perry had previously worked at Anglo-Scottish alongside Derek Meddings. He moved on to Sapphire Films' 1955–60 ITC series *The Adventures of Robin Hood*, where the production secretary was Sylvia Thamm, moonlighting from AP Films during the company's thin period of work prior to Lew Grade agreeing to finance *Supercar*. Sylvia recommended that Perry interview for a job on the *Supercar* crew, and he was accepted onto the team as a clapper loader. Perry remained with the Andersons up until the end of production on *UFO* in 1970, eventually directing both puppets and live actors.

The second series episodes were edited by Gordon Davie, remaining from the first series, and John Kelly—the two alternating episodes. Kelly would not remain in the editing suite for long, graduating himself to directing episodes of *Fireball XL5* and *Stingray*. These two were joined by an uncredited assistant editor who was new to AP Films. David Lane would become one of the most important figures in the Anderson creative team, staying with Gerry Anderson right to the end of *Space: 1999* and beyond, working on some of his unrealised 1970s movie projects and returning in the 2000s for *New Captain Scarlet*.

Lane had been working as an assistant editor on the 1961 Rank-ITC co-production *Ghost Squad*, which was unexpectedly cancelled after only thirteen episodes. His former employers arranged for an interview with Gerry Anderson, who needed a first assistant editor for the second series of *Supercar*. David Lane passed the interview successfully, and a long working relationship was born. So successful was Lane that when the crew was being assembled for *Fireball XL5*, Gerry called Lane (who was back working for Hammer Films at this point) to ask him to become one of the editors (along with Gordon Davie and Eric Pask) on *Fireball XL5*.

With George Murcell unavailable for the voice recording for the second series of *Supercar*, actor Cyril Shaps was brought in to perform the roles of Masterspy and Professor Popkiss. Born in London in 1923 of Polish ancestry, Shaps had been a voice artist from the age of twelve, performing in radio advertisements for Radio Lyon and Radio Luxembourg—stations in Europe beaming English language commercial programming to Britain. After the war, during which he lectured on Art and Literature for the Royal Army Education Corps, Shaps won a scholarship to RADA. Generally seen in small roles, he was a character actor *par excellence*. Although Cyril Shaps' stock in trade tended to be grandfathers and Rabbis, his acting range was enormous, so much so that the change in voice artist went completely unnoticed by even the most attentive of viewers.

Another major change that viewers would not have noticed was the purchase of AP Films by Lew Grade's ITC. This represented the ultimate statement of confidence by Grade in the potential AP Films had to make products that could be widely and profitably exported, particularly to the American market that ITC was especially keen to sell programmes to. AP Films made some of the most American-looking shows of any company ITC was associated with. There was nothing about *Four Feather Falls* or *Supercar* that suggested that these programmes were made in England. AP Films was making Americana in miniature.

While AP Films represented a potentially fruitful investment for Lew Grade's company, what was the attraction of the deal to Gerry Anderson and his board of directors? Although the financial aspects of the deal would undoubtedly have been attractive, there were other considerations; joining the ITC production empire meant getting Grade's total support for AP Films' series. This had obvious advantages both with getting the shows seen on the regional and often fractious ITV network. It also assured access to ITC's established export network and contacts with both the American television networks and the syndication market.

On the other hand, it was advisable not to cross such a powerful figure as Grade. His opposition could prevent AP Films' series being shown during the weekends in London or in the large Midlands market on weekdays. The deal worked for both parties, and Gerry Anderson worked with Lew Grade for the next fifteen years.

Supercar certainly proved popular, being widely seen in the US—if not on one of the networks, at least in syndication. In Britain, the series was seen around the ITV regions from January 1961 until New Year's Eve 1968, when Scottish Television ended a repeat run. Granada Television, which by this time served the north-west of England seven days a week, ran the series one last time in a sporadic run from January 1971 to July 1973. From then on *Supercar* was seen no more, at least until the era of the VCR.

Supercar remains one of the most fascinating and charming of the Supermarionation series. In some ways this is because there were no ground-rules as to what the series had to be, so it could develop organically in ways that might not have been intended at the outset. The series clearly wants to be an action series based around its high-tech vehicle, something of a cross between a Spitfire and a family saloon, seen in the opening credits climbing, diving, and performing aerobatics, then diving into the sea and emerging again at high speed.

This original concept is married to the Woodhouse's *Beaker's Bureau* idea, and it is clear that Dr Horatio Beaker is the most fully realised character at the start of the series, and many early episodes are built around him. It is interesting to compare the first two episodes of the series, 'Rescue' (the first episode has no onscreen title, but is known by this name in all existing paperwork) and 'Amazonian Adventure'. Episode one spends a long time introducing Supercar and the cast of characters, test pilot Mike Mercury eventually convincing Professor Popkiss and Dr Beaker to let him use the craft to rescue the stranded Jimmy and Bob Gibson.

Supercar does not have a set purpose—it is a revolutionary test vehicle being developed in secret by the team at Black Rock Laboratory, but with no apparent purpose and with no client. It is not being made for the military, although they would no doubt love to get their hands on it as it is far more advanced than anything they have—the series was set in the then-present day of 1960 to 1962.

By the time of the second episode, Beaker is the star of the show. Mitch the Monkey is ill with a tropical disease, so Beaker and Mercury go to the Amazon rainforest to find the only plant that can cure him. There they are captured by a tribe of head-hunters, the disconcerting sight of a set of shrunken decapitated heads must have been unusual in a children's programme even in 1961. What comes across clearly is how much the Woodhouse brothers love writing for Beaker. His dialogue, filled with technical terminology and what would become the show's catchphrases ('satisfactory—most satisfactory' and 'well, now who's a fool?') is genuinely hilarious, as is his interplay with Mike Mercury, voice artists David Graham and Graydon Gould playing the comedic aspects for all they are worth. Gould, faced with the potentially thankless task of being *Supercar*'s straight man, injects a surprising amount of ironic humour into his role and tends not to get the credit he deserves.

We see Beaker change from being unwilling to risk Supercar on unnecessary or frivolous missions to becoming a rather keen adventurer. By the time of episode seven, 'Grounded', in which Mike proposes traveling along the ground at high speed in a damaged Supercar, Beaker's response is very revealing: 'Lunatic! Absolutely lunatic! But rather fun.' He even gains a cousin, Felicity Farnsworth, and an amusing running gag in which we see Beaker conducting what we think are highly dangerous scientific experiments, then discover he's actually cooking.

Although Beaker gains the most screen time and most of the best dialogue, what is created in *Supercar* is a sense of family—interestingly, more so than in *Thunderbirds*, in which the main characters actually are family. Popkiss and Beaker are the mother and father of the Black Rock Laboratory team: it becomes apparent as the series progresses that Popkiss handles most of the domestic chores such as cooking and often stays home while Beaker gallivants around in Supercar. Beaker, meanwhile, is so totally wrapped up in his incredibly varied scientific work (he's a true polymath) that he gets lost in his workaholic world of research. Mike Mercury acts as a surrogate son for the pair, and as a heroic big brother figure for Jimmy Gibson, who spends all his time with this group of adults, despite the fact he has a pretty heroic big brother of his own, Bob Gibson.

Despite the lack of a fixed purpose for *Supercar* and the characters in the series format, the series has the confidence to introduce a regular pair of villains, but not feature them in every episode. Masterspy and Zarin are used relatively sparingly, giving their appearances more impact. They seem to be broadly based on the actors Sydney Greenstreet and Peter Lorre, who were paired in a series of films by Warner Brothers after their success in the 1941 film *The Maltese Falcon*, the plot of which is echoed in Masterspy and Zarin's first episode, 'The Talisman of Sargon'. This would not be the first time Peter Lorre was referenced in an AP Films production, Robert Easton producing a deadly accurate impression of the actor's distinctive voice for the character of Agent X20 in *Stingray*.

Supercar's humour is occasionally of a type that programme-makers would avoid today. Aside from the occasional racial stereotype, such as the head-hunting South American Tuaga tribe in 'Amazon Adventure', there are a few plot devices that would certainly attract the attention of broadcasting standards regulators today. The aforementioned 'Amazon Adventure' presents us with the sight of decapitated heads, while other episodes show us unhealthy high-jinks such as Mitch the Monkey inside a working washing machine filling with suds, and Mike Mercury electrocuting Dr Beaker on Supercar's hull for fun.

The second series of *Supercar*, which was written by Gerry and Sylvia Anderson, has a few changes of emphasis. The Andersons tended to give Professor Popkiss more to do; their first series script 'Flight of Fancy' gave him both a sister, Heidi, and a first name, Rudolph. Heidi returns during the second series in the bizarrely self-referential episode 'Precious Cargo', in which the Popkiss' wine supplier in France turns out to be a monstrous tyrant, oppressing his young ward Zizi, an overworked Cinderella figure. She dreams of being rescued by Supercar and its team, which she had read about in a comic strip—and here we were thinking that Supercar was absolutely top secret. The Anderson's scripts tended towards the odd or experimental: in a highly unusual act for its day of 'breaking the fourth wall', the episode 'Transatlantic Cable' sees Popkiss talking directly to the audience, while the final episode, 'King Kool', is the oddest of all, featuring a gorilla who is a star jazz drummer.

Key Episode

Episode 23: 'The Lost City'
Written by Gerry and Sylvia Anderson
Directed by Alan Pattillo
First UK broadcast Saturday 17 June 1961 (ATV London)

Mike, Beaker, Jimmy, and Mitch set off in Supercar on an expedition to the South Pole, but are drawn off-course into a crash-dive by an unknown force. Supercar lands in the Amazon jungle, in the ruins of an ancient city. Here they discover the secret base of Professor Watkins, who disappeared from London ten years previously and was thought to be dead. With the help of his robot servants, he has been plotting to aim a nuclear missile at Washington, D.C.

With *Four Feather Falls*, the AP Films team mastered the art of concise storytelling—the not inconsiderable skill of telling a satisfying tale in fifteen minutes flat, including opening and closing credits. With *Supercar* a new approach had to be found to fill the extra screen time required for a twenty-five-minute series. Early episodes come across today as being technically accomplished, but a little slow-paced. Alan Fennell was called in with a view to writing for a projected third series of *Supercar*, which was ultimately abandoned. His critique of the episodes that he was shown was that the scripts were 'too technical'. Some first season scripts certainly fall into the trap of emphasising the testing of the then-new *Supercar* over telling a story.

'The Lost City', produced towards the end of the first *Supercar* productions block—episode twenty-three of twenty-six—took a different approach. Gerry and Sylvia Anderson's script pares the story down to its absolute basics, stripping out all extraneous detail and building the story around several action climaxes. Although this was not ultimately to be the model for *Supercar*'s second block of episodes, 'The Lost City' can be seen to have had an impact that reached much farther. The pattern was set here for the basic episode structure of AP Films' next two series, *Fireball XL5* and *Stingray*.

The episode even looks somewhat different from most *Supercar* stories, with Mike Mercury looking far more like he's wearing a uniform than normal, with peaked hat and dark glasses. This was the image of Mercury most often seen in merchandising for the series, whereas we'd generally seen him on-screen either hatless or in a very unflattering helmet.

The episode starts with what in today's jargon we'd call a 'cold opening', pitching us straight into the action, with Supercar suddenly forced into a crash dive. This episode continues in this manner; most previous stories built their plot up slowly to an action climax, but 'The Lost City' gives us peril right from the first sequence. Scenes then follow on from one another with the pacing of a '30s movie serial, action taking precedence over explanation.

The structure of the story works around three key action scenes:

1. Supercar being thrown off course into a crash dive.
2. One of Professor Watkins' robots menaces Jimmy, who is alone in Supercar.
3. Supercar chases Watkins' atomic missile.

Other scenes exist merely to propel the characters to the next situation as quickly as possible. *Fireball XL5* and *Stingray* also tended to be structured in three acts—they are hardly unique series in working this way. Writers in the era seem to have worked out that three is the optimum number of dramatic situations that can be fitted into a twenty-five-minute episode.

It works like this:

1. Our heroes discover a threat from an outside source. In 'The Lost City' it is Professor Watkins in the Amazon, in *Fireball XL5* it could be Planet 46's Subterrains, or in *Stingray* the Altanteans from 'The Invaders'. The fact that all three examples involve outsiders or alien races is a handy storytelling shorthand—their motive is, at heart, invasion.
2. One or more of our heroes are captured, enabling the plot to progress to the final stage, as our heroes escape from captivity and defeat this week's threat.

In *Fireball* and *Stingray*, as a general rule, the villains are handed over to the judicial system. The *Supercar* regular cast are a group of independent explorers and scientists and in 'The Lost City' the justice meted out to Watkins is both poetic and rough. In the context of *Supercar*, Waktins' fate of being killed by his own missile might seem rather harsh. It might be argued, though, that Masterspy's average scheme is on a fairly small scale, with the ultimate object of making a bit of spare cash. Watkins, on the other hand, was going to kill millions of people by blowing up Washington, D.C., for no readily apparent reason. His fate is suitably apocalyptic—we last see him shaking with fear as he awaits death. Serves him right.

'The Lost City' is a rare *Supercar* episode that actually includes SF elements beyond the appearance of the flying car itself. Professor Watkins' underground lair is impressively realised, with the air of the base of a James Bond villain, some two years before the first Bond movie was released. The major SF aspect to the story, though, is the robot army that runs the base. By modern standards these are somewhat clunky and comedic-looking, not helped by the usual problems faced by the puppeteers in making the marionettes walk convincingly. It is interesting to note that when the same robot puppets were reused in the *Fireball XL5* story 'The Granatoid Tanks', they stayed firmly behind the controls of their armoured vehicles and were not seen to walk.

'The Lost City' was not to be the template for future *Supercar* stories. Instead of pacy thrills, the series seemed to choose a more whimsical and self-referential route; for example, Beaker could often be heard singing the show's theme song, which he could never remember the words to. Even this is tried out in 'The Lost City', with Beaker humming a section of the show's incidental music. What this episode demonstrates is the ability of AP Films to experiment within an established format with a view to improving the current show and developing the next one. By the time the last first-run *Supercar* episode was screened in April 1962, the company was already in production on *Fireball XL5*, having proved here that they could handle the pace and style needed to move Supermarionation on to the next level.

9

Lew Grade

Lew Grade was the great showman of ITV, making him the perfect figure to see the commercial possibilities of Supermarionation. The attitudes of British broadcasting at the time meant that his abilities and the advantages of having someone like this within British entertainment were often looked down upon. Today, Grade is quite properly regarded as a legendary figure in the history of post-war British entertainment.

Grade was born on Christmas Day 1906 in Tokmak, Ukraine, as Lovat Winogradsky. His parents, Isaak and Olga, took the family to England in 1912 to escape the persecution often visited on Jewish communities at the time. The young Lovat found his name unilaterally changed to Louis by immigration officials. He was a natural scholar and a hard worker, blessed with a photographic memory and a flair for mathematics.

At the age of fifteen, Louis joined the clothing industry, learning the trade quickly and soon setting up his own company. Despite working long hours he maintained a very active social life; he loved to dance, so much so that he became a champion Charleston dancer. This gave him the impetus to become a professional dancer, going under the name Lew Grad, though a newspaper misspelling caused him to change this to Lew Grade.

Lew toured Europe for the next five years, at the same time recommending promising acts to his agent friend Joe Collins, father of Joan and Jackie Collins. Tiring of the physical demands of dancing, he decided to go into the talent agency business himself, and he and Joe Collins formed a partnership. His two brothers, Leslie Grade and Bernard Delfont, were also very successful theatrical agents, and Lew broke up with Collins in 1943 to run Leslie's agency when the latter was called up for military service.

When Leslie returned from war service in 1945, he and Lew formed a formal partnership, and the Lew and Leslie Grade Agency became transatlantic, booking major American acts for UK appearances. His extensive contacts put Lew Grade in a powerful position to put together a consortium to bid for an ITV contact when commercial television was being formed in 1954. The resulting bidder, the Independent Television Corporation, included major cinema owners and theatrical impresarios. Surprisingly, the consortium was so high-powered that the regulatory authority deciding the merits of the various bids, the Independent Television Authority (ITA), feared that an entertainment monopoly was being created.

Instead, ITC was advised to become a maker of programming to the ITV companies. With half a million pounds in the bank and nothing to spend it on, Lew Grade swung into action, funding British-based American producer Hannah Weinstein's *The Adventures of Robin Hood*, which became an immediate smash hit and proved very successful also in the US.

Ironically, the ITA's attempts to avoid an entertainments monopoly backfired, leaving ITC in an even stronger position than they would have been had they been granted a broadcasting licence in the first place. One of the franchise winners, the Associated Broadcasting Development Group, formed by the Norman Collins/Sir Robert Renwick/C. O. Stanley consortium, found that their funding arrangements had collapsed. ITC offered a fifty-fifty merger, which the ITA had little choice to accept, lest they find themselves in the highly embarrassing position of having one of its main companies implode before the new network even began broadcasting. Lew Grade and ITC were now in the highly advantageous position of being both a producer of filmed programming and controlling the ITV contact to broadcast to the English Midlands during the week, plus the prime contract to broadcast to London during the weekends. The new company was to be called ABC—the Associated Broadcasting Company.

One of the other consortiums granted an ITV broadcasting licence also found itself in dire financial straits; the Kemsley-Winnick group clearly did not have the funds to continue, and their licence was withdrawn. One of the losing bidders, the Associated British Picture Corporation, reluctantly agreed to take over the contract to broadcast to the English Midlands and North of England during the weekend. ABPC was a major film producer, part owned by Warner Brothers and owning Elstree Studios. It also owned one of Britain's largest national cinema chains, ABC, and objected to another ITV broadcaster operating under this name. This resulted in a legal battle with the Grade consortium, which had to change its name to Associated Television, better known as ATV.

The worldwide success of *The Adventures of Robin Hood* was an indicator of what was to come for ITC. The company launched a series of costume adventure series, aimed at a younger audience, including *The Scarlet Pimpernel* (1955) and *The Buccaneers* (1956). Modern day adventure series followed, keeping the half-hour format, including *The Four Just Men* (1959) and *Danger Man* (1960) the latter starring Patrick McGoohan. Another American hit series did not come until *Fireball XL5*, which was picked up by the NBC network and screened coast-to-coast. Other live-action hits followed, with *The Saint*, initially rejected by the networks, becoming a big hit in syndication. The series was eventually bought by NBC and upgraded from monochrome to colour, running from 1962 to '69. The spy series *Danger Man*, retooled as a gadget-filled one-hour series, was also a big American hit for ITC from 1964 to '66, where it was known as *Secret Agent* to differentiate it from the half-hour version.

Always at the heart of this success was Lew Grade. He had an eye for talent and let them get on with what they did best, with minimal interference from him. Once the shows were produced, Grade used his abilities, not only as a showman, but as a world-class salesman, to ensure that his company's products were seen throughout the world. He was acknowledged for his efforts in 1969, when he was knighted, becoming Sir Lew Grade. In 1976 he was honoured once again, becoming a life peer, Lord Grade of Elstree.

By this time, Lord Grade's time at ITV was coming to an end, as he was reaching the company's mandatory retirement age of seventy. Still full of ideas and energy, ITC began to concentrate on film production, which took vital funds away from its television series and was partially responsible for the cancellations of *Space: 1999* in 1977 and *Return of the Saint* in 1979. A series of expensive feature films that failed to make their money back, particularly *Can't Stop the Music* and *Raise the Titanic* in 1980, led to Lord Grade selling his stake in ITC. The new owners asset-stripped the company, ending its long history of television production. Grade, however, remained an active film and television producer virtually until his death on 14 December 1998 at the age of ninety-one.

10

Fireball XL5

'*I wish I was a spaceman, the fastest guy alive.*'

Produced by Gerry Anderson
Created by Gerry and Sylvia Anderson
Music composed, arranged, and conducted by Barry Gray
Title music arranged by Charles Blackwell, vocal work by Don Spencer
An APF Television Production.
Made in association with ATV
An ITC World Wide Distribution
30 × twenty-five-minute episodes
First broadcast Sunday 28 October 1962 (ATV London)

Steve Zodiac and the crew of the World Space Patrol craft Fireball XL5 travel
the universe to protect Earth and keep the cosmos safe from hostile races.

Supercar was an established hit on both sides of the Atlantic, but even as the
last thirteen episodes of the extended episode commission were being filmed,
Lew Grade was asking for new ideas from Gerry Anderson. What emerged was
a proposal that meant expanding the SF elements of *Supercar* to a full-blown
space opera, set 1,000 years into the future. Its name was Century 21.
  Some of the details of the proposal were altered in the adaptation of the idea
to its final screen form; for a start, it was eventually established that the action
took place a mere 100 years from the 1962 in which the series was being made.
  The series was set in a future in which mankind was colonising other
planets, and encountering alien races both friendly and hostile. For protection,
the World Space Patrol had been formed, with a fleet of spaceships able to

travel quickly from planet to planet in order to keep the peace. The new show was to have three heroes—the handsome and brave captain of the ship Steve Zodiac, the beautiful and resourceful Doctor of Space Medicine Venus, and the science expert Professor Matthew Matic. They were joined on their adventures by Robert the Robot, a Perspex see-through robot who acted as the ship's autopilot, and Zoony, Venus's pet lazoon introduced in the show's fourth episode, 'Space Magnet'.

The actual name of the ship our heroes would travel round the universe in was up for debate at this point, as was the name of the series itself. Century 21 was eventually dropped as the series name during pre-production for the initial name of the World Space Patrol craft, *Nova X 100*. Thankfully, inspiration struck after someone saw a tin of Castrol XL engine oil, and the final name of both spaceship and series was born—*Fireball XL5*.

With one of the aims of *Supercar* being to cut down on the number of scenes of characters walking, *Fireball XL5* took the idea a stage further by giving the characters Jetmobiles to get around on when they had to travel shorter distances. These were a SF update on the motor scooters that had achieved wide popularity among teenagers in '50s and '60s Europe. They proved such a good way of getting characters from place to place over medium distances that the idea was reused in the next two Supermarionation series, *Stingray* and *Thunderbirds*.

The main form of transport for our heroes was, of course, Fireball XL5 itself, which in contrast to the relatively compact Supercar was designed to look huge and impressive. Like Supercar, it was designed by Reg Hill with the largest, 7-foot-long version being made by Bill James. Described as being over 300 feet long, Fireball would occasionally land on planets, but more often the front end of the ship would detach as a scout craft—this was named Fireball Junior.

The opening credits sequence to each episode laid down a statement of intent to the audience for what they were about to see. The deep, thunderous tones of Barry Gray's music introduces a redesigned company logo announcing that this is 'An APF Television Production Filmed in Supermarionation'. Although this term for the company's puppet processes had been introduced in later episodes of *Supercar*, far more of a feature is made of it here. Now Supermarionation had its own logo, echoing the famous one designed by 20th Century Fox for its Cinemascope anamorphic widescreen process.

Copyrighted special production processes such as Cinemascope and Cinerama, with their own logos, were a film industry tactic to combat the growing popularity of television. It is somewhat ironic and amusing therefore to see a television company in the early 1960s using exactly the same strategy to make its productions stand out from the crowd. Each episode of *Fireball XL5* aimed to be a miniature SF film, and it had an opening sequence to match.

The use of music and logos helped to create a real sense of anticipation as Steve and Venus set off on their Jetmobiles to enter Fireball. This part of the opening sequence is ingeniously done; as we see them approach the ship, suddenly they look tiny against the vastness of Fireball, which is shown in sections, filling the television screen and shot from below to loom over the camera. As the pair arrive in the ship the music ends for now, replaced by the sound of the ship's roaring engines as Fireball sets of along its launch rail, given extra impetus by a rocket sled in a very clever and realistic launch procedure.

Barry Gray's opening theme music is a bravura example of having ones cake and eating it, presenting a two part theme that is at first accomplished in the traditional Hollywood orchestral style, then presents a second movement that is much more fast-paced and uses more 'SF' instrumentation. The music opens with a deep, thunderous flourish from the orchestra's brass section, somewhat reminiscent of Max Steiner's score for *King Kong* (1933) or even Akira Ifukune's mighty theme from the 1954 Japanese film *Godzilla*—films with huge, threatening protagonists. As Fireball's engines prepare to spark into life, Gray's music builds to a huge crescendo, to be replaced by the mighty roar of the engines as the ship sets off on its rocket sled. As Fireball sets off into space, the music sets off on an entirely different track; pacier and using Barry Gray's favoured electronic instrument, the ondes Martenot.

In a way, the music reflects the twin aims of the series, of being a large-scale adventure series (albeit in miniature), and also a lighter, fun show for all the family. In contrast, the end theme goes all-out for fun, and in the process broke Supermarionation out of its youthful fan base and into the wider public consciousness.

'Fireball', written by Barry Gray, is a terrific song with a lyric that acts as a metanarrative for the series in interesting ways, taking the point of view of the young viewers of *Fireball XL5* who wished that they really were handsome adventurers zooming around the universe—the fastest guy alive with a heart like a fireball. Australian singer Don Spencer was chosen to perform the song, which was a much more conventional pop number than *Supercar*'s theme.

The song has a noticeably lighter touch to its orchestral pop sound than some of Barry Gray's other efforts in this area (though his Adam Faith pastiche 'I've Got Something to Shout About' featured in the *Stingray* episode 'Titan Goes Pop' is good fun). One reason for this was the employment of arranger Charles Blackwell to work on the song. Blackwell, aged only twenty-two at the time, was making a name for himself as a top pop arranger, starting his work with the legendary producers Joe Meek and Robert Stigwood. Being able to attract an in-demand talent such as Blackwell and his production partner Stigwood for the end theme of a children's television series demonstrates that AP Films were suddenly operating in a much bigger league.

'Fireball' proved a popular single, staying in the charts for eleven weeks and peaking at No. 32. This was quite an achievement, as the BBC, whose light programme still dominated music radio in Britain, usually steered clear of granting significant airplay to any records associated with advertising or commercial television.

Another audible change in *Fireball XL5* was the recruitment of some new voice artists to join the returning Sylvia Anderson and David Graham at the show's Sunday morning recording sessions. Taking place at GHW Gate Recording Theatre, near Borehamwood railway station, some 16 miles from AP Films' Slough studios, the actors would usually record the dialogue for three episodes at a time.

Steve Zodiac's voice was provided by Canadian actor Paul Maxwell. Born in 1921, Maxwell studied at Yale and became an actor while in America. He found television work in series including *Dragnet* and *Alfred Hitchcock Presents*, as well as cult horror movies *Blood of Dracula* (1957) and *How to Make a Monster* (1958). Maxwell, whose wife was Scottish, moved to England in the early 1960s and quickly became in demand on filmed television series such as *Danger Man* and *Ghost Squad*, which were always on the lookout for new North American performers. After *Fireball XL5* Maxwell provided the voice of Captain Paul Travers in the 1966 film *Thunderbirds Are Go*, and played Captain Ashton in the *Thunderbirds* episode 'Alias Mr Hackenbacker'. He also provided voices for *Captain Scarlet and the Mysterons*, and can be seen in person as Lt Jim Lewis in the *UFO* episode 'Subsmash'.

A second voice artist skilled in providing different accents was needed to join David Graham. This berth was filled by John Bluthal, who had arrived in the UK from Australia in 1959. He was originally born in Galicia, Poland, in 1928, his family moving to Australia in 1938 to escape the threat of the Nazis. Bluthal studied drama at the University of Melbourne, then acted on radio and in variety theatre. He moved to England in 1959 and quickly began working with the most prominent names in British comedy, including Sidney James and Eric Sykes. He established what was to be a long professional association with Spike Milligan, with whom he had appeared in the 1958 Australian television special *The Gladys Half Hour*. In a long career, John Bluthal is probably best known to audiences today as Frank Pickle in the popular 1990s BBC sitcom *The Vicar of Dibley*.

The final new voice artist introduced to the *Fireball XL5* cast was none other than Gerry Anderson himself, who provided the only puppet voice he would ever perform—Robert the Robot. Robert's very limited vocabulary was produced by passing Gerry's voice through a device invented to allow people who had had their larynx removed to communicate.

The recording sessions would, naturally enough, take place before filming began on the puppet stages for the episodes in question, since the recorded dialogue was needed so the puppets could perform their mouth movements. Five puppeteers were now used to operate the puppets—Christine Glanville, John Blundall, Mary Turner, and Eddie and Yvonne Hunter. A close-knit group, they would perform puppet productions between their work on the Supermarionation series under the name The Company of Five Productions.

The process of writing *Fireball XL5*'s thirty-nine episodes was carried out on a more regular basis for a dramatic series than had been *Supercar*, which was largely written by the Woodhouse brothers and the Andersons. For *Fireball XL5*, as with future shows, the Andersons stepped back from writing to a large extent, instead taking on the role of script supervisors. Gerry would largely take this responsibility, working with the team of three writers who provided all but the two stories provided by Gerry and Sylvia themselves. As it turned out, these would become some of the most illustrious writers to work on an Anderson series.

Alan Fennell first met Gerry Anderson when he was working for the children's publication *TV Comic*, which sent him to negotiate (successfully, as it transpired) for the rights to run a *Supercar* comic strip. The two men got along well and Fennell, already an experienced writer of comic strips, was drafted onto *Fireball XL5*'s writing team. Alan Fennell spent his entire career as a professional screenwriter working on Anderson productions, mainly because it was not his major interest. Despite being one of the main providers of scripts for *Fireball XL5*, *Stingray*, and *Thunderbirds*, his heart remained in publishing.

With his deep understanding of the Supermarionation series and background in comics, Fennell was a natural choice to edit City Magazines *TV Century 21* (later simply *TV21*). There he established the publication's unique style, mixing a semi-newspaper style with regular comic stories based largely on the Supermarionation shows. As well as his writing duties on *Stingray* and *Thunderbirds*, which coincided with his 1965–67 tenure on the comic, Fennell also wrote many of the *TV21* stories, including many for the *Stingray*, *Lady Penelope*, and *Thunderbirds* strips. After leaving *TV21* he retained some of his links to television writing, providing two scripts for Century 21's *UFO* and writing novelisations of the 1968–73 series *Freewheelers* and the film *Digby, The Biggest Dog in the World* (1973). Alan Fennell would return to the world of Gerry Anderson in the 1990s, publishing new Supermarionation-themed titles when there was an explosion of interest in the shows.

Anthony Marriott was an actor who had worked on the repertory stage and had been a member of the well-regarded BBC Repertory Company, as well as making a few small television appearances. He had written an episode of the ITC/Rank co-production *Ghost Squad* before providing eleven scripts for *Fireball XL5*—his only work for the Anderson series. Marriott's reputation, as well as his great success, rests on two productions. *Public Eye*, created by Marriott with Roger Marshall, was a long-running series about a down-at-heel, but honest private detective; it was made by ABC Television (subsequently Thames) between 1965 and 1975. His other success was with the even longer-running stage play he wrote with Alistair Foot—*No Sex Please, We're British*; this ran for a record-breaking 6,761 performances (more than double the previous record holder) on the West End stage.

Interestingly, the third member of *Fireball XL5*'s writing team had a similar background to Anthony Marriott. Dennis Spooner first submitted scripts to AP Films for *Supercar*, which remained unused when production ended on that series and *Fireball XL5* began. The Andersons were convinced of his abilities, and Spooner was a key writer on the next three Supermarionation shows. After forming a writing partnership with future scriptwriter Tony Williamson when the two were stationed together with the RAF during their National Service, Dennis Spooner became a comedy performer. Meeting with little success, he turned to writing, selling scripts to popular comedy actor Harry Worth. He also broke into dramatic writing, firstly with Granada Television's soap opera *Coronation Street* in 1960 and also Associated-Rediffusion's popular detective series *No Hiding Place*, which ran from 1959 to 1967.

He was still writing comedic scripts during this period, but made the decisive break to work exclusively in drama after *Thunderbirds* when he became story editor on *Doctor Who* on the later William Hartnell seasons. After this, Spooner wrote fourteen episodes of ITC's *The Baron*, then co-created *Man in a Suitcase* with Richard Harris, after which he formed a partnership with Monty Berman to create other filmed adventure series for ITC. This made Dennis Spooner a key figure in late '60s and '70s filmed adventure series; for Lew Grade, Spooner and Berman made *The Champions* (1968), *Department S* (1969), *Randall and Hopkirk (Deceased)* (1969), *Jason King* (1971), and The *Adventurer* (1972). When the Spooner and Berman run of series came to an end, he even wrote for the Andersons again, supplying scripts for *UFO* and *The Protectors*, plus linking scenes for the *Space: 1999* compilation film *Alien Attack* (1976).

With a large number of episodes to produce to meet a projected October 1962 airdate, episodes were filmed in pairs, which meant that two directors of photography were needed, John Read alternating episodes with Ian Struthers. On *Supercar*, Struthers was listed as lighting cameraman, while Read was director of photography—in normal filmmaking parlance, the two terms are interchangeable.

The editorial department was now beefed up to three editors, who worked on alternate episodes in order to cut the footage produced at the Ipswich Road studios into their own finished form. Theses editors were Gordon Davie, Eric Pask, and David Lane, the latter replacing Bill Harris who was now promoted to *Fireball XL5*'s team of directors.

Four directors were employed on *Fireball XL5*, Bill Harris alternating episodes with Alan Pattillo, David Elliott, and John Kelly. Each director would have been almost constantly in some stage of filming an episode—either in pre-production, shooting, or post-production, due to the highly efficient production schedule introduced by AP Films for *Fireball XL5*.

In order to have enough episodes ready for broadcasting on the projected airdates, a system was introduced so that three production units were always filming, with episodes produced in pairs. The Ipswich Road studios had two puppet stages working in tandem. Broadly speaking, one set contained the permanent sets that were seen in virtually every episode—such as the *Fireball XL5* cockpit—while the other contained sets that would be needed for a specific story. While work was taking place on the puppet sets, Derek Meddings was directing the model unit on a separate stage, working on scenes containing Fireball itself and other models. Directors not actively working on the puppet stage would either be preparing their work for the next episode to go onto the studio floor or in the editing suite with one of the three editors. In this way an incredibly efficient production line was established, allowing one episode per week to be shot and sent for editing.

Like the later *Star Trek*, it is useful to think of *Fireball XL5* in terms of it being a Western in disguise. *Star Trek* was sold to its network, NBC, as 'Wagon Train to the stars', invoking the almost legendary 1957–65 Western television series. *Fireball XL5*'s sales pitch mentions that Earth has grown overcrowded and humanity is spreading out to populate the rest of the universe. Although little is made of the crowded Earth idea in the series episodes, it does not take a great leap of imagination to link this idea to the migration west of American settlers in the nineteenth century. If we look at the series in these terms, it becomes immediately apparent why some of the alien races Steve Zodiac and co. encounter might not be too pleased when Fireball and its all-human crew arrive on their doorstep.

Steve Zodiac is the (very) square-jawed, tall, and brave hero, very much like a non-singing Tex Tucker with a space pilot's licence. It is interesting to note that when Steve is sent back in time to the American West by Professor Matic's time machine in the episode '1875', he immediately looks and feels right at home as the Sheriff.

The French-accented Venus is a welcome reminder that the crew are working for the World Space Patrol—it is good to have at least one non-American regular character. European characters were a common feature of the American West, and were often seen in the classic Hollywood Western movie, often as the saloon bar gal. For the most famous example of this character see Marlene Dietrich as Frenchy in 1939's *Destry Rides Again*. In the '60s, children's television was not quite ready for this type of character, so Venus, a Doctor of Space Medicine, gets to act in clearly delineated gender roles of the era in which the series was made. She gets to do all the cooking for the men of the ship, even if the meals are largely in the form of pills.

Professor Matthew Matic is the closest link of all *Fireball XL5* has to the Western genre, David Graham giving him a voice similar to that of Western character actor Gabby Hayes. This allows the series to pull off an early version of a trick that was repeated eleven years later with *Space: 1999*'s Victor Bergman—the most technically knowledgeable character is the most warm and human person on-screen.

While *Four Feather Falls* made itself accessible by being a miniature version of the Westerns that were filling the late '50s television schedules, *Fireball XL5* used the character types of the Western in order to add warmth and familiarity to a SF series being made at a time when there were not many space-set series on the air.

Fireball XL5 was first screened in the UK on Sunday 28 October 1962, six months after the final episode of *Supercar* was first seen by London viewers. The series was an immediate hit with British youngsters, and was seen regularly on repeat showings even into the 1970s, when British television had moved to colour broadcasting and most monochrome series had been banished from the airwaves. It was seen regularly in most ITV regions until 1972, and was used occasionally as filler for runs of two or three episodes in the Granada TV region as late as August 1974. Surprisingly, the series returned for a round of repeat screenings across almost the whole ITV network from January 1985, giving the series an afterlife far longer than any previous AP Films series.

However gratifying their success in Britain was, for ITC it was just the icing on a very profitable cake. Their attempt to make a thoroughly American-style series in Slough had paid off; the series allowed Lew Grade to achieve something neither he, nor any other British television executive had managed before—to sell a series to one of the American networks. NBC ran *Fireball XL5* on Saturday mornings from 1963 to 1965, making its original broadcast run the most successful Supermarionation series by some way. AP Films had hit the big time.

Key Episode

Episode 3: 'Planet of Platonia'
Written by Alan Fennell; Directed by David Elliott
First broadcast Sunday 20 January 1963 (ATV London)

Like many of the best SF stories, 'Planet of Platonia' has a story that takes the sort of situation one might read about in the morning paper and updates it into a new setting. In this case Fireball travels to Platonia, a planet entirely made of platinum, which on Earth is a scarce metal. Earth needs platinum for various industrial purposes, while Platonia is desperately short of other minerals Earth can supply. The ruler of the planet, Bizan, needs to make a trade deal so that his people can be supplied with minerals (it is also hinted that water—or 'Refresher Liquid' as it's known on Platonia—is also rare and valuable), but also to prevent his enemies taking power.

Bizan's position is even more precarious than he thinks, as we soon learn that his most trusted aide, Volvo, is a traitor. An attempt to kill Bizan with a bomb is made at his palace, the fifth assassination attempt in as many weeks. Fireball's mission is to safely transport Bizan to Earth for the trade talks—if any harm comes to the ruler it would mean war, as Bizan's rival, Ginerva, wants to conquer Earth. It should be mentioned here that David Graham's vocal turn as Volvo is a *tour de force*—obsequious, devious, and threatening, sometimes in the same sentence.

As this is an early episode of *Fireball XL5*, the launch of the ship (or 'blastaway', as Steve Zodiac puts it) is still treated as a major event, Fireball being filmed from various angles looming over the viewer before we see it hurtle down its launch rail in stock footage from the opening credits sequence, complete with the shadow of the engine smoke being seen on the studio backcloth. Other things we notice include Professor Matic's rotating desk. Like World Space Patrol's revolving headquarters building in Space City, this serves no real purpose except to add movement and visual interest to the scene.

Another consequence of this being an early episode in the series' run is that as many of the show's technical features as possible are used. Thus Steve, Venus, and Robert the Robot fly to the planet's surface on Fireball Junior, leaving Matthew to orbit Platonia on the main body of Fireball. They travel the rest of the way to Bizan's palace on their Jetmobiles, and later in the story we also see the jetpacks the crew use to move when undertaking a spacewalk, which had also been seen in the previous two stories.

The Fireball crew are not the only ones with gadgets at their disposal, as Steve and Venus are treated to a huge seven-course banquet by Bizan, each course arriving on a conveyor belt. Having overeaten, Steve goes to bed, but struggles to sleep, convinced that some harm will come to Robert, who is guarding Fireball Junior. He's right—Volvo has disabled Robert with an electronic device and put a time-bomb into the robot.

Here we learn that Steve Zodiac is tougher than we think. Spotting Volvo getting away, he shoots him with his ray gun, waking him up on board Fireball Junior to question him. Steve is convinced that Volvo has planted a bomb on board the ship, but cannot find it and Volvo is not saying where it is. Volvo is taken onto Fireball XL5 in space, putting him in as much danger as they are. The bomb is due to explode in thirty minutes, and Volvo finally cracks with only moments to spare. Steve must carefully remove the bomb from inside Robert and takes the smoking device (it must have an old-fashioned chemical timer) to an ejection tube. As Steve undertakes the delicate task, we see sweat on both his and Volvo's faces.

Volvo is put into Fireball's Space Jail, but escapes and ejects into space, where he is to be met by a fighter craft launched from Platonia. If both the fighter ship and the sequence detailing Fireball's destroying it with an interceptor missile look suspiciously familiar, this is because the entire sequence is made up of stock footage from the show's pilot episode 'Planet 46', the only change being the footage of the fighter being optically flipped.

Steve dons a jetpack (and presumably takes an oxygen pill, which in *Fireball XL5* allows characters to breathe in space) and retrieves Volvo, who is now stranded in space. We learn that Ginerva was piloting the fighter ship, and with his death the rebellion is at an end.

This is the first episode of *Fireball XL5* in which we see a relatively friendly alien race, and it is very much to the series' credit that, within the limitations of a twenty-five-minute children's series, quite an interesting and complex political situation is described. Platonia's ruler is friendly towards Earth, but partially for his own ends in order that he can sign a trade deal that will secure his position. One is reminded of various Middle Eastern nations where rulers were (and still are) kept in power with the support of powerful western nations they supply with oil. We never see Bizan's political rival Ginerva—or indeed any of the rest of the planet's population apart from the treacherous Volvo—but it is clear that if Ginerva has any sort of popular support, then the colonising forces of humanity are not welcomed by the whole population. This is still an improvement on the reception the Fireball crew got from the alien races seen in the first two episodes—the hostile and fascistic Subterrains from 'Planet 46' and the memorably creepy Suventian Brain from 'Hypnotic Sphere'.

As well as the political aspects of the story, there is much to admire about the production, which is symptomatic of the improving production standards of the series compared to *Four Feather Falls* and *Supercar*. The presence of so many alien races give the puppet sculptors free reign to create imaginative facial features and make the protagonists of the series look genuinely alien.

The interior of Fireball not only looks realistically technical and practical, as did the Black Rock Laboratory in *Supercar*, but it is also very attractively designed. The cockpit is minimal, but the expanse of glass all around the pilots seats give an impression of space (both in terms of room and outer space) and movement. Professor Matic's revolving desk, as already mentioned, adds visual interest and movement and is also enlivened by the presence of a huge and rarely used television screen in the background, plus a smaller screen that he actually uses.

The star of the show design-wise, however, is the Fireball XL5 lounge. In its attempt to look as streamlined and modern as possible, this naturally is the very epitome of mid-century modern design, using strong lines and stripped down of extraneous ornamentation. The centrepiece of the design is a curved double sofa (later seen in the *Thunderbirds* episode 'Brink of Disaster') surrounding a circular table on which stands a large lamp shaped in cones and curves. This use of curves echoes the curved lines of Commander Zero and Lt Ninety's desks in the World Space Patrol control room and of Professor Matic's rotating desk. Everything else in the room, from the star-patterned carpet to the bookshelf, chairs, and picture frames, is made up of straight lines. This cleverly helps to draw the eye to the centre of the room, where the characters and action of the scene usually is.

Over its long run of episodes, *Fireball XL5* could often be comedic or sometimes just plain silly, but in this early, quite serious story, the series demonstrates that Supermarionation was maturing. It was becoming able to tell more complex tales in a way that was still accessible to the youngest of viewers.

11

Derek Meddings

One of the greats among British film technicians was Derek Meddings. He was born on 15 January 1931 into a film industry family; both his father and stepfather were technicians at Denham Studios (master carpenter and head electrician respectively). His mother was secretary to the famous film producer and studio boss Alexander Korda, one of the most powerful men in the pre-war British film industry.

The young Derek was desperate to break into the film business, but there were few job opportunities above the menial level for people with neither experience nor qualifications. Instead Derek went to art school, to which he was far more suited then a traditional academic education. This approach paid off, and he was hired to provide lettering for the titles of films made at Denham, including changing the titles of Westerns to Spanish, Italian, and German. This allowed him to demonstrate his painting talents, as the new titles had to have a background image matching the original. Soon his abilities as a painter were noticed and Derek became a scenic artist, painting backdrops to scenes shot in the studio.

It was while at Denham that he met the Canadian Les Bowie, who was not only a scenic artist, but also a brilliant matte painter, who had revolutionised techniques for the production of matte artwork. The two got on well and Bowie liked Meddings' work enough to offer him the chance to head the Matte Department of Anglo Scottish Films, a company making adverts for television and cinemas that Bowie had his own production unit within. While there he also got into producing special effects—both model work and floor effects (effects that take place on the actual sets being used by the actors). Bowie and Meddings were kept busy, not only in the booming commercials market, but also on both feature films, Meddings assisting Bowie on his effects work for Hammer's horror output.

When AP Films began pre-production on *The Adventures of Twizzle*, Les Bowie was the obvious person to approach to produce sets for the series. He was unable to accept, but recommended Derek Meddings for the job. Derek's commitments became greater when Les Bowie left Anglo Scottish for a commission to work on the Disney adventure movie *Swiss Family Robinson* in 1960—Derek took over Bowie's old unit. Ironically, when Bowie returned to the UK he set up his own company and undercut Anglo Scottish on most jobs they went for.

Young, keen, and talented, Derek was ideal for the work at AP Films, and the company would fit its shooting schedule around his availability. After finishing his day's work with Anglo Scottish, he would travel across to AP, first at Islet Park, Maidenhead, then at Ipswich Road, Slough, and work through the evening (often until 1 a.m. or 2 a.m., including weekends).

Derek finally joined the AP Films staff full time towards the end of production on *Four Feather Falls*. He had been invited to join several times before, but only agreed when the company agreed to match what he was being paid by Anglo Scottish. With the company's next production, *Supercar*, requiring a much wider range of model effects than any of their previous puppet series, the previous arrangement was no longer practical as Derek's skills with models were needed on a full-time basis. From Anglo Scottish, Derek also recruited Brian Johnson to work as his assistant.

An absolutely vital member of the AP Films/Century 21 team, by the time *Fireball XL5* went into production his responsibilities expanded from designing model effects to helping Reg Hill design vehicles. As the studio expanded and its productions became more complex, Hill took on more productions responsibilities—his function as art director was taken on by Bob Bell for the puppet sets and Derek Meddings for model design. This process was to be repeated a few years later during the production of *Thunderbirds*, when Derek asked Mike Trim to design vehicles as the company was making several productions simultaneously. By this time Derek was running three effects stages and had a staff of fifty under him.

With the closing of Century 21 Studios at the conclusion of production on *UFO*, Derek Meddings provided effects for two films released in 1972: the Copenhagen-shot British dystopian SF production *ZPG* (or *Zero Population Growth*) and the Alistair Maclean adaptation *Fear is the Key*. On the latter film he worked with production designer Syd Cain, who was impressed with Derek's work and asked if he would be interested on working on the next project Cain was signed up for—the James Bond film *Live and Let Die* (1973).

For *Live and Let Die*, Derek shot the bombing of villain Dr Kananga's poppy fields in miniature and also the floor effects, including the absurd finale of Kananga's distended, oxygen-filled body rising to the ceiling and exploding. Other films in the series gave Meddings rather more scope for his model skills. *The Spy Who Loved Me* in 1977 took the model effects of Bond movies to a new level with its submarine-swallowing oil tanker SS *Liparus*. The Meddings miniature models, which had been getting larger for added realism ever since *UFO*, were by now huge. The *Liparus* was some 63 feet long and shot in the real ocean, as opposed to a studio water tank, during a four-month shoot in the Bahamas.

For the next Bond movie, *Moonraker* (1979), the impeccable model work was achieved using remarkably simple methods—vapour trails on a space shuttle were formed by filling the model with salt and letting it fall out of the bottom of the rocket. The climactic space battle was filmed my masking off different areas of the negative and exposing the required section, then winding the film back in the camera and working on action taking place in the next section. One shot saw the process being repeated over 100 times. This incredibly painstaking process gave results with a very high picture quality and saved huge amounts on lab costs for process work.

Between these two James Bond productions came another huge international production, *Superman: The Movie* (1978), based in Britain at least in part to take advantage of the large talent base of model and effects technicians. This represented some of Derek Meddings best work for the cinema, creating the film's scenes of a devastating earthquake and the destruction of San Francisco's Golden Gate Bridge by taking advantage of natural light on the backlot at Pinewood. For this film Derek Meddings and the rest of the effects team, including Les Bowie, won a Special Achievement Academy Award. Sadly, Les Bowie died during the production of the film.

Meddings also provided model effects for *Superman II* (1980) and returned for what would be his final James Bond movie for the next fourteen years, *For Your Eyes Only* (1981). His effects here achieved the greatest compliment of all—invisibility; his model effect to create the illusion of a helicopter flying through a warehouse was undetectable to even the sharpest eye.

In the late 1980s, he finally set up the independent effects company he'd first planned in the early '70s in the wake of the closure of Century 21. The Magic Camera Company was hired by director Tim Burton to provide the visual effects for his 1989 re-envisioning of *Batman*. Meddings remained convinced that the former animator and lifelong visual effects enthusiast Burton approached him for the film because he had been a childhood fan of *Thunderbirds*.

He continued to work on major films throughout the 1990s. Illness slowed him down for a while in this decade, but Derek was back to his best form for the James Bond 'comeback film' *Goldeneye* in 1995. Sadly, Derek Meddings died suddenly of a heart attack while the film was in post-production, ending an incredible era in British special effects production that was appreciated around the world.

12

Stingray

'*Stand by for action!*'

Produced by Gerry Anderson
Created by Gerry and Sylvia Anderson
Music composed, arranged, and conducted by Barry Gray
Title music arranged by Charles Blackwell, vocals by Don Spencer
An APF Television Production in Videcolor
Made in association with ATV
An ITC World Wide Distribution
39 × twenty-five-minute episodes
First broadcast Sunday 4 October 1964 (ATV London)

The people of Earth are protected from often hostile undersea races by the World Aquanaut Security Patrol. Its flagship is the submarine Stingray, crewed by Captain Troy Tempest and Lt 'Phones' Sheridan. They are accompanied on their missions by Marina, daughter of friendly undersea ruler Aphony.

It is a measure of how much confidence Lew Grade had in the popularity of AP Films' productions that he agreed to *Stingray* being shot in colour. This was not the first time ITC had made colour programming, but *Stingray* has the distinction of being the first British dramatic television series to be made entirely in colour, before even ITC's major live-action successes *Danger Man* (which was being revived as a one-hour series with high production values at around the same time) and *The Saint*, which had yet to secure a sale to the vital American network market.

The order for thirty-nine episodes of a colour series meant that AP Films' rented premises on Ipswich Road were no longer adequate, and larger new studios were acquired elsewhere on the Slough Trading Estate, some half a mile away on Stirling Road. Extensive conversions were made including three larger stages (two for puppets and one for model effects), its own screening cinema, and additional space for the art department, which also maintained its own base of operations nearby on Edinburgh Avenue.

Although *Stingray* has what is commonly referred to as a pilot episode, it did not serve the same purpose as a traditional pilot. These are primarily a sales tool, designed to sell a series concept by showing potential backers and broadcasters how it might look like on-screen. The first episodes made by AP Films and Century 21 were always very similar to the rest of the series for the simple reason that once Lew Grade had approved the format of any new series Gerry Anderson pitched to him, he trusted the company to get on and make it.

For the first three quarters of its pilot episode, generally known by the title 'Stingray', the world of *Stingray* is deadly serious. The format is very similar to *Fireball XL5*, with the World Space Patrol replaced by the World Aquanaut Security Patrol, manned by Captain Troy Tempest and Lt 'Phones' Sheridan. Troy has long suspected that undersea races exist, and are responsible for the destruction of the submarine Sea Probe. He discovers he is correct when his command Stingray, a sleek atomic powered submarine of revolutionary design, is attacked by a mechanical fish and the pair are held hostage by Titan, the undersea tyrant.

So far so serious, with male-dominated situations of peril underscored by Barry Gray's dramatic music; then Marina shows up and everything changes. Besides serving the useful plot function of freeing our heroes and enabling their escape, the beautiful woman from under the sea (looking rather like Brigitte Bardot) attracts the attention of Troy Tempest. Suddenly the emotional palate of the series has grown larger in ways that *Fireball XL5*—and especially the all-male environment of *Supercar*—never attempted—romance is in the air. It seems clear from the ending of the episode, as the Troy Tempest puppet's 'smiler' face allows him to beam from ear to ear, that Stingray's captain is more than somewhat enamoured of Marina. The trouble is, he is already dating Atlanta Shore, the Assistant Controller of WASP (World Aquanaut Security Patrol) headquarters Marineville and daughter of Marineville Commander Sam Shore, Troy's boss.

The difference in tone this gives to the series is thrown into sharp relief by the difference between the series opening and closing theme songs. The opening theme is a rollicking call to 'Stand by for Action' with pounding tom toms and a forceful brass section matched with shots of a leaping and diving Stingray unleashing sting missiles at a mechanical fish. In contrast, the end theme, sung by Gary Miller, is pure romantic balladry, the credits rolling alongside a miniature romantic saga of Troy Tempest and Marina approaching each other at the bottom of a coral sea. The pair then enjoy a romantic picnic on the beach, followed by a meal at a romantic, candle-lit restaurant. The pair then looks out to sea, Troy now in a red tuxedo and with eyes only for Marina. Marina then swims back from whence she came, while Stingray patrols the depths.

This difference was often seen in the episodes themselves, some episodes being quite simplistic action dramas, while others explored the romantic triangle between Troy, Marina, and Atlanta. Thus 'Treasure Down Below' works very well—Phones buys a treasure map while on shore leave, while Troy gets in trouble with Atlanta when she learns that he has taken Marina out when they are supposed to have a date that night. When the Stingray crew finds itself near the advertised location of the treasure, it is sucked into a whirlpool, where a hostile undersea race awaits.

This story, from the pen of the comedically inclined Dennis Spooner, is in contrast to the simplistic adventure tale 'The Big Gun' from Alan Fennell, who was responsible for far better stories elsewhere in the series. During this episode, the hostile undersea race is responsible for destroying islands using a submarine-looking floating army tank. For no reason that is explained onscreen, the undersea race's Mighty Leader next orders the craft to destroy the west coast of the United States. Stingray foils the plot after discovering the race's underwater city in the deepest part of the ocean and then destroys it with sting missiles. This action is actually carried out by Marina, despite the fact that Stingray is not under any threat at the time. An entire civilisation has been destroyed with hardly a second's thought.

Thankfully, simplistic militarism of this sort is rare in *Stingray*. Perhaps the familiarity of a format so similar to that of *Fireball XL5* caused writers Fennell and Spooner, who wrote all but three of the thirty-nine scripts, to have some fun with *Stingray*. At times strong doses of comedy, fantasy, and satire were added to the mix, resulting in some of the most successful episodes of the series. Alan Fennell's 'Titan Goes Pop' sends up the concept of pop stardom, as the visit of singer Duke Dexter to Marineville results in such heavy security precautions that Titan decides that he must be kidnapped as he is of such great importance.

Dennis Spooner's story 'Stand by for Action' sees Marineville being used for a movie about the WASPs, with Troy Tempest being played by Johnny Swoonara—Troy himself having failed the audition. This allows for some fun to be had at film stardom, with *Fireball XL5*'s Steve Zodiac puppet being taken out of storage to appear as Swoonara. Steve Zodiac always looked like a caricature of the handsome, all-American hero and *Stingray*, with its move towards slightly more realistic puppets, plays with this amusingly.

'Star of the East' sees Alan Fennell having fun with the figure of the Far Eastern dictator, in this case El Hudat, whose hold on his country is less firm than he thinks. This episode worked so well that Fennell wrote a sequel, 'Eastern Eclipse', featuring Ali Khali, El Hudat's twin brother who overthrew him in the first story. Fennell also penned 'Raptures of the Deep', which mocks the figure of jazz hipsters and their impenetrable lingo, shortly before the Beat Boom made them an endangered species. 'Tom Thumb Tempest' is another Fennell story, which sees Troy, Phones, and Marina miniaturised. This was the latest in a series of episodes in Supermarionation series in which the puppets interacted with life-size props and even animals. *Supercar*'s 'Calling Charlie Queen', written by Gerry and Sylvia Anderson, was the first story to use this plot device, followed by *Fireball XL5*'s 'The Triads'—an Alan Fennell script. The Andersons were clearly enamoured of this idea, which returned as a key element of the format of their 1969 series format *The Secret Service*.

For *Stingray*, an entirely new group of actors were recruited to provide the character voices. Troy Tempest's distinctively warm, attractive voice was provided by Don Mason, who was born in St Thomas, in the Ontario province of Canada. This lies on the shores of Lake Erie, only a two-hour drive from Detroit, over the US border. This put Don squarely in that belt of Canada in which the accent of the populace is pretty indistinguishable from American, giving him some professional advantages. As a part of the Commonwealth, British law allowed Canadians to work in the UK with relatively few restrictions. It made sense for Canadian actors to try their luck in Britain, where their work had the chance of being seen by a much larger audience than in the relatively small Canadian market.

Strangely, Don's few known credits during the British phase of his career tended to have him cast as air crew. Thus in the 1957 ITC war series *O.S.S.* he appeared in one episode as a co-pilot—his pilot was none other than David Graham. In the BBC Studio 4 production *Flight into Danger* from 1962 he was a first officer, and in the same year's play 'Course for Collision', a part of the BBC's *Suspense* strand, he was again a co-pilot. Both plays were written by Arthur Hailey, who was to hit the jackpot in 1970 when his novel *Airport* was filmed to great popular success. 'Course for Collision' is of particular interest, as its cast also features *Supercar*'s Graydon Gould and *Crossroads to Crime*'s Harry Towb. Mason's looks were hard to categorise, which can be fatal for the career of a character actor. Thus, Don Mason's most famous role in the UK was as Troy Tempest in *Stingray*, the James Garner looks of Tempest meshing perfectly with Don's mellifluous voice. On his return to Canada, Mason specialised in voice work, often for cartoons.

Ray Barrett provided the voices of Commander Shore, his assistant Lieutenant Fisher, and Titan, the tyrant of the depths. Equally adept at American, English, and Australian accents, Barrett was born in Brisbane, in the Australian state of Queensland in 1927. He started his career on radio, first in Brisbane and then Sydney, becoming the first actor to be put under exclusive contract to the Australian Broadcasting Corporation. In 1958, Barrett moved to the UK. Regular work came in 1960 when he became a regular as Dr Don Nolan on ATV's popular soap opera *Emergency-Ward 10*, alongside his fellow Australian Charles Tingwell who went on to provide voices for *Thunderbirds* and *Captain Scarlet and the Mysterons*. This increased Barrett's profile considerably and he was seen regularly on TV series such as *Armchair Theatre*, *The Avengers*, and *Z-Cars*, plus films including the Edgar Wallace B-features *Time to Remember* (1962) and *To Have and To Hold* (1963). He was not conventionally handsome, but Barrett's large build and pockmarked features, a result of severe teenage acne, gave him a rough-hewn appeal that worked equally well for both tough heroes and menacing villains. He was re-hired by AP Films to provide voices for their next series, *Thunderbirds*, for which he provided the voices for The Hood and John Tracy, in addition to a host of guest character voices. His profile was further raised in 1964 when he was cast as detective Peter Clarke in the final series of the ATV crime series *Ghost Squad*, replacing original star Michael Quinn as co-lead alongside Neil Hallett.

Robert Easton provided the distinctive Texan drawl of Lieutenant 'Phones' Sheridan, co-pilot of *Stingray*, and the perfect impersonation of German-born Hollywood star Peter Lorre, which formed the voice of Titan's Surface Agent X20. Robert Easton was born in 1930 in Milwaukee, but grew up in San Antonio, Texas. He first displayed his talent for vocal dexterity by purposely taking on the local accent as the slow Texan drawl helped to disguise his stutter. Easton took up acting from 1945, with roles including a regular part on the original 1952–61 radio version on *Gunsmoke*. He also began to turn up in small, often uncredited film and television roles during the 1950s. One notable part at the back end of this period was as 'Sparks' in the 1961 film *Voyage to the Bottom of the Sea*, a precursor to *Stingray*'s Phones.

In order to escape typecasting in country bumpkin roles, Easton had worked on his vocal range, developing an ear for different accents. When in 1961 he moved to the UK with his English wife, he acted in films and television series while studying Phonetics at University College London. When the Eastons returned to Hollywood after three years, preventing him from lending his voice to other Supermarionation productions, fellow actors were impressed by Robert's by now trained abilities with accents and asked him to teach them. Soon, Easton's acting was joined by a burgeoning second career as a voice coach. He remained in work as a character actor for the rest of his life, but Easton was widely acknowledged as the best voice coach in the business.

Probably the best known performer to be cast for voice roles in *Stingray* was Lois Maxwell, taking over what had been Sylvia Anderson's role as the main female voice artist she had enjoyed in *Supercar* and *Fireball XL5*. In fact it is surprising just how few female speaking parts there are in *Stingray*, the other regular woman seen on-screen being the mute Marina. Lois Maxwell had become very well known by the time *Stingray* had started production in early 1963 through her appearance in the first James Bond Film, *Dr. No*, in 1962.

The new Stirling Road studios were operating several stages at once, two for puppets and one for model effects, while other episodes were being prepared for shooting. Ted Wooldridge was in charge of lighting the special effects shots, as he had for *Fireball XL5*. Missing from the crew of *Thunderbirds*, Woolridge returned in the same role for *Captain Scarlet and the Mysterons*.

John Read was credited as director of photography for the entire series, and also as lighting cameraman for a third of the episodes. The arrangements for shooting the episodes were unusual, as the other two lighting cameramen, Paddy Seale and Alan Perry, doubled up as camera operators for the episodes they were not lighting. Alan Perry was John Read's regular camera operator, while Paddy Seale did the same task for Julien Lugrin's episodes and vice versa. Alan Perry had, of course, been with AP since *Supercar*, progressing from being a clapper loader to camera operator on *Fireball XL5*.

Paddy Seale had also gained a promotion from special effects camera operator on *Fireball XL5*, which is indicative of AP Films' willingness to promote from within the ranks and give new talent a chance. Seale remained as lighting cameraman for *Thunderbirds*, alternating with Julien Lugrin, and lit six episodes of *Captain Scarlet and the Mysterons*. He was also the lighting cameraman for the puppet unit on the feature film *Thunderbirds Are Go*. He remained with the Anderson puppet series until the end, alternating lighting duties with Julien Lugrin on *Joe 90* and *The Secret Service*. Seale's non-Anderson work included the 1976 Anglo-German television series *Star Maidens*, which employed much of the crew that had worked on *Space: 1999*'s first season. In the 1980s he worked for Gerry Anderson once again, lighting episodes of Anderson-Burr's *Terrahawks* and *Dick Spanner*.

In the editing suite, David Lane returned with Eric Pask from the *Fireball XL5* team, the pair now cutting episodes on a rota basis along with Harry MacDonald. MacDonald was to return as one of the main editors on *Thunderbirds* and *Captain Scarlet and the Mysterons*. He returned for three episodes of *Joe 90*, and again for Century 21's live-action series *UFO*, editing eight of the first block of seventeen episodes.

Joining the *Stingray* sound department was music editor Tony Lenny, gaining his first screen credit. He would return as one of the sound editors working on *Thunderbirds*, before going off to enjoy a distinguished career in this field. He became sound editor on major productions such as the 1979 ITC series *Return of the Saint* and was BAFTA nominated in 1985 for his work on the Merchant Ivory production *A Room with a View*. Before this he worked as both editor and director on Anderson-Burr's *Terrahawks*. Sadly, his very promising career was cut short by his death in 1990, shortly after the production of *Bullseye*, starring Michael Caine and Roger Moore.

In a bizarre co-incidence, Gary Miller, performer of *Stingray*'s end theme 'Aqua Marina', was the second singer associated with an AP Films series to die tragically young. Gary Miller was born Neville Williams in Blackpool, the famous seaside resort on England's north-west coast, in 1924. His period of chart success lasted from the mid to late 1950s, starting with a No. 13 cover version hit in 1955 of the American folk song 'The Yellow Rose of Texas', which had been an American hit in the same year for Mitch Miller (no relation). Gary Miller's biggest hit came the following year, when his version of the theme song from the ITC television series *The Adventures of Robin Hood* reached No. 10 in the UK pop charts, outselling a release of the song by Dick James, who performed the song on the series itself.

'Garden of Eden' reached No. 14 for Miller in 1957 and 'Wonderful, Wonderful' was a minor hit the following year, reaching No. 29. This was followed by a No. 14 hit version of 'The Story of My Life', the Burt Bacharach and Hal David composition that *Four Feather Falls*' Michael Holliday took to No. 1 in February of 1958. As with 'The Yellow Rose of Texas', this highlights what was a common practice in the British music industry at the time; a big American hit would be covered by multiple British artists in the hope of having a hit record before a deal could be made to release the original in the UK. Other versions of 'The Story of My Life' were released in 1958 by Alma Cogan, Dave King, and popular American singer Guy Mitchell, trying to beat the original hit by Marty Robbins into the shops.

The hits became less frequent after 1958, despite a steady stream of singles from his label, Nixa, a subsidiary of Pye. Even 'Aqua Marina' failed to chart on its 1964 release and this was his last single release until 1967. For *Stingray*, Miller sang both 'Aqua Marina' and the commercially released version of the opening theme, his lead vocal backed by the Mike Sammes Singers. When Troy Tempest was heard to sing 'Aqua Marina' in a fantasy sequence during the episode 'Raptures of the Deep', it is Miller's vocals that are heard. He also provided the singing voice for Duke Dexter in the episode 'Titan Goes Pop', performing Barry Gray's 'I've Got Something to Shout About' as an amusing pastiche of Adam Faith.

From 1964, Miller concentrated on acting, becoming a popular television performer through appearances including being a regular panellist on the music review panel show *Juke Box Jury*. He was also acting on the West End stage, in the musical *She Loves Me* at the Lyric Theatre on London's Shaftesbury Avenue opposite Gary Raymond and Rita Moreno. This was based on the same Miklos Laszlo play as the hit 1998 film *You've Got Mail*, starring Meg Ryan and Tom Hanks.

Miller made his television acting debut in the 1965 ITC police series *Gideon's Way* in the episode 'The Great Plane Robbery'. This reveals Gary Miller to have been a confident and natural actor, playing Len, one of a gang of gold robbers led by George Baker. In something of a coincidence, 'The Great Plane Robbery' was written by Alun Falconer, the screenwriter of AP Films' *Crossroads to Crime* and features George Murcell, who appeared in that film and went on to provide the voices of Masterspy and Professor Popkiss in the first series of *Supercar*.

His acting career continued with a part as Secret Agent VO3 in the stage play *Come Spy with Me*, which opened in 1966 and starred female impersonator Danny La Rue. By this time Miller's health was starting to deteriorate and he was replaced for several months by his understudy Craig Hunter due to heart trouble. He returned to his role and in 1968, while *Come Spy with Me* was still running, was also cast in *The Saint* episode 'The People Importers', this time as Slater, part of a people smuggling racket. Before production was completed Miller suffered a fatal heart attack, aged only forty-four—his role of Slater was completed using a double.

Over the years, *Stingray* has tended to somewhat live in the shadow of *Thunderbirds*, the unprecedented success of which has obscured just how successful its predecessor was. *Stingray* represented the point at which the merchandising effort behind the series reached a whole new level. This was coordinated by AP Films own merchandising company, Century 21 Merchandising, headed by Gerry Anderson's old national service friend Keith Shackleton. Among the many variations of model Stingrays that were available—on wheels powered by friction motor, remote controlled with lights and a siren, or even an inflatable plastic model—plus annuals, jigsaw puzzles games, and dozens of other variations on the Stingray craft, characters and imagery, two sets of products have stood out over the years.

Firstly came the brilliant idea of presenting adventures of the Anderson series in audio form. An entire programme of releases was produced through Century 21's own record label in an unusual format—7-inch vinyl records designed to be played at 33⅓ RPM. This made the releases more affordable, and also a decent length. This even became a part of the format of the records: '21 Minutes of Adventure'. Three Stingray adventures were released; firstly the interactive 'Into Action with Troy Tempest', followed by 'A Trip to Marineville', in which Troy Tempest takes young Johnny (voiced by Sylvia Anderson) on a special trip to the WASPs headquarters. The final Stingray release, 'Marina Speaks', gives a rather unconvincing explanation as to why Marina and Aphony are mute.

Century 21 Merchandising's second great marketing coup was the creation of the comic *TV Century 21*, for several years in the mid to late 1960s the most popular comic in Britain by some considerable margin. It should not be forgotten that when this publication made its initial, huge impact on the buying habits of British youth, its lead strip was not *Thunderbirds*, which had yet to be aired, but *Stingray*.

Stingray was a major hit series. The next trick for AP Films was to work out how they were going to follow it up.

Key Episode

Episode 29: 'Titan Goes Pop'
Written by Alan Fennell
Directed by Alan Pattillo
First UK broadcast Sunday 6 December 1964 (ATV London)

Marineville is visited by Duke Dexter, a pop star with a fanatical and enormous female following. The security arrangements are so extensive that X20 concludes that Dexter must be the most important person ever to have visited Marineville. Titan orders that he be kidnapped and taken to his palace in Titanica.

Despite Dennis Spooner being the comedy specialist among *Stingray*'s writers, the award for the funniest episode in the series goes to Alan Fennell's 'Titan Goes Pop', a fascinating and wildly entertaining spoof of the phenomenon of the pop superstar. As one of the last thirteen episodes of *Stingray*, the episode starts with a riot of colour and sound with the blue of the huge aquatic explosion and blazing red colour of the AP Films and Videocolor logos. This version of the opening credits sequence replaced the original, which cleverly started out in monochrome and reverted to colour when the picture zoomed out to Commander Shore in Marineville Tower.

As the episode itself starts we see a Duke Dexter concert, being watched by the regular cast members on television. The way that Dexter is presented is very interesting in terms of the cultural references that it makes, some of which might be missed by younger viewers. Duke's raven black quiff of hair and heavy eyelids reference, of course, Elvis Presley. The Presley influence can also be seen in Dexter's stage gear of shiny gold shirt and trousers with contrasting blue neckerchief. Elvis single-handedly popularised the use of glittery colours and bright pinks in his stage outfits, particularly with his gold *lamé* suit, created for him by Nudie Cohn in 1957.

While Elvis introduced the phenomenon of the rock and roll star with massive, all-encompassing fame and the attendant hoard of screaming fans, musically the influences are from elsewhere. The music is far lighter than anything Elvis ever recorded and Gary Miller's vocals are more reminiscent of Buddy Holly or, from a British perspective, Adam Faith. There is a gag in Dexter's first scene, as he appears on television, where his guitar amplifier smokes and then explodes. Given the rather sedate nature of the guitar sound, even by the standards of the day, this joke has dated somewhat, but it does get across just how loud and raucous rock and roll music sounded to grown-ups who were raised on pop music rooted in jazz and show tunes.

The way by which we first see the regular characters encounter Duke Dexter is also of interest. Troy, Phones, Atlanta, and Commander Shore are watching a television broadcast of Dexter's hit 'I've Got Something to Shout About' at the Shore's Marineville apartment. Ostensibly they are together to play cards, but in reality they form a family unit, each mirroring popular attitudes to pop stardom. Despite giving the impression of enjoying the show while it was on, grumpy dad Sam Shore expresses his disapproval while his daughter Atlanta (looking awfully glamorous in a sparkly gold roll-top jumper) is clearly a big Duke Dexter fan. Troy and Phones, Sam's surrogate sons, are aware of Duke and his enormous fan base, but utterly bemused by the phenomenon.

In the real world Duke Dexter's stardom would have been brief, swept into history like the jazz hepcats of Alan Fennell's earlier *Stingray* episode 'Raptures of the Deep' by the rise of blues influenced beat groups—that's showbiz.

Meanwhile, back at the plot, the visit of Duke Dexter to Marineville is the source of some great jokes. Firstly, Titan's Surface Agent X20 sees the enormous security precautions being taken, but as the messages to do with it are in code he has no idea what they are for. Fortunately, the minute preparations for Dexter's visit are declared top secret, yet details are still splashed all over the press—including the WASPs own newspaper, *The Marineville Observer*.

X20 rushes to inform Titan of the news, which results in some of the best dialogue in the entire series:

> 'And so, your majesty, with my great cunning, using all the experience I have gained working as a surface agent, I have discovered that Duke Dexter is visiting Marineville.'
>
> 'Excellent! Excellent! How did you find out?'
>
> 'Well… I read it in the newspaper.'
>
> 'Brilliant! So Duke Dexter is coming to Marineville. Who is Duke Dexter?'
>
> 'My investigations are still continuing, but one thing is for sure. With the secret measures and all the activity I've seen, he is the most important person ever to have visited Marineville.'

As a result of this conversation, Titan decides that Dexter must be taken to Marineville. Besides being central to the plot, this part of the episode displays how far these two characters have drifted by this point in the series from their original functions as serious villains. Ray Barrett's mock-Shakespearean delivery of Titan's lines sounds irresistibly like one of Peter Sellers' *The Goon Show* characters, especially when teamed with Robert Easton's X20, whose Peter Lorre-inspired tones always had comedic possibilities.

Other scenes are almost as funny. Troy acts as a decoy so the real Duke Dexter can safely reach Marineville Tower. We never see the fans, we just hear their screaming, while the sight of Troy running from them is the funniest visual image in the episode. Troy arrives in the control room covered in hand prints and kisses, his clothes torn.

Disguised as 'Agent X' from WASP Security, with pink make-up to disguise his fishy complexion and clothed in a wig, stripy jumper, and jeans, X20 gets into Marineville and has Duke taken to his house on the island of Lemoy for safety. Once there, he drugs Duke's drink and takes him to see Titan in his palace on Titanica. Titan concludes that Duke is causing so much chaos among the surface-dwellers that Titan himself could not do better, once again he drugs him and sends him back to Lemoy. Having worked out that 'Agent X' was a fake, and Duke having turned up unharmed, Commander Shore thinks that his disappearance was a publicity stunt, and the concert goes ahead.

The episode closes as Titan and X20 watch the Marineville concert on television, the undersea tyrant delighted at what he sees, echoing some of the fears of the more apocalyptic commentators of the '50s and '60s at the effects of popular culture on society: 'They're in a state of frenzy. He's driving them mad. If he keeps this up they'll be ready to be conquered in no time at all. Success at last!'

13

Thunderbirds

'Thunderbirds Are Go!'

Produced by Gerry Anderson (executive producer on series two)
Created by Gerry and Sylvia Anderson
Music composed and directed by Barry Gray
An APF Television Production in Videocolor
Made in association with ATV
32 × twenty-five-minute episodes
First broadcast Thursday 30 September 1965 (ATV Midlands)

Millionaire ex-astronaut Jeff Tracy runs International Rescue from his private Pacific island, sending his sons out on dangerous rescue missions using revolutionary craft designed by the genius Brains.

The first rescue in the history of *Thunderbirds* was a real one. Late on Friday 24 October 1963 the iron miners of the Lengede-Broistedt mine, in Lower Saxony, part of what was then West Germany, would have been planning their weekends when disaster struck. Half a million cubic metres of water burst into the mine tunnels. Seventy-nine miners escaped, but a further fifty were trapped underground. An incredibly complex and technically challenging series of three rescues were performed over a period of two weeks as the world's media looked on.

A long and difficult rescue was mounted, the last man being rescued fully two weeks after the mine flooded, the rescue of the last eleven men entering popular German culture as the '*Wunder von Lengede*'—'the Miracle of Lengede'. Over 450 journalists from the world's press were present for the finale of this true-life drama, among their rapt audience was Gerry Anderson. The Lengede mine rescue gave him an idea—what if there was an organisation dedicated to performing seemingly impossible rescues? International Rescue was born.

A new project was needed in the near future to present to Lew Grade as AP's follow up to *Stingray*. Time and space was needed to develop the basic idea away from the pressures of the studios in Slough, so the Andersons retired to their Portuguese holiday home to create the company's next series.

What emerged was a mixture of the original rescue organisation idea with the SF spin on the format of the popular Western series *Bonanza*. This series, hugely popular in both the UK and America, featured the adventures of middle-aged widower Ben Cartwright, running his huge ranch The Ponderosa with his three sons. Each son had a different mother, so the three were highly contrasting in looks. The puppet of the Tracy brothers' father, Jeff Tracy, was specifically designed to resemble actor Lorne Greene, who portrayed Ben Cartwright for fourteen seasons from 1959 to '73.

Warned that the new series would be the most expensive that AP Films had yet produced, Lew Grade backed *International Rescue* (as the project was then known) without hesitation. The script for 'Trapped in the Sky' and the series specification were passed to the production team, so sets could be designed, Derek Meddings could set about designing the craft (at this point named Rescue One, Rescue Two, etc.) and the puppet designers could bring the Andersons' characters to life.

During pre-production, Gerry had a flash of inspiration; he recalled the name of a United States Air Force training field mentioned in letters home from his RAF pilot brother Lionel during the war—Thunderbird Field. The name had always struck Gerry as being atmospheric, and now it occurred to him that Thunderbirds would be a great name for the new series and the rescue craft.

The Thunderbirds Craft

In a brilliant stroke of creativity, Derek Meddings, who had by this point taken over complete responsibility from Reg Hill for vehicle design, came up with the idea of basing the look of each of the five Thunderbird craft in some way on the number it had been assigned.

Thunderbird 1

Thunderbird 1 was a sleek design suggesting both a rocket and a conventionally-powered aircraft, reflecting its primary purpose of reaching the site of any disaster first. Although its main function was command and control, its huge pulling power could often be used during rescues. The craft also contained

Scott's Mobile Control Unit, a communications base he set up once at the danger zone in order to coordinate rescue efforts.

Thunderbird 1's long, thin design, which was upright on take-off, alluded to the aircraft's great speed and the number one. The take-off routine of Thunderbird One, like those of the other four rescue vehicles, worked on the 'transforming room' idea that had worked so successfully on Surface Agent X20's dining room-cum-communications hub in *Stingray*. Always wearing the same blue lapel-less jacket and dark blue polo-neck jumper (in the first season episodes this was a sure sign that Thunderbird 1 was about to be launched), Scott stands against a section of wall, grabs two lamps behind him, and the whole section revolves. This reveals Thunderbird 1, and Scott is taken to the craft on an extending platform. While Scott is changing into his uniform, Thunderbird 1 is transported on rails down to its launch pad, somehow turning round in the process so that its identification lettering is always facing the camera. Meanwhile, on the surface, the Tracy Island swimming pool slides to one side, and Thunderbird 1 launches vertically through the resulting gap.

Thunderbird 2

Thunderbird 2, with its massive, bulbous body and rear-mounted jet engines resembles the number two turned on its side. This was a huge carrier craft, which was able to carry rescue equipment to the danger zone in a series of pods held in its centre. This enormous green craft, with its distinctive forward-facing wings, soon became a favourite of the production crew visually, and when the series was eventually seen by the public this verdict was enthusiastically confirmed. Thunderbirds' model units did not find the heavy model used for most of the flying sequences easy to work with—there was a knack to 'flying' the model smoothly, and during take-off sequences a crew-member was often at hand out of camera range in case a string broke and the model fell. During the making of the episode 'Terror in New York City', the original model was damaged by fire in an effects sequence. A temporary repair was affected by model shop crew, including Mike Trim, but ultimately a second model of Thunderbird 2 was constructed. Many people, including both eagle-eyed viewers and members of the production crew, could see that the new version was a slightly different shape.

The launch of Thunderbird 2 is one of the series' enduring, classic sequences. Always wearing a brown waistcoat and olive green collarless shirt (in the first series, at least), Virgil stands against a large painting of a rocket launch. This pivots from the bottom, causing Virgil to slide backwards onto a container which slides down a chute. Pausing to turn him the right way round, Virgil is then transported down into Thunderbird 2's hangar, sliding through an entry hole at the top of the cockpit and straight into the pilot seat. While Virgil is changing into his International Rescue uniform, the correct pod containing the rescue equipment required for the mission is positioned under Thunderbird 2, which lowers down onto the pod and locks it into place. The craft then taxis forward, leaving the hangar through an entrance created when the whole side of the mountain underneath the Tracy Island observation deck lowers itself. Famously, the rows of palm trees either side of the path leading to the launch area swing out of the way.

Thunderbird 3

Thunderbird 3's unusual arrangement of three rocket motors is, as you may have gathered by now, due to it being assigned the number three. Derek Meddings' inspiration came from the basic design of the Soviet Soyuz rockets, which, unlike NASA's Mercury and Apollo rockets, had their motors outside of the main body. This gave the Soyuz a very distinctive look compared to the American spacecraft, but one that many viewers at the time might have been less familiar with. The creative genius of Meddings, of course, gave Thunderbird 3 a look all of its own, with a distinctive orange colour scheme, central stabilising fins, and the three motors attached to the main fuselage by struts. The collar around the top part of the craft is part of the docking mechanism that allows access between the ship and Thunderbird 5.

A Thunderbird 3 launching was always something a bit special on *Thunderbirds*, as it did not occur in every episode, unlike the launch sequences of Thunderbirds 1 and 2. Thunderbird 3's pilot (Alan or John), and any auxiliary crew, descend to Thunderbird 3's hangar on the sofa in the Tracy's living room, which is replaced by an exact duplicate. When it reaches ground level, the sofa then travels on rails to the bottom of the craft, where it is lifted upwards into Thunderbird 3's cabin. When ready, the ship launches through an unusually-shaped structure known as the Round House. One factor that helps make the Thunderbird 3 launching so effective is that the model used for many of the shots was some 6 feet tall. This allowed the director of the launch sequence to move the camera up and around the model, making the launch look highly cinematic.

One aspect of Thunderbird 3, which it would appear the producers were not happy with, is the interior of the craft. Many of the interior shots of Thunderbird 3 in the first series episodes came from stock footage from 'Sunprobe'—the first episode in which Thunderbird 3 is sent on a mission. The pilot's cabin is painted a rather unpleasant yellow, and the pilot's console resembles an old cinema organ as opposed to the sleek and technical look of the other craft. For the second series episodes the launch sequence for the feature film *Thunderbirds Are Go* was used. The smaller frame size of the Techniscope format used for the films meant that the picture quality was noticeably reduced when blown up to the televisual format. The interior of the craft was also completely redesigned for *Thunderbirds Are Go*, with a more silver-effect colour scheme. The 1966-model Thunderbird 3 also gained upgraded pilot and co-pilot seats, it only seems fair that a crew facing several gs worth of pressure on launching should at least have headrests.

Thunderbird 4

Thunderbird 4 was a miniature submarine used for undersea rescues, which was usually transported to the rescue site by Thunderbird 2. As with Thunderbird 2, the inspiration for Thunderbird 4's body-shape came from taking the craft's assigned number and putting it on its side. The result was a miniature submarine often compared, partially due to its yellow colour-scheme, to a Reliant Robin car. Actually, this fits in with one of the most interesting aspects of Supermarionation design and formats—its use of domestic settings transforming into futuristic control centres, plus car-like aircraft (Supercar) and submarines (Thunderbird 4). This gave the imaginations of the young audiences of the Supermarionation series an enormous kick; even if you had no Thunderbirds toys, your own house or parent's car could be a piece of Thunderbirds equipment.

Unlike the other *Thunderbirds* rescue craft, Thunderbird 4 generally required a method of transportation to get it to the danger zone. Usually this was Thunderbird 2, carrying Gordon Tracy in the miniature submarine in Pod 2, dropping the pod into the sea so it can carry out its rescue mission. Thunderbird 4 is no mere pod vehicle; in 'Terror in New York City', Thunderbird 2 has been shot down by a World Navy ship, mistaking it for a hostile craft. To help make up for their mistake, they ferry Thunderbird 4 to New York to help save two journalists trapped in a flooding underwater cave.

Thunderbird 5

Thunderbird 5 had two design inspirations—from above its basic shape resembles the number 5, fitting in with Derek Meddings' basic design idea, but he also took ideas from his own design for Tracy Island's Round House, through which Thunderbird 3 is launched. Uniquely among the Thunderbird craft, Thunderbird 5 is never directly involved in rescues, instead being a manned communication satellite. When *Thunderbirds* was made in the mid-1960s the idea that anyone in the world can broadcast a call on any frequency to International Rescue sounded pretty far-fetched. Today, however, the idea sounds quite achievable, and not unlike the methods used by security agencies to detect terrorist plots. The interior of Thunderbird 5 is very stylishly achieved, dominated by two items—the wording 'International Rescue' curved around the inside cabin, which served no real purpose, but looks fabulous, and the miniature (in real life) reel-to-reel tape player through which John Tracy listens to rescue calls. This was a commercially available piece of equipment, made in Japan and available under various different names, including the Acme Model 1500 and the Homey HR 408-a. This was widely available in the UK at the time of *Thunderbirds* production, including at the Woolworths chain stores. Thunderbird 5 is usually manned by John Tracy during the episodes, but he shares duties on the satellite with Alan on a rota basis.

Voice Artists

With its large cast of regular characters, *Thunderbirds* had the biggest cast of voice artists yet seen on a Supermarionation series. Ray Barrett returned from the *Stingray* voice cast to lend his wide range of accents to John Tracy and The Hood; additionally, he provided a voice to a wide range of secondary characters, including Tin-Tin's old flame Eddie Houseman in 'End of the Road' to a hilarious Dame Edith Evens impression as The Duchess of Royston in 'The Duchess Assignment'. David Graham was also back in harness, providing the shy, stuttering voice of Brains, the genius who designed the Thunderbirds rescue craft, plus the faux-posh cockney accent of Parker—safecracker, chauffeur, and manservant to International Rescue's London Agent Lady Penelope. A wine waiter at a pub in Cookham (frequented by Gerry Anderson) suggested the voice of Parker, which was immediately adopted by Graham with great enthusiasm. David Graham was, of course, a genius voice artist, and provided the voices for a huge range of characters during the run of *Thunderbirds*.

Also returning to the *Thunderbirds* voice cast, after not providing any character voices for *Stingray*, was Sylvia Anderson. She provided the voices for many of the female characters needed for individual episodes, as well as the upper-class tones of Lady Penelope Creighton-Ward. So associated has Sylvia Anderson become with the role that one might be surprised to learn that she was not, in fact, the first choice for the part. Gerry Anderson was keen to recruit sometime *Carry On* star Fenella Fielding, possessed of a famously seductive, husky voice. Denise Bryer, who had provided voices for *The Adventures of Twizzle* and *Four Feather Falls*, also recorded tests for the part. Eventually the role went to Sylvia Anderson, it is claimed after a certain amount of persuasion on her part.

The rest of the performers hired to give voice to the *Thunderbirds* characters were new to the Anderson series. David Holliday, who provided the distinctively husky tones of Virgil Tracy, was an actor largely known for appearing in musical theatre. He travelled to England to play the male lead role of Tony in Leonard Bernstein and Stephen Sondheim's musical *West Side Story* in 1958. The actor remained in London for some years afterwards in stage productions and was still based in London when the role of Virgil was being cast. Unfortunately, by the time *Thunderbirds*' second series and the two feature films were recording the vocal tracks, Holliday was unavailable, due to his stage career increasingly taking him overseas—he appeared in the musical *Dearest Dracula in Dublin* in 1965, and in 1967 was performing in Copenhagen in a production of *Annie Get Your Gun*, played entirely in Danish (Holliday having to learn his lines phonetically).

David Holliday recommended his friend from the *West Side Story* cast Matt Zimmerman for the part of Alan Tracy, the last of the *Thunderbirds* roles to be cast—Ray Barratt voiced Alan's single line of dialogue in 'Trapped in the Sky'. Matt was born in Ontario, Canada, but grew up in New York. He won a scholarship and travelled to the UK to learn the craft of acting at LAMDA, the London Academy of Music and Dramatic Art. There he studied alongside future *Captain Scarlet and the Mysterons* and *UFO* star Ed Bishop. Matt was still acting in *West Side Story* when *Thunderbirds* was being cast, and was cast as Alan Tracy on the spot by Sylvia Anderson, who thought he looked like the puppet—fortunately, she also liked his youthful, American-accented voice. As the series developed, Alan turned out to be the plum role in the series, with script editor Alan Fennell developing his romance with Tin-Tin.

Hastings-born Peter Dyneley had already made a career out of being able to play acting roles in virtually any accent required of him. He was especially adept at American accents, and had even performed an entire lead role as an entirely convincing American in the 1959 American-Japanese co-production *The Manster*, in which his character grows an extra head. This co-starred Dyneley's wife, former Rank starlet Jane Hylton, who also appeared with her husband in the BBC-TV espionage series *The Mask of Janus*. This series, in which Dyneley featured as spymaster Commander Hastings, was his 'day job' while he was recording *Thunderbirds* episodes with the rest of the voice cast on a Sunday. The series was reformatted slightly in its second season, and was given the slightly racier title *The Spies*. Although Peter Dyneley was not used again as a voice artist by Gerry and Sylvia Anderson after *Thunderbirds*, he was cast in the role of NASA liaison David Poulson in their film *Doppelgänger*, shot in 1968, the year after Thunderbird 6. Unfortunately, after the producers and director Robert Parrish saw the rushes of the scene between Dyneley and Patrick Wymark it became clear that the two actors were physically too similar and the part of Poulson was recast with Ed Bishop.

Shane Rimmer was appearing in a variety stage show in Leeds when he got a call to travel down to London to perform a voice audition for *Thunderbirds*. The Canadian writer and actor got his start in show business as a radio presenter and as part of a vocal singing group. It was as a solo singer that Shane first came to England, recording several singles. Shane's acting career first took off when he was cast as part of a nuclear bomber crew in the film *Dr. Strangelove or: How I Learned to Stop Worrying and Love the Bomb*, shot in 1963 and released in January 1964. The cachet of appearing in a Stanley Kubrick film meant that Shane suddenly found himself in demand as an actor, and at the time *Thunderbirds* was casting he had just come off a run in the BBC's magazine-based soap opera *Compact*.

In addition to providing the voice for Scott Tracy, *Thunderbirds* also gave Shane Rimmer his start as a writer, creating text for promotional materials aimed at the American market and also linking material (which he also voiced) for when the episodes were split into two parts, a format in which they were occasionally screened during the 1960s. Although he would occasionally provide voices for future shows, Shane's major contribution to future Anderson series would be as a writer. A friend of script editor Tony Barwick, he provided scripts for *Captain Scarlet and the Mysterons*, *Joe 90*, and *The Secret Service*, plus the later live-action detective series *The Protectors*. He also had major acting roles in two episodes of *The Protectors* and the *Space: 1999* episode 'Space Brain'.

Christine Finn shared the female character voice roles with Sylvia Anderson, as well as playing the regular characters Tin-Tin and Grandma Tracy. Receiving her acting training at LAMDA, Finn was born and raised in India, moving to Britain in 1946, shortly before India gained its independence. She was spotted as a potential actress while working in a clerical role for the BBC, then she was trained professionally. After graduating she acted regularly on stage and television, with occasional film roles. In 1957 she became a regular actress in ATV's hospital-based soap opera *Emergency-Ward 10*, but Christine Finn's most notable television part was in Nigel Kneale's *Quatermass and the Pit*, which first aired in December 1958 and January 1959. In the years following *Thunderbirds*, she ceased appearing on stage, and her television career ended in 1969 with an episode of Paul Temple, starring *Captain Scarlet* voice actor Francis Matthews.

With David Holliday unavailable for the second series of *Thunderbirds* and for the recording sessions for the two *Thunderbirds* movies, actor Jeremy Wilkin was recruited to play the part of Virgil Tracy. Wilkin's background made him perfect for the trans-Atlantic appeal of *Thunderbirds*—he was British-born, but had immigrated to Canada after graduating from the world-famous acting school RADA. By 1963 Wilkin had returned to Britain and was picking up regular acting roles on television, including the lead role in the 1965 ABC television series *Undermind*. In addition to *Thunderbirds*, Wilkins provided voices for *Captain Scarlet and the Mysterons*, *Joe 90*, and *The Secret Service*. He also had a small role in *Doppelgänger* and was a regular member of the Skydiver crew in *UFO*. His last appearance in an Anderson series was in *The Protectors* episode 'Route 27', the final episode in that series production order.

Some other voice roles were filled later in the *Thunderbirds*' run by uncredited actors, most notably John Tate, a British-based Australian actor and the father of future *Space: 1999* star Nick Tate. For some of the second season episodes, two members of the *Thunderbirds Are Go* voice cast provided character voices—Australian actor Charles Tingwell and *Fireball XL5*'s Steve Zodiac himself, Paul Maxwell. Both actors would return to provide voices for *Captain Scarlet and the Mysterons*.

The Tracy Brothers were, like their inspirations the Cartwrights, designed to be contrasting in looks, which was helped by the contrasting styles of the puppet designers, John Brown, John Blundall, Christine Glanville, and Mary Turner. The general direction of puppet design in the Anderson series between *Four Feather Falls* and *Stingray* had been towards more realism. Thus, while *Fireball XL5*'s Steve Zodiac looked like a caricature of a handsome Hollywood leading man, *Stingray*'s Troy Tempest was just plain handsome, in the manner of film star James Garner. Most of the puppet sculptors went along with this, chief puppeteer Christine Glanville designing Thunderbird 1 pilot Scott Tracy to look like the young Sean Connery.

John Blundall, who would go on to be one of the mainstays of British theatrical puppetry, took a different view. He had always tended to design the more unusual puppets, such as *Fireball XL5*'s Robert the Robot and Zoonie the Lazoon. For *Thunderbirds*, Blundall created three puppets for the regular cast that took a radically different approach, but still managed to fit in with the overall look of the series—Grandma Tracy, Kyrano, and, most memorably of all, Lady Penelope's manservant, the safecracker, ex-convict, and chauffeur Aloysius Parker. Mary Turner was given the job of designing Parker's employer, Lady Penelope Creighton-Ward. This took several attempts to gain the approval of Sylvia Anderson, until the idea was hit upon to make the character look as much like Sylvia as possible, without her knowledge.

The puppets were also technically more advanced than the previous versions. Initially introduced in *Stingray*, different heads for each character with a variety of expressions; for *Thunderbirds*, this idea was expanded on even more, with 'smiler and 'frowner' heads, as well as heads with blinking eyes (usually used when the characters were falling unconscious), developed alongside their normal expression heads.

It soon became clear that *Thunderbirds* would entail far more model effects work than any of the previous Supermarionation series. With this in mind, a visual effects second unit was set up. In normal film-making parlance, a second unit tends to be dedicated to filming sequences not requiring the main cast members, such as stunt sequences and insert shots. In the case of *Thunderbirds*, however, directors Brian Johncock—who was soon to change his surname to Johnson—and Ian Scoones were producing work equal in importance and quality to that of Derek Meddings' main visual effects crew.

Johnson did not stay with the series for its entire length, however. At MGM-British Borehamwood Studio, the renowned director Stanley Kubrick was setting up his mammoth production of Arthur C. Clarke's *2001: A Space Odyssey*, which would eventually premiere in April 1968. Initially, he enquired if Gerry Anderson might be able to handle the effects for the film, but with the heavy production schedule of his own series this was clearly impossible. Instead, Kubrick poached Brian Johnson from AP Films along with one of his assistants, Roger Dicken, with the promise of being able to work on a highly prestigious film on a huge budget, plus a healthy pay rise compared to what the Anderson studios were able to pay. Ian Scoones was joined by Shaun Cook to complete directing the remaining effects work of the second unit.

For the second, shorter series of six episodes, there were some changes of personnel on *Thunderbirds*, as these stories were being produced in tandem with the feature film *Thunderbirds Are Go*. Derek Meddings had been billed as supervising special effects director from episode two onwards, as so many effects stages were operating at the same time. For the second series, with Meddings busy on the film, Jimmy Elliot was drafted in to direct model effects for the television series along with Shaun Whittacker-Cook.

Bob Bell was similarly tied up with work on the *Thunderbirds Are Go*, and became supervising art director on the final six *Thunderbirds* episodes, his assistant Grenville Nott was promoted to art director. Nott stayed in this role for the next Supermarionation series, *Captain Scarlet and the Mysterons*. Also added to the art department team were two designers, Keith Wilson and John Lageu, who worked on both the film and television versions of *Thunderbirds* simultaneously. Wilson worked on interiors such as rooms the characters might find themselves in, while Lageu, whose background was in technical design, worked on sets such as aircraft cockpits. Keith Wilson stayed with the Andersons right up until *Space: 1999*, taking over as production designer on that series. Lageu left Century 21 during the production of *Captain Scarlet and the Mysterons* and worked on some of the later Hammer films. This included in 1969 working as assistant art director to Scott MacGregor on Hammer's 'Space Western' *Moon Zero Two* (1969).

AP Films proved to be an entry point to the film industry for many young talents. As with writers, experienced film effects technicians proved unwilling to join AP Films, which was still regarded as less prestigious than film assignments. The company instead recruited for new staff as its workload grew by advertising in newspapers, attracting art school graduates such as Alan Shubrook and Roger Dicken. Young and keen, they soon became highly skilled and were far cheaper to employ than more experienced staff. The film business was at this period notoriously difficult to break into, partially due to the fact that it was a union closed shop, meaning that no one without a film union membership card could be employed, and one could not get a union membership without having been employed by a film studio—Catch-22. The technical needs of the Supermarionation productions were so specific that AP Films could get new recruits accepted into one of the film unions with little difficulty as they would not be putting existing members out of work.

The extra workload caused other changes to be made in the company's working methods. Gerry and Sylvia Anderson were forced to step back from their traditional role as script editors. From this point on both Gerry and Sylvia Anderson performed far less writing on the shows, and writer and director Alan Pattillo was hired as *Thunderbirds*' script editor. This involved commissioning scripts and dealing with writers, as well as his existing duties writing and directing episodes. Pattillo began putting his mark on the direction of the series, developing the characters of Lady Penelope and Parker in order to broaden *Thunderbirds*' appeal and story opportunities.

This became a priority for the production when Lew Grade finally saw 'Trapped in the Sky' in December 1964, unexpectedly throwing the production schedule for the series into chaos. Famously, upon seeing the episode in its original twenty-five-minute format, Grade was so impressed and delighted that he immediately ordered that the series be made into fifty-minute episodes. This was thrilling for Gerry and Sylvia, but brought immediate problems—nine episodes were in various stages of production, while a further ten scripts were either written or at an advanced stage.

A new writer was brought in to work with Gerry and Sylvia Anderson on expanding these stories to the new length—Tony Barwick. Barwick became script editor for the next three Supermarionation series and worked with Gerry Anderson for the rest of his career, ending with the abortive 1992 animated series *GFI* (*G-Force Intergalactic*). The shooting of the new sequences was fitted in among the already stretched crew's workload, and it took seven months before the series shooting schedule was able to return to some form of normality. The *Thunderbirds* schedule was already tight; as with all the series made since *Fireball XL5*, episodes were being shot in pairs, two puppet crews filming scenes for different episodes simultaneously on the AP Films stages.

Alan Fennell and Dennis Spooner, who had written almost the entirety of *Stingray*, returned to script many of the *Thunderbirds* adventures. Fennell was especially important to the production in its early stages, scripting four of the first five stories and supplying ten scripts in total. Pattillo himself wrote five scripts for the first series and two for the shorter second block of episodes. With the series now being made in a longer format, it was vital that more writers were recruited. There was still a certain amount of resistance among experienced screenwriters to work on what was regarded as a children's puppet series. This meant that two writers with no previous credits found themselves working on *Thunderbirds* scripts, with great success. Engineer Donald Robertson's 'Edge of Impact' was his first ever script to be filmed, and he was asked to write three further adventures. Similarly, Martin Crump's 'Operation Crash-Dive' was his first ever screenwriting job and he later wrote one of the best-loved of all *Thunderbirds* stories—'The Duchess Assignment'.

Especially impressive, regarding the production of *Thunderbirds*, is how many new talents came to create some of their best work all at the same time. This is especially true of Barry Gray, whose music, in the form of his orchestrations of Roberta Leigh's songs, was prominent right from the start. For *Thunderbirds*, Gray wrote the stirring 'Thunderbirds March', which would have been achievement enough for most composers, but he produced at the same time a seemingly endless stream of thrilling music for the episode scores. Most famously, this includes the music that underscores the series of clips from the upcoming episode, originally composed to accompany the rescue of Fireflash in 'Trapped in the Sky'.

It is impossible to underestimate the contribution that Gray's music makes to the Supermarionation series. On *Fireball XL5* and *Stingray*, there is an extent to which the visuals are perceived as being larger in scale than they actually are due to Barry Gray's majestic scores, and his masterful ability as an arranger to make relatively small orchestras sound huge. With *Thunderbirds*, the scale and the visuals and the music come together to produce often quite intoxicating results, not least on the opening credits of each episode. Although there were triumphs still to come, it is arguable that Barry Gray reached his peak as a composer on *Thunderbirds*, at exactly the point Supermarionation reached its peak of popularity.

It was still possible for compositions for earlier series to be used for *Thunderbirds* as required, as a library of Gray music had now been formed, replacing the occasional use of compositions by Edwin Astley music in *Supercar* when nothing else suitable was available. 'March of the Giant Oysters' from the *Stingray* episode 'Secret of the Giant Oyster' was used from time to time in *Thunderbirds*, while the sea-bound *Thunderbirds* episode 'Danger at Ocean Deep' was almost entirely scored using suitably nautical-sounding compositions from *Stingray*.

One thing Gray was unable to achieve to general satisfaction was an end theme song, an element that had been such a success for *Fireball XL5* and *Stingray*. His song 'Flying High', sung in a vaguely Everley Brothers style by Gary Miller, was replaced as the *Thunderbirds* end theme at a late stage of production by a version of the 'Thunderbirds March'. This last-minute decision helped seal the tune, quite possibly Barry Gray's masterpiece, in the popular imagination. 'Flying High' was eventually heard on *Thunderbirds*, played by video disc jockey Rick O'Shea in the episode 'Ricochet'.

Opening Credits and Logos

The rituals involved with watching television can sometimes be overlooked, but are vitally important to the viewing experience. Most important of these is the opening credits sequence (with hard-pressed television producers having to tell a story in a mere forty-two minutes, these are sadly today much reduced). *Thunderbirds* has an opening credits sequence far longer than anyone would attempt today, but so thrilling and well-designed as to be an undisputed classic of the form. The thrill of hearing voice artist Peter Dyneley intone the countdown '5-4-3-2-1', his tones suggesting both approaching doom and the thrill of a new mission is an integral part of the sheer joy of watching an episode of *Thunderbirds*.

It should be said that television station transmission departments did not always share audience's love of the Anderson opening sequences. It was highly unusual for the first image to be seen on a TV show to be of such importance as the '5' in the *Thunderbirds* countdown, or *Stingray*'s 'Stand By for Action', and these were often accidentally clipped off TV showings. The introduction of the Century 21 Television Logo solved this problem to an extent, but it is notable that Anderson series post-*Thunderbirds* did not have such openings, and often featured pre-credits sequences.

The Anderson series themselves were ahead of their time in their use of logos and typography during an era when this was an extreme rarity on British television. From *Fireball XL5* onwards, each series announced its title in an instantly recognisable form, which was then used on comics, merchandising, and books. By the time of *Thunderbirds*, this had gone beyond typography to a more complex, specially designed logo, making creative use of the typeface Playbill, with each letter appearing slightly behind the one on front, giving the effect of the word retreating into the distance.

Thunderbirds, the Swinging '60s, and the White Heat of Technology

One only has to compare the portrait of Britain presented the last time AP Films made a production set in Britain (their 1960 B-movie *Crossroads to Crime*) to the sleek, confident Britain seen in *Thunderbirds* to see how differently the country was able to present itself over the space of a mere five years.

Quite unexpectedly Britain had, by the mid-1960s, become one of the most fashionable places in the world. The increasingly popular image of Britain was of a young, colourful, vibrant place—which many who actually lived there might have struggled to recognise. This was a version of Britain (or, to be more exact, London and the Home Counties) cleaned up and presented for export. What better medium in which to display this not-quite-real fantasy Britain than puppetry—in which nothing is real. *Thunderbirds* was thus able, for the first time in a Supermarionation series, to express something of the country in which it was made.

Thunderbirds also expressed something about changing attitudes towards the possibilities presented by technological change. From *Supercar* to *Stingray*, technology is seen as an opportunity, opening up new worlds for humanity—a common feature of SF. This was a particularly prevalent opinion in Britain at the time, as future Prime Minister Harold Wilson predicted in a famous 1963 speech, 'a Britain that would be forged in the white heat of a scientific revolution'. In *Thunderbirds*, our relationship with science and technology is more problematic than in previous Supermarionation series—technology is both the problem and the solution.

Thus for every atomic irrigation plant making the Australian desert green (as seen in 'The Mighty Atom'), there is a figure such as The Hood ready to cause disaster in order to steal its secrets. Humanity can invent a beautiful Pacific-Atlantic Monorail ('Brink of Disaster'), but if it is run by a penny-pinching crook, such as Warren Grafton, then safety standards will be compromised and lives will be put in danger. Even the elements can turn against us, such as the monsoon in 'End of the Road' and the lightning strikes in 'Lord Parker's

'Oliday' and 'Brink of Disaster', as if the gods wish to remind us who is really in charge. But in the right hands, such as those of Jeff Tracy and his sons, technology is also our greatest defence, a protective hand encircling the planet, as depicted in International Rescue's own logo.

The writers of *Thunderbirds* had the knack of producing stories, which keyed into popular concerns of the day, cleverly projecting them forward, magnified to epic proportions, into the then-future of the twenty-first century. To paraphrase the science-fiction author Philip K. Dick, if fiction asks 'what if…?' science fiction says, 'My God, what if…?'

'Trapped in the Sky' concerns a stricken airliner at a time when the annual trip to Butlin's was being replaced with trips to sunny Spain via air travel. Air travel still retained an air of aspirational glamour at this time, but with the added *frisson* of danger provided by the dire consequences of an air crash. A spate of crashes involving the British-made de Havilland Comet jet airliners in 1953 and 1954 (as a result of which the phenomenon of metal fatigue was discovered) were still relatively fresh in popular memory at the time. Air Terrainian's opulent lounge area and spacious seating offered a rather more attractive proposition than today's endless queueing and body searches. It is also worth noting that 'Trapped in the Sky' appeared some five years before the huge success of the star-studded Hollywood thriller *Airport* made this type of story fashionable.

Donald Robertson's later story 'Path of Destruction' also plays on fears around transport and perceived dangers of foreign travel. Increasingly huge articulated lorries were rumbling along British roads, terrifying the residents of the smaller towns that they occasionally had to pass through—the country's motorway network was still being developed. This was reflected in a story about Crablogger One, a huge, mobile, atomic-powered (naturally) tree-felling machine. Its crew is felled on a logging trip to South America when they make the mistake of trying the local food—prepared in a memorably squalid restaurant kitchen—leading to the entire crew being knocked out by food poisoning. In a splendid example of SF's magnification of effects, the danger of a large commercial vehicle inconveniencing local traffic is transformed into the rather more dramatic scenario of an out-of-control nuclear-powered wood pulp factory about to destroy an entire town.

The dangers inherent in nuclear power generation were becoming more apparent by the mid-1960s. What was presented even five years earlier in *Supercar* as being a relatively safe and vaguely futuristic source of unlimited power was now increasingly seen as a potentially huge danger. Dennis Spooner's 'The Mighty Atom', in its original half-hour form, demonstrated its writer's comedy instincts in a story about a surveillance device disguised as a white mouse. Expanded to fifty minutes of screen time, an extended sub-plot is added in which The Hood's attempts at industrial espionage in a nuclear-powered water desalinisation plant almost results in an atomic holocaust wiping out large parts of Australia.

This plot strand also fits in with the popular genre idea of science running out of control, and the linked notion of the disastrous results of man interfering with nature. This often represents SF at its most politically conservative, sending messages that 'there are things mankind is not meant to know' and that scientists should not 'act like gods'. *Thunderbirds* retained a balance between highlighting the dangers of scientific advances (without which the series would have struggled to come up with plotlines) and the sheer joy it takes in the opportunities and physical beauty of futuristic technology.

The nearest *Thunderbirds* comes to this type of story is Alan Pattillo's 'Attack of the Alligators!', which recycles H. G. Wells' famous story *Food of the Gods and How It Came to Earth* from 1904. A chemical designed to make animals grow to enormous size, thus solving world food shortages (not the best thought-through of schemes—can you imagine how much a giant cow would eat before being turned into an enormous number of burgers?) is accidentally released into a swamp, resulting in the local alligators growing to huge, menacing size. 'Attack of the Alligators!' is one of the best-remembered *Thunderbirds* episodes, the sight of live animals threatening to eat the regular cast members provided a thrilling new dimension to the series. This is only slightly undercut by the fact that the giant alligators are portrayed by rather cute young specimens of the breed.

The '60s trend towards urban regeneration is given a SF spin in the spectacular Alan Fennell-scripted 'Terror in New York City'. The faces of British cities were being changed as unsuitable slum housing and beautiful Victorian architecture alike were swept away in the cause of modernity. Fennell's spin on this trend was a scheme to move the iconic Art Deco Empire State Building to allow the surrounding area to be redeveloped. In typical *Thunderbirds* fashion, the scheme results in disaster when the ground gives way beneath the building as it is being moved. Television reporter Ned Cook and his cameraman fall into the resulting cavern, their rescue from an underground cave filling with water is decidedly reminiscent of the German mining disaster, which originally inspired *Thunderbirds*.

Shopping habits were changing along with the skyline of Britain's cities, as more people began shopping in supermarkets, tiny by today's standards, and department stores as opposed to using specialist shops for each type of purchase. Alan Fennell's 'City of Fire' takes this idea to its logical conclusion, inventing the Thompson Tower, a 350-storey tower block, so tall that it reaches above the clouds, on which any product produced anywhere on Earth can be purchased. Of course, in reality when shopping centres arrived they were built outwards, rather than upwards, possibly because of the awful warning presented here, in which a careless woman driver (a piece of sexist stereotyping, which now seems very dated) is the cause of a fire, which results in the entire structure burning to the ground.

Perhaps the most direct reference to mid-1960s events in *Thunderbirds* comes with the episode 'Ricochet', which updates the British craze for pirate radio stations in the mid-to-late 1960s to the space age. Jeff Tracy's objections to the pirate video pop music station KLA (fifteen years before MTV began broadcasting in the US), which operates from a manned satellite orbiting the Earth, are very similar to the arguments against the pop music stations operating from fishing boats just outside British coastal waters in the 1960s. They were seen by officialdom as a danger to shipping lanes, and as using a bandwidth that might interfere with that used by emergency services. The pirates were adored by the huge teenage, music-loving audience, which was largely not served by the BBC's radio stations. While real-life stations such as Radio Caroline were occasionally forced off the air by their ships taking in water, station KLA is damaged when a renegade rocket launch is self-destructed near its unregistered location.

Space also provided *Thunderbirds* with one of its best-loved episodes in the form of 'Sun Probe', in which writer Alan Fennell and a splendid production take an unpromising idea and produce magic. The unlikely central notion of the episode takes America's efforts to mount a manned flight to the moon and extends it a hundred years into the future, when the first manned flight to the sun is launched.

The mission of Project Sun Probe is for three Solarnauts to fly close to the Sun, send a probe to collect a section of material thrown off by it, then turn around and return to Earth. Radiation from the Sun prevents the retro rockets from working, so Thunderbird 3 must launch to send a signal to activate them before Sun Probe's air conditioning packs in and the crew are fried—it is never explained how the signal can get through the Sun's radiation. From a plot that amounts to 'three men strapped to a giant fridge can't find reverse gear' comes a *Thunderbirds* classic. This is partially because the episode had to be expanded from twenty-five to fifty minutes, in the process of which a subplot was added in which Thunderbird 3's retros also fail and the rescue craft, with Alan, Scott, and Tin-Tin on board, also threatens to crash into the Sun.

End of the Road: The Cancellation of Thunderbirds

Incredibly, the 1960s *Thunderbirds* phenomenon lasted only two years from the broadcast of the first episodes. The major reason for this was that the expected deal for the series to be screened on US network television failed to happen. In some ways the deal collapsed because Lew Grade was simply too successful as a salesman. So impressed were the networks with the sample episodes and by Grade's sales pitch that all three bid for the series. Eventually the amounts of money being asked for the series became so high that one of the networks dropped out. The others, thinking that their competitor knew something they did not, got cold feet and backed out themselves. The moment that happened, *Thunderbirds*' moment had passed. That great opportunity when *Thunderbirds* could truly have swept the world and have become a global phenomenon was gone in the blink of an eye.

The world's greatest salesman, Lew Grade, had gambled big and lost big. However, it is exceptionally remarkable with how far he managed to take a series as far out of the ordinary as *Thunderbirds*. American television executives were (and remain) notorious for liking the familiar—genres, actors, and music had to be similar to what was currently popular. SF was traditionally seen as being either a children's genre, via cheaply made series such as *Space Patrol* (shown on Saturday mornings from 1950 to 1955) or suited to anthology series such as *The Outer Limits*, which ran from 1963 to 1965.

Episodic SF was something new; Irwin Allen was one of the first to find true success with his series *Voyage to the Bottom of the Sea* (which began airing from 14 September 1964) and *Lost in Space* (which premiered almost exactly a year later). *Star Trek* was still in pre-production at this point at Desilu Studios. The idea of a one-hour dramatic puppet series aimed at a family audience was completely outside of the experience of network television. Considering how close Lew Grade came to selling *Thunderbirds* to a US network demonstrates just how good a series it was and how convincing he was as a salesman.

By television standards, *Thunderbirds* was a very expensive and complex series to produce, and American sales were vital to making the series profitable. Despite the sale of the series to countries as far afield as Australia and Japan, America was by far the biggest television market—network television was the one place where the serious money was. Although *Thunderbirds* was seen in the US, it was sold to individual local stations for far smaller amounts of money than the networks would have paid.

This was the chain of events that led to a fateful meeting between Gerry Anderson and Lew Grade towards the end of production on *Thunderbirds'* first twenty-six-episode season. Anderson expected a straightforward meeting to confirm that the newly renamed Century 21 Productions could go on to produce more episodes. Instead, he was shocked to learn that Grade would find it easier to sell a new series than more episodes of *Thunderbirds*. Instead, ITC would back a shortened, six-episode second series and finance a feature film of *Thunderbirds*, but he wanted a new series format.

For the first time in their professional relationship, Gerry Anderson had no new ideas to pitch to Lew Grade—he had to go back to the drawing board. What he eventually came back with was not only quite unlike the previous Supermarionation series, it was different to anything seen on television before.

Key Episode

Episode 25: 'The Cham-Cham'
Written and directed by Alan Pattillo
First UK broadcast 24 March 1966 (ATV Midlands)

If 'Trapped in the Sky' represents the peak of *Thunderbirds* as a pure action-adventure format, 'The Cham-Cham' is the best representative of the series that *Thunderbirds* became during its thirty-two episode run. It is a series still in love with technology, probably more so than ever, with the beautiful RTL-2 military plane at the heart of the plot along with the titular Cham-Cham device itself. This is an absurdly large machine (how on Earth does Olsen sneak it into his hotel room?), which allows him to encode data in musical form.

The series is by this point given a lighter atmosphere by strong doses of comedy, along with elements of espionage. James Bond was a huge global success with the September 1964 release of *Goldfinger*, while *The Avengers* was on the cusp of breaking out into international fame with its mix of action, comedy, and a strong female co-lead.

One can see on-screen the confidence the whole production had at the time, which gives it a real cinematic air, possibly more so than the two *Thunderbirds* movies—the film *Thunderbird 6* is actually in some ways similar to this episode, but at fifty minutes 'The Cham-Cham' is far tighter and more entertaining. What it also shows is that, for the first time, a Supermarionation production could present glamour convincingly on-screen. This represents a triumph for the series' art director Bob Bell.

'The Cham-Cham' represents what one might refer to as Supermarionation Mk 1 (the progression from *The Adventures of Twizzle* to *Thunderbirds*, before the radical stylistic change of *Captain Scarlet and the Mysterons*) at its peak. Everything about the production works perfectly. The script, which borrows its central idea of a band unknowingly passing secret information in musical form from the 1963 *Sentimental Agent* episode 'All That Jazz', is paced perfectly. This is despite the fact that there is a distinct lack of actual rescuing or use of the *Thunderbirds* craft until the later stages of the episode. The episode so successfully brings the audience into the world of Paradise Peaks that we even forgive the episode its occasional moments of silliness (such as Parker floating to Earth in Mary Poppins fashion, using his umbrella as a parachute).

The episode also demonstrates how central to the success of the series Lady Penelope and Parker had become, and how the writers had become more comfortable in portraying their relationship. They seem rather formal in their scenes during 'Trapped in the Sky', while 'The Perils of Penelope'—the first episode that really showcases the pair—suffers more than most in its conversion from twenty-five minutes to fifty. 'The Cham-Cham', on the other hand, has the air of a story that was written from the start around Lady Penelope and Parker's unique relationship.

There were triumphs to come in the careers of Gerry and Sylvia Anderson and the AP Films/Century 21 team, but, looking back, 'The Cham-Cham' can be regarded as the absolute pinnacle of what they achieved with puppetry.

14

Thunderbirds at the Movies

By the mid-1960s, the Hollywood movie studios were struggling for survival. Their decline began with a 1948 Supreme Court antitrust court decision, which forced them to divest themselves of their cinema chains. These were highly profitable and provided the studios with a guaranteed outlet for their films, effectively locking out most independent producers. The studios were further hamstrung by the rise of television as a mass medium and their carrying of expensive overheads, such as studio facilities and backlot—in an era when films were increasingly made on location.

The major exception to this story of decline and near-extinction was United Artists. UA was formed in 1919 by film superstars Mary Pickford, Douglas Fairbanks, and Charles Chaplin along with D. W. Griffith, Hollywood's most esteemed film director. The original idea was that the company's four founders would gain complete control of their careers and productions, but by the early 1950s United Artists was virtually moribund. The company was revived in 1951 by Arthur Krim and Robert Benjamin with a business model radically different to the Hollywood norm. It would have no production facilities of its own, instead funding independent producers and distributing the results through cinema chains now freed from their ties to the Hollywood major studios.

The idea was an immediate success, and by the 1960s the company was casting its net beyond America, funding and distributing productions from the vibrant European market that was increasingly making much of Hollywood's output look staid and old-fashioned. This paid dividends in a big way when UA backed three phenomenally successful film series—The James Bond movies, Sergio Leone's 'Man with No Name' Spaghetti Westerns, and The Beatles' films. Originally the latter was a wheeze, whereby the cheapest possible film was made in order to generate the guaranteed success of a soundtrack album for United Artists Records. The band's first film, *A Hard Day's Night*, was unexpectedly both a critical and financial success.

By 1966, United Artists was the most successful studio in Hollywood, and came to the door of the newly rechristened Century 21 Productions in search of their latest hit film series. The film was financed by Lew Grade to the tune of £250,000 before United Artists came on board, such was his faith in *Thunderbirds*, and the American studio was convinced that it had another major hit franchise on its hand.

Efforts were made to make the film version of *Thunderbirds* stand apart from what could be seen on television. Naturally the film was made in colour, and for most audiences worldwide this would be the first chance to see the craft and characters in colour outside of the pages of *TV21* comic, since colour television broadcasting was largely confined to the US in 1966. A widescreen process was also chosen for *Thunderbirds Are Go*, as was common for major productions of the era. Traditionally, the widescreen image had been produced by having the image squeezed onto a 35-mm frame by means of an anamorphic lens, then 'un-squeezed' using a similar lens on the projection equipment. The original anamorphic lenses had disadvantages, though, and were particularly poor at close-ups. This made anamorphic widescreen impossible to use on a Supermarionation production, which was largely shot over very short distances.

Techniscope, introduced by Technicolor's Italian subsidiary in 1960, produced wide images in a different way, splitting the almost square 4:3 ratio image into two wider frames. However, there were problems with image quality; half the amount of film was used, which saved money, but meant that the potential picture quality was also reduced by 50 per cent. Vitally, close-ups were possible in Techniscope, as it used traditional camera lenses.

Thunderbirds Are Go is a film utterly in love with its technology, which can, to modern eyes, rob the film of pace. It should be remembered, though, that in 1966 there was nothing else like this on the world's cinema screens. The narrative opens with an extended sequence of Zero X's main body, its lifting bodies, and its landing craft being assembled on the runway, the crew briefing and eventual lift-off to the first manned expedition to Mars. Not surprisingly, things start to go wrong (this is *Thunderbirds*, after all). The Hood is on board Zero X, taking pictures of the craft's internal workings, and his foot gets caught in the wing flap mechanism, jamming the elevator controls. This causes Zero X to go out of control. Both the crew and The Hood manage to escape the resulting crash into the ocean.

This sequence, which takes up the first fifteen minutes of the film, is extremely well-done and extremely well-directed by David Lane (chosen to direct the film by Gerry Anderson when first choice Alan Pattillo turned down the assignment, having tired of working with puppets). A second mission is prepared, but this time International Rescue is called in to handle the security arrangements—Jeff agrees after much deliberation, and the Thunderbird craft swing into action.

As the film was shot in a different aspect ratio to the television series, the familiar stock footage of Thunderbirds 1, 2, and 3 being launched had to be reshot. This meant that some inconsistencies were ironed out, such as Thunderbird 1's apparent change of position while on its way to the launch pad. Also, Thunderbird 3's interior was totally redesigned. The original set, designed for the episode 'Sun Probe', footage from which was then reused when the craft was seen subsequently, was an ugly yellow colour with a spectacularly unsuitable cockpit. This was replaced by a much more futuristic design using a great deal of chrome. Naturally, Lady Penelope and Parker are called in, Penelope undercover as a magazine reporter.

The second launch takes place, but only after Lady Penelope foils an attempt to replace one of the crew members with a The Hood, wearing a mask (was he really going to wear that thing for the entire mission?). This is actually quite a good idea, as the scenes of the launching are intercut with International Rescue's foiling of the second sabotage attempt, avoiding pointless repetition. We also learn that FAB 1 can travel on water using a built-in hydrofoil, and, during an extended sequence of the car shooting down The Hood's military helicopter, we see that Zero X has already taken off.

Forty minutes into the film, things start to go wrong with the narrative. There is a very long sequence of Alan dreaming about going to the Swinging Star nightclub with Lady Penelope, where Cliff Richard Jr and the Shadows are playing. Eventually the story picks up again, as Zero X lands on Mars, but by this point the film's narrative has stopped dead for a full fifteen minutes, leaving an aching chasm at a crucial point in *Thunderbirds Are Go*.

In an interesting precursor to the events of *Captain Scarlet and the Mysterons*, the Zero X crew make the mistake of blowing up bits of the planet's surface. In the process, they unleash giant, fireball-spitting Rock Snakes, forcing the Martian Exploration Vehicle to make a swift getaway and blessing the film with a much-needed action sequence. The film's structural problems return, as Zero X now has six weeks before it returns to Earth, which again prevents the film from developing a strong narrative.

When the craft does return, one of the lifting bodies designed to allow Zero X to land fails, causing the ship to be damaged, including the crew escape unit. Alan is put on board the undercarriage of Zero X in an attempt to repair the circuit for the escape unit before Zero X crashes on the town of Craigsville. Eventually, he has to complete the circuit by hand. This is possibly a sign that new ideas for Thunderbirds were running short, as this sequence is extremely similar to the climax of the series episode 'Operation Crash Dive'.

To the surprise of all concerned, *Thunderbirds Are Go* was a resounding failure at the box office. It was released in time for Christmas 1966 with an enormous publicity campaign, but audiences stayed away in their droves. It is possible that some of United Artists publicity posters for the film did not help as they included the warning that 'Adults over 16 should be accompanied by children', working against the Anderson's insistence that *Thunderbirds* was for the whole family.

Despite this setback, United Artists retained its faith in *Thunderbirds* as a movie franchise. The studio had experience with developing film series and knew that some patience was required. Though profitable from the start, the James Bond films had not become a global phenomenon until *Thunderball*, the fourth film in the series, at which point the first three films became very hot properties indeed.

The costs involved should also be taken into account. *Thunderbirds Are Go* cost £250,000, while *Thunderbird 6* was granted an increased budget of £300,000. Although this was more than the budget of the television series, it was a relatively tiny amount of money compared to the amount being spent on the average Hollywood film. The then-current James Bond film *You Only Live Twice* (which cost rather more than the average) cost $10.3 million and took $111 million at the box office. Even this amount, which (adjusted for inflation) dwarfs the amount taken by most hit films, was regarded as a disappointment compared to the $141 million taken by *Thunderball*, the previous film in the series. The small cost of the *Thunderbirds'* films in relation to the potential rewards shows why United Artists were minded to give it a second chance.

The result was *Thunderbird 6*, a very different style of film to *Thunderbirds Are Go*, with more in common to the series episode 'The Cham-Cham'. That had been an end-of-season special, during which the production tried its hand at a more light-hearted production with the air of a Hollywood musical. Here the approach was spread across an entire film. *Thunderbird 6* melds two storylines into one overall plot—The New World Aircraft Corporation agrees to build Brains' design for a twenty-first century equivalent of an airship. Instead of being held aloft by gas, Skyship One has an anti-gravity device, and moves slowly, in conditions of great luxury, rather than making a fetish of speed. Lady Penelope, Parker, Alan, and Tin-Tin travel on Skyship One's maiden test flight around the world, while Brains remains on Tracy Island, ordered by Jeff Tracy to work on designs for a new Thunderbird craft. Jeff is convinced that such a craft is necessary, despite having no idea what it might actually do.

The cruise of Skyship One is a trap, however. The real crew has been murdered, replaced by villains who are recording every word the International Rescue personnel say, as part of a plot by The Hood, who wants to capture Thunderbirds 1 and 2.

The luxurious, peripatetic nature of *Thunderbird 6* puts the film in a tradition of filmmaking particular to the 1960s. As television replaced radio and film as the primary form of public entertainment in America, the finances of the major film studios became tied to mega-productions, many of which left their traditional studio bases far behind in an attempt to show audiences things they had never seen before. This trend can be seen to have begun with Mike Todd's 1956 production *Around the World in 80 Days*, which became the model for such films. Huge successes could be had with this strategy—spend big and the rewards could be just as huge. Stanley Kramer's *It's a Mad, Mad, Mad, Mad World*, for example, cost a then-huge $9.4 million in 1963, but grossed $60 million.

Other such hits followed, mixing action, outdoor settings, and comedy. With studio finances growing ever-more stretched, the limits of this approach were demonstrated in 1967 at Warner Brothers Studios, while *Thunderbird 6* was being filmed in Slough. A huge $13 million was lavished on the musical *Camelot*, a three-hour commercial disappointment hoping to repeat the success of the *Sound of Music*, which had broken box office records ever since its 1965 release. It was to be the last film studio head Jack Warner produced—he sold the company soon after.

Thunderbird 6 is a beautiful-looking film, meticulously produced with that special, luxurious sheen only seen in the most expensive 1960s films. Somehow, though, the delicate balance of comedy, drama, and action that made *Thunderbirds* work had been lost. Most of the running time is given over to Lady Penelope, Parker, Alan, and Tin-Tin's world cruise. These four characters allowed the writers of the television series to take *Thunderbirds* beyond basic rescue stories—the rescues that were once at the heart of the episodes now seemed like add-ons and it is notable just how little dialogue Scott and Virgil Tracy have in both films.

Even when Thunderbirds 1 and 2 finally see some action, they are dwarfed by Skyship One, repeating the same basic error made by *Thunderbirds Are Go*— the Thunderbird craft themselves no longer look impressive, being diminished by the huge size of Zero X and Skyship One. The whole point of Thunderbird 2 is that it is huge and dominates the screen, but Derek Meddings' new designs for the films were long and slim like the screens they were designed to fill. The squat Thunderbird 2 was designed to fill a television screen.

Even the puppets had been redesigned for the films, losing some of their character in the process. It is often thought that the new-style, correctly proportioned puppets being used on the *Captain Scarlet* sets while *Thunderbird 6* was being shot were a huge change from *Thunderbirds*. A comparison between the earliest *Thunderbirds* episodes and the two films reveals that the puppet style had changed considerably in that time. The Alan, Scott, and Virgil puppets all look rather different to the versions created for the first season of the television series.

It is possible that, despite being the creators of *Thunderbirds*, Gerry and Sylvia Anderson were not the best people to write the films. Besides not featuring the Thunderbirds craft and key regular cast members enough, *Thunderbird 6* struggles to maintain a consistent tone. The murders of the real Skyship One crew are quite brutal, their bodies being tossed overboard while the ship is in flight. The climactic shootout between the International Rescue personnel and the villains also seems unnecessarily violent. Thunderbirds 1 and 2 also seem armed to the teeth, suddenly obliterating The Hood and his henchmen when it transpires they've fallen into a trap.

The result was that, despite the new, lighter, and more colourful approach taken by *Thunderbird 6*, the film had the same disappointing box office results as its predecessor on its release in July 1968. United Artists patience was finally worn thin and *Thunderbirds* had reached the end of the road—for now, at least.

15

Other Worlds: British '60s SF Beyond the Andersons

What remains truly remarkable about the AP Films/Century 21 output is just how different and against the grain it was compared to what other British filmmakers were producing at the time. Even the SF films coming out of Britain were, with some interesting exceptions, quite unlike the futuristic worlds coming out of Slough Trading Estate.

The 1960s British SF movies, broadly speaking, fit into three categories. The biggest budget productions were in a sort of proto-Steampunk style, inspired by the great success of films based on Jules Verne's *Twenty Thousand Leagues Under the Sea* in 1954 and H. G. Wells' *The Time Machine* in 1960. As the '60s progressed, this fitted in well with a growing interest in Victoriana, which was incorporated into the visual arts as a vital component of psychedelia. Film producers began a long series of pictures inspired by Wells and Verne.

Examples of British participation in this trend include *Mysterious Island* (1961), *First Men in the Moon* (1964), *Jules Verne's Rocket to the Moon* (1967), *City Under the Sea* (1965), and *Captain Nemo and the Underwater City*. This last example seemed rather anachronistic on its 1969 release, but it was only a few years until producer John Dark started a new cycle of releases with his 1975 hit *The Land that Time Forgot*.

Secondly, there were SF/horror crossovers. It remains in the eye of the viewer where these fall on the SF/horror spectrum, but it can be argued that the best known of these is Hammer's 1967 adaptation of Nigel Kneale's BBC serial *Quatermass and the Pit*. Other examples tended towards the low-budget, such as *Curse of the Fly* (1965), the second sequel to the 1958 film *The Fly* with its original star Vincent Price long gone. Another American co-production was Herman J. Leder's 1966 *The Frozen Dead* with imported star Dana Andrews, well past his commercial peak and cast in the opposite of his normal heroic type as a Nazi scientist. Planet Film Productions made a pair of horror/SF crossovers, *Island of Terror* (1966), starring Peter Cushing and Edward Judd, plus *Night of the Big Heat*, released the following year, which featured both Cushing and Christopher Lee. These were produced by Tom Blakeley, the son of Mancunian Films proprietor John E. Blakeley, who had great success in the North of England making films with comedians such as Frank Randle and a young George Formby (before Rank made him a national star). Despite their obvious low production values, Planet Films productions have developed a loyal cult following over the years.

Some of the cheaper films in this sub-genre are genuinely very good, with *The Projected Man* (1967) providing some legitimate chills and an interesting window into a more progressive attitude towards censorship of sexual content. Quickly elevated to classic status was Michael Reeves' *The Sorcerers* from the same year.

The final strand of British SF filmmaking was the alien invasion sub-genre, which Gerry himself had been involved in with his sound work on *Devil Girl from Mars* (1954), and which the Anderson productions took on board with *Captain Scarlet and the Mysterons* and *UFO*. This style of film achieved a major commercial breakthrough with Hammer Films' adaptations of Nigel Kneale's *The Quatermass Experiment* (1955) and *Quatermass 2* (1957) both directed by Val Guest, a close friend of the Andersons. The success of these two productions not only set Hammer on the road to the worldwide success of their Frankenstein and Dracula films, but also inspired a slew of low-budget alien invasion movies. Robert S. Baker and Monty Berman quickly bought the rights to another television SF serial and made *The Trollenberg Terror* (1958), while even Merton Park—more used to making Edgar Wallace B-pictures for Anglo-Amalgamated—got in on the act with their 1966 release *Invasion*. Also gracing cinemas in the years leading up to *Captain Scarlet and the Mysterons* were *Unearthly Stranger* (1963) and John Gilling's *The Night Caller* (1965). Both were stylish, intelligent, low-budget productions that were eagerly snapped up by American distributors, which perhaps gave Century 21 Productions a clue that this might be a profitable route to take when they were planning their follow-up to *Thunderbirds*.

16

Captain Scarlet and the Mysterons

'This is the voice of the Mysterons. We know that you can hear us Earthmen.'

Executive producer Gerry Anderson
Produced by Reg Hill
Format by Gerry and Sylvia Anderson
Music composed and directed by Barry Gray
A Gerry Anderson Century 21 Television Production
An ITC World Wide Distribution
32 × twenty-five-minute episodes
First broadcast Friday 29 September 1967 (ATV Midlands)

When a Martian expedition destroys an alien city, mistaking a harmless scanner for a weapon, an incredible force is unleashed, which promises to destroy all life on Earth. These are The Mysterons, a formless people with the power of retro-metabolism—they can create a duplicate of any person or object, but first they must destroy the original. Defending the Earth is Spectrum, a semi-secret military organisation run from Cloudbase—a floating aircraft carrier. The Mysterons kill two Spectrum members, Captain Black and Captain Scarlet, but after a fall from a high building, Scarlet leaves the Mysterons control, but retains his special powers—he is virtually indestructible. Captain Black remains at large under Mysteron control, and helps to coordinate their plans for the destruction of all human life on Earth.

The first screening of *Captain Scarlet and the Mysterons* was actually on 29 April 1967 in the London area. This was unbilled and unscheduled, as part of a colour test transmission and introduced to the world AP Films' new identity. The name had been outmoded since the departure of Arthur Provis from the company in 1960, and was replaced by a new title. This was A Gerry Anderson Century 21 Television Production, a new identity accompanied by a splendid animated logo and musical 'sting' by Barry Gray. The production company at the heart of the Anderson empire now had a name in line with its associated publishing and merchandising arms. Perhaps more importantly, the Gerry Anderson name was front and centre as the possibility became real that in Gerry, Britain might have its own equivalent to Walt Disney.

After the company logo came the opening credits, which made it clear to audiences that they were seeing something completely new and different from the newly renamed company. Ironically, this involved returning to some imagery from *Four Feather Falls*, as the camera pans down a dark alley, taking the point of view of a stalking gunman. The camera then pans quickly to reveal our hero, spot lit by hissing arc lamps. There is the sound of gunfire as Scarlet is strafed by machine-gun fire, but it has no effect on him. Scarlet raises his pistol and shoots his attacker, and with the sound of Barry Gray's distinctive seven beat timpani refrain, Scarlet's name appears on-screen—'One man fate has made indestructible. His name—Captain Scarlet'.

A second, even creepier credits sequence soon follows as the secondary characters in Captain Scarlet's large recurring cast are introduced. With eerie music in the background, the green twin circles with which the Mysterons presence is indicated floats across the Spectrum characters. Meanwhile, like some kind of malign railway station announcer, the deep, booming Voice of the Mysterons broadcasts to Spectrum a clue as to what their latest plot is to destroy all human life on Earth.

Interestingly, the voice of the Mysterons is a specially treated and lowered version of the voice of Donald Gray, and still quite recognisably the same as the voice of Colonel White. This is fitting, since we trust Colonel White as the wise leader of Spectrum, and it becomes clear from the events of the opening episode that the Mysterons are not simply evil because they are aliens. In some ways Spectrum and the Mysterons are mirror images of each other, defending their respective civilisations from what they perceive as a deadly threat.

The history of Supermarionation can be described as a constant attempt to expand the scope of what could be achieved via puppetry. With 'The Cham-Cham', and even more so in the *Thunderbirds* feature films, the production team pushed Supermarionation into achieving a genuine air of Hollywood glamour. When Gerry and Sylvia Anderson devised the format for *Captain Scarlet and the Mysterons* they attempted to make key elements of the new series as different to *Thunderbirds* as possible. In the process, Supermarionation was completely reinvented and a new set of genre archetypes were mined for inspiration. The puppet form had been used for comedy, SF, action adventure, and glamour—now it was going to be genuinely creepy. Scarlet was now going to bring zombies and the paranoid atmosphere of *Invasion of the Body Snatchers* to a young television audience.

Captain Scarlet and the Mysterons was to be very different to any of the previous Anderson puppet series, which had attempted to balance thrills with comedy. This would be, by far, the most serious production in tone of any Supermarionation series. This was partially due to the subject matter of the series, in which death was bound to happen in every episode. It might also be regarded, however, as an inevitable result of the new, realistically proportioned puppet designs. It was now possible to make puppets containing a lip-synch mechanism, but with a head in proportion to the rest of the body, however, they proved difficult to make display emotion.

This meant that most episodes of the series were very serious indeed. It is interesting to note that, unlike the *Stingray* and *Thunderbirds* puppets, none of the puppets created for *Captain Scarlet and the Mysterons* had 'smiler' variations made. The puppets were only really convincing when being serious, and any attempt to introduce a lot of movement into their actions would destroy the illusion of realism.

This effected every part of the production. The voices chosen were also very serious—actor Francis Matthews was asked to play Captain Scarlet using his Cary Grant voice, but this sometimes had the effect of making his vocal performance stiff and monotone. The scripts similarly tended far more towards the grimly serious than had previous series. Comedy relief was now a rarity— even the endings of the episodes usually featured a heroic entreaty to continue the fight against the Mysterons rather than attempting to give the audience a stress-relieving chortle.

On the subject of puppet design, it is also notable that Captain Scarlet is the last Supermarionation series to attempt to portray strong female characters. Spectrum's cadre of female fighter pilots—The Angels—were a key part of the series format, even given their own separate merchandising range. The series failed to feature them strongly as individuals though, a major problem being that the smaller puppet heads made it difficult for the sculptors to create female characters with interesting, memorable faces. The Angels remain memorable as a group, but not individually.

It is worth noting that the only female regular characters in the final two Century 21 puppet series, *Joe 90* and *The Secret Service*, are elderly housekeepers whose faces were much easier to sculpt memorably than younger women. These were hardly characters designed to drive the narratives of the series they featured in—the heady days of Lady Penelope, aristocrat and International Rescue secret agent, suddenly seemed a long time ago.

The look of Supermationation was also transformed for the new series. With the multiple vehicles of International Rescue being such a key part of the appeal of *Thunderbirds*, Derek Meddings and Mike Trim designed an array of vehicles and aircraft for Spectrum. The Spectrum craft represent one of the high points in sustained design excellence for the Anderson series, with a seemingly endless array of beautiful vehicles to allow Spectrum to defend Earth against the Mysteron threat.

The two most popular designs were Meddings' Spectrum Pursuit Vehicle (or SPV) and Angel Interceptor fighter aircraft. The former was a vehicle positioned at some point between a car and an armoured tank, designed to travel over any terrain with five sets of wheels, plus a caterpillar track array at the rear for emergency traction. Uniquely, the SPV was driven with the driver facing backwards and viewing the road via a television screen, steering the car the opposite way to normal. This allowed the vehicle to be designed with no windscreen, which, along with its large front bumper, gives the SPV a tough, hard-wearing look. SPVs are kept hidden in secret locations throughout the world, requisitioned by Spectrum officers as required.

The Angel Interceptors, which were launched from the flight deck of Spectrum's floating headquarters Cloudbase, represented a design of some visual delicacy. Derek Meddings managed to create an aircraft that looked like it could sting, rather than a bulky fighter-bomber. This was helped by the decision not to allow the audience to see rockets emerging from the plane, which *Fireball XL5* and *Stingray* had proved was a difficult effect to achieve convincingly. Instead the Angel Interceptor's missiles were launched from within its body—we only saw the flash of the missile launch and then its explosive impact. The planes were piloted by an all-female squad of pilots, codenamed Angels—Destiny, Symphony, Rhapsody, Melody, and Harmony.

Back on the ground, Spectrum agents' standard road transport was the Spectrum Patrol Car, a sleek, shark-like red saloon car capable of speeds up to 200 mph. This was designed by Mike Trim, as was the more rarely seen Maximum Security Vehicle—a bullet-proof vehicle designed to transport threatened personnel in safety; this was highlighted in the second episode of the series, 'Winged Assassin'. Much of the vehicle design work in *Scarlet* was carried out by Trim, as Derek Meddings was busy with designing for *Thunderbird 6*, the feature film that was being produced at the Stirling Road studios in tandem with the new television series. Thus, Mike Trim was also called upon to design the Spectrum Passenger Jet, with its idiosyncratic reversed rear fin, and the Spectrum Helicopter, with another distinctive rear-end design feature in the form of a turbo-fan.

The superb vehicle designs for *Scarlet* were turned into big-selling toys with the Airfix plastic construction kit of the Angel Interceptor selling in huge numbers for many years, as did the die-cast models of the SPV and SPC—even the Maximum Security Vehicle proved popular for the company, complete with 'radioactive isotopes' for it to transport.

Derek Meddings' role on the effects of *Scarlet* were also limited by his commitments on *Thunderbird 6*, leading him to take the title of supervising visual effects director. The day-to-day effects work was performed by three units—two main units directed by Shaun Whittacker-Cooke and Jimmy Elliot, and a third directed by Peter Wragg who was dedicated to filming flying sequences.

Set design on the series also looked more modern and sleek than on previous series. Bob Bell, busy as art director on *Thunderbird 6*, was working as supervising art director, with Keith Wilson and John Lageu performing many of the set designs. As on the later *Thunderbirds* episodes and the two feature films, Lageu designed the more technical vehicle and aircraft interiors, while Wilson worked on sets. The interior sets for Cloudbase remain particularly impressive, both stylish and highly detailed with ground-breaking use of see-though coloured Perspex.

The Spectrum uniforms were also modern and stylish. Later *Thunderbirds* episodes had shown an increasing awareness of modern fashions, most notably Lady Penelope's Mondrian dress, based on a design by Yves Saint Laurent, though the Tracy boys also looked increasingly like they'd been shopping in Carnaby Street boutiques. For *Captain Scarlet and the Mysterons*, Sylvia Anderson was highly influenced by Pierre Cardin's SF-themed Cosmos collection. The basic Cardin design was adapted into a slightly more military look by Keith Wilson. Also added were epaulettes, which lit up when a radio message was incoming on the uniform's hat-mounted radio, a design feature first mooted during the development of the WASP uniforms for *Stingray*.

Most of the *Thunderbirds* writers had moved on to other projects, or were not professional writers and resumed their original careers. Dennis Spooner was story editor on *Doctor Who*, while Alan Fennell was busy with his publishing activities, with *TV21* comic reaching its peak of popularity. Alan Pattillo had turned down the offer to direct the first *Thunderbirds* feature film, and it was little surprise that he left the company after working on *Thunderbirds*' second series.

Pattillo's screenplay idea for *The Avengers* episode 'The Bird Who Knew Too Much' was accepted, and turned into a finished script by that series associate producer Brian Clemens in 1967. He then found regular employment as a sound editor on feature films before joining the crew of the ITC filmed detective series *Strange Report* as editor. He worked extensively, though not exclusively, as an editor from this point on, working on many films and TV movies, yet occasionally returning to contribute to Anderson productions. He wrote one episode of *Captain Scarlet and the Mysterons* and one of *UFO*, 'The Square Triangle'. In 1976 he edited the *Space: 1999* episode 'The Mark of Archanon', and in 1983 directed four of the first six episodes of *Terrahawks*, helping set the style for the series.

It fell to script editor Tony Barwick to assemble a new team of writers for *Captain Scarlet and the Mysterons*, which proved to be no easy task—Barwick eventually wrote more than half of the thirty-two episodes himself. Many of the writers working on *Scarlet* had no previous experience in screenwriting, or indeed any credits afterwards. Seven of the new writers contributed only a single script to the series—this total does include Pattillo and Leo Eaton, who directed his own script 'Place of Angels'. Shane Rimmer, who had previously written promotional material for *Thunderbirds*, joined the writing team and would regularly provide scripts for the final three puppet series.

Always keen to recruit from within, Century 21 promoted several crew members to regular directors for the new series, creating the basis of the directorial team that would also helm the next two series. To set the style, two old hands were in charge of the first two episodes, Desmond Saunders directed the opening episode before taking on the role of supervising director, while the second episode was directed by David Lane, who then moved on to direct the feature film *Thunderbird 6*.

Brian Burgess returned to direct half a dozen episodes before taking on a different role on the series, replacing Harry Ledger as visual effects production manager. After *Captain Scarlet and the Mysterons*, he became a highly successful production manager and producer on feature films and for American television.

Burgess was replaced on the *Scarlet* team of directors by Leo Eaton, promoted from the rota of four assistant directors employed on the series—his first task as director was on his own script, 'Place of Angels'. He stayed on as a director for *Joe 90* and *The Secret Service*, and was hired for the crew of *UFO*'s first production block in 1969, working on six episodes. Subsequently, Eaton has had a very long and successful career as a producer, director, and writer of documentary films for both adults and children.

Alan Perry was promoted from his role as camera operator to director, starting with episode five, 'Manhunt'. Ken Turner had been assistant director to David Lane on *Thunderbirds Are Go*, and was then added to the *Captain Scarlet* director's roster; starting with 'Operation Time', the sixth episode to go into production, he was to direct seven episodes in all before moving on to direct episodes of both *Joe 90* and *The Secret Service*. Both Perry and Turner were to go on to direct episodes of Century 21's live-action series *UFO*, along with David Lane. Turner in particular developed a bold visual style, which suited the more *outré* aspects of that series down to the ground.

The final member of the *Captain Scarlet* directorial team was the most experienced director ever to work on the Supermarionation productions. Aged forty-nine when he was working on the series, Robert Bryce Lynn was an older head among the young, recent directorial graduates. He was from a show business background, the son of well-known comedic actor Ralph Lynn. Robert began his film career in 1936 as an assistant cameraman, working his way up to the position of assistant director; he worked for Hammer on their famous horror productions *Dracula* (1957) and the *Revenge of Frankenstein* (1958—co-starring Francis Matthews). He had also directed extensively for television on filmed series such as *Dial 999* for Harry Alan Towers and two Rank/ITV co-productions—*Interpol Calling* and *Ghost Squad*. He had directed a series of thrillers for Harry Alan Towers in South African locations prior to joining Century 21. The next time that Lynn worked with Anderson was in 1976; this was on the second series of *Space: 1999*, for which he was assistant director for ten episodes, and directed two further stories himself.

The production had three lighting cameramen working on episodes, long standing crew member Julien Lugrin alternating episodes with Paddy Seale. Seale left after episode eleven, returning for *Joe 90*, and was replaced by

Ted Catford. Often known as Teddy Catford, he was a highly experienced cinematographer who had worked extensively in documentary film-making, often on training films and public information films for the government communications agency, the Central Office of Information.

The Stirling Road studios of Century 21 Productions were running two puppet unit crews at once to keep up with the demands of production on *Captain Scarlet*. Most episodes directed by Robert Lynn and Ken Turner were photographed by lighting cameraman Julien Lugrin, with Nick Procopides and Derek Black as camera operators. Brian Burgess and Alan Perry's first two episodes were photographed by Paddy Seale, with Ron Gallifant and Alan McDonald as camera operators. Ted Catford took over as lighting cameraman from Seale, with Alan McDonald acting as camera operator, Ron Gallifant was replaced by his counterpart from episode seventeen, Ted Cutlack.

Interestingly, the final three episodes of the series, 'Attack on Cloudbase', 'Inferno' and 'The Inquisition', share most of the same crew. With Lew Grade having asked for a new series concept instead of more episodes of *Captain Scarlet*, it seems that production was being wound down for the final three stories, the last of which was a flashback episode with only eleven minutes of new material required. Key crew members were preparing for the new Supermarionation series, which would enter production with barely a break from the final episode of *Scarlet* wrapping production. This was for *Joe 90*.

Voice Artists

The traditional weekend recording session time had been abandoned for the new series. This had allowed actors with regular stage or filming engagements to still fit in their commitments to the current Supermarionation series. The effect this change had on *Captain Scarlet* was that it had the largest voice cast of any of the AP Films/Century 21 series to date, some actors only voicing characters for a few episodes. Neil McCallum, a Canadian actor who had provided voices for *Thunderbirds Are Go*, only contributed to three episodes, while Paul Maxwell, returning from *Fireball XL5* and *Thunderbirds Are Go*, left the voice cast after episode twelve. Also leaving after episode twelve was legendary Australian actor Charles 'Bud' Tingwell, who had previously lent his vocal talents to the second series of *Thunderbirds* and *Thunderbirds Are Go*. Jeremy Wilkin was also rehired, proving his versatility in a wide variety of voice roles and accents throughout the series, while the familiar and distinctive voice of Shane Rimmer was also heard from time to time playing minor characters.

Also joining the cast was Australian actor Gary Files, who would become one of the mainstays of the Supermarionation voice cast for the final three series of their run. Born in Melbourne, Australia, Files left for Canada in 1959 to attend the National Theatre School in Montreal, staying to establish a promising theatre career. At the time *Captain Scarlet and the Mysterons* was being produced, Files was in the middle of a four-year stay in England before resuming his career in Canada and finally settling back home in Australia.

Sylvia Anderson returned to vocal duties, but not in the same capacity as the other series. *Captain Scarlet and the Mysterons*, in fact, employed the largest contingent of female voice artists of any Supermarionation series. At the start of the recording sessions, Sylvia, voicing the regular character of Melody Angel, was joined by Janna Hill, playing Symphony Angel, and Liz Morgan, who lent her vocal talents to Destiny, Rhapsody, and Harmony Angels. From episode fifteen, Harmony Angel was recast, the Chinese character was voiced by Lian Shin for her final appearance.

The main characters in the series were performed by the same actors throughout the thirty-two episodes of the series. Captain Scarlet himself was voiced by forty-year-old Francis Matthews, who had started acting in repertory in Leeds, then learned his craft 'on the job' in other rep companies elsewhere in Britain after serving in the Royal Navy. He was best known at the time for his film career, which saw him feature in the Hammer horror movies *The Revenge of* Frankenstein (1958) and *Dracula, Prince of Darkness* (1966), as well as starring opposite iconic horror star Boris Karloff in *Corridors of Blood* (1958). Before being cast as Captain Scarlet, Matthews had acted opposite comedy duo Morecambe and Wise in their first two films for Rank, *The Intelligence Men* (1965) and *That Riviera Touch* (1966), Eric Morecambe becoming a close friend. Subsequent to recording vocals for Captain Scarlet, Francis Matthews achieved international fame when he took over for television the role of Francis Durbridge's urbane author and sleuth Paul Temple.

With *Captain Scarlet and the Mysterons* being repeated often over the following decades, Francis Matthews found the part something of a mixed blessing, keeping him in the spotlight in later years, but finding the reaction of fans during convention appearances with 'that little red doll' somewhat mystifying.

Scarlet's partner on his Spectrum missions, Captain Blue, was voiced by Ed Bishop, who would go on to be one of the most beloved of actors in Anderson series. Aged thirty-five in 1967, Edward Bishop (as he was billed at this point in his career) was born George Victor Bishop in Brooklyn, New York. He graduated in Theatre Arts at Boston University, diverting from his intended career in banking. Serving in the US Army, he became a disc Jockey at the St John's Newfoundland station VOUS, and did his first amateur acting with the St John Players. He gained a Fulbright Scholarship to study acting in England at LAMDA from 1957 to 1959. He had intended to return to the US, but found he liked the British acting community and decided to stay in England.

Changing his first name to Edward to remove any confusion with an established actor with a similar name, he soon became a popular member of the community of British-based American actors. He had provided voices for a puppet production before, being hired by Roberta Leigh and Arthur Provis for their unsold 1964 pilot for SF series 'Paul Starr'.

In the period Ed was recording his part for *Captain Scarlet and the Mysterons*, he also appeared in two SF productions shot at MGM-British Borehamwood: Stanley Kubrick's *2001: A Space Odyssey* (1968) and Montgomery Tully's *Battle Beneath the Earth* (1967). The latter was a much smaller production, made in order to further utilise the huge cave set built for 'Fall Out', the final episode of ITC's series *The Prisoner*. After production ended on *Scarlet*, Ed was hired again by the Andersons to replace Peter Dyneley in *Doppelgänger* after he was found to be too similar in looks to Patrick Wymark, with whom he shared most of his scenes. A year after *Doppelgänger* wrapped, Ed was hired as the star of Century 21's first live-action television series, *UFO*.

The head of Spectrum, Colonel White, was voiced by veteran South African actor Donald Gray, upon whom the actual puppet was based, with the addition of white, swept-back hair. Gray, who was aged fifty-three when the series was being produced, was born Elred Owermann Tidbury in Cape Province, South Africa. Aged nineteen, he won a competition held across the English-speaking world to win a contract with Paramount Pictures. He appeared in several Paramount Productions during 1934 in uncredited small parts before leaving for England, as he would have had to take American citizenship to remain. Eventually Gray began landing bigger film roles than he had been offered by Paramount, replacing James Mason in the lead of *Strange Experiment* (1937) and appearing in Alexander Korda's huge 1939 production *The Four Feathers*, directed by his brother Zoltan Korda.

When war broke out, Gray, who was appearing in repertory theatre in Aberdeen at the time, joined the Gordon Highlanders, later gaining a commission to The King's Own Highlanders. In 1944, he was injured in action in France by a German anti-tank shell and had to have his left arm amputated. Post-war he overcame his disability and resumed his acting career in both South Africa and Britain, working for the BBC, both as part of the Corporation's Radio Repertory Company and as a continuity announcer. From 1955 to 1961, Donald Gray starred in his most famous role, as one-armed Private Detective Mark Saber in the series that appeared on the American network ABC and later NBC under various titles. As this was a production of the Danziger Brothers' notoriously cheap production outfit, it is doubtful Gray achieved any great wealth from the show's 156-episode run. Thus, by 1967, he remained a famous name, but was available for work.

Guyanan Cy Grant provided the voice of Lieutenant Green, Spectrum's communications officer. The multi-talented Grant was probably the highest profile black television performer in Britain at the time. After serving in the RAF as bomber crew and spending much of the Second World War in a German prisoner of war camp, Grant studied law and became a qualified barrister. Unable to find work in the legal profession, he instead turned to acting to make some money while he found work in law. Grant was a natural performer, appearing as part of Laurence Olivier's Festival of Britain Company in London and New York. He also sang calypsos and other Caribbean folk songs, adding to his successful film and television acting career by becoming the first black performer to appear regularly on British television, on the BBC's nightly news programme *Tonight*. There for two-and-a-half years, he sang calypsos with lyrics about current events. Stepping down from this role to escape typecasting, Cy Grant remained very well-known to the general public and was an ideal choice to play the first black character to appear regularly in an Anderson production. This was especially notable in an era when British television rarely had black characters in recurring roles. Following the production of *Captain Scarlet and the Mysterons*, Cy Grant was cast in the small role of a doctor in the Century 21 film *Doppelgänger*.

Barry Gray's music for *Scarlet* tends to have a 'smaller' sound to it than in previous Anderson series, attempting less bombast and more subtlety. Some pieces were performed by an orchestra as small as four people, while at times the number of musicians was expanded to as many as sixteen. As previously noted, earlier series (particularly *Supercar* and *Fireball XL5*) saw the visuals 'leaning' on the music to lend the series a sense of being a larger-scale production. By 1967, the visuals had reached such a peak of realism that this was no longer necessary, allowing Gray to experiment with different sounds to join with the general air of change and development in the creation of the series.

Another aspect of the music that was experimented with was the series theme tune. The opening to the episodes had no theme music whatsoever, beyond some atmospheric stings to accompany the moody, film noir-esque opening sequence. The familiar *Captain Scarlet* theme music was only heard at the end of the episodes, initially in an instrumental version performed by Barry Gray's orchestra. Interestingly, this included a section when the name 'Captain Scarlet' was intoned using an electronically enhanced voice. This was the only remaining on-screen evidence for an earlier version of the series format in which Captain Scarlet was reanimated in the form of an android.

For the second half of the series, the theme tune was replaced by a different version, this time with lyrics, performed by the pop group The Spectrum— a British band signed by RCA Records. The band had never made a great deal of impact in the United Kingdom, but two of their singles went to number one in Spain. There was a desultory attempt to push the band as a sort of British equivalent of The Monkees, with a short-lived comic strip of the band's fictional adventures in *Lady Penelope* comic, which lasted from January to May 1968. The band, which had previously sported a Carnaby Street mod look, were photographed extensively wearing Spectrum uniforms for *Captain Scarlet and the Mysterons*' publicity.

The nearest thing The Spectrum ever had to a UK hit single was their version of The Beatles' 'Ob-la-di, Ob-la-da', which did manage to score a number one hit in West Germany. Individually, the band members were very talented—drummer Keith Forsey went on to become a highly successful songwriter ('Flashdance' and 'Don't You Forget About Me'), producer, and soundtrack composer.

Key Episode

Episode 2: 'Winged Assassin'
Written by Tony Barwick
Directed by David Lane
First UK broadcast Friday 6 October 1967 (ATV Midlands)

'This is the voice of the Mysterons. We know that you can hear us Earthmen. You will pay for your unprovoked attack on our complex on Mars. We will be avenged. We will assassinate the Director General of the United Asian Republic.'

Captains Scarlet and Blue are sent on their first mission since Scarlet was removed from the influence of the Mysterons, to protect the life of the Director General of the Central Asian Republic, who is visiting England. Spectrum puts into action a complex plan to protect the Director General and transport him safely to London Airport, using a decoy lookalike. The real Director General is sent to the airport in a converted petrol tanker, but, in the middle of the Atlantic, airliner DT-19 is developing engine trouble...

No episode of *Captain Scarlet and the Mysterons* expresses the horror of the series concept better than 'Winged Assassin'. The episode treads a fine line between adult themes and suitability for the young audience that the Supermarionation series had previously attracted with great skill, and it provides a genuinely thrilling climax.

As in many episodes of the series, 'Winged Assassin' sees apparently ordinary people and objects drawn into the conflict between Earth and the Mysterons. Thus, a businessman dictating a report on his garden is also a Spectrum agent and an oil tanker is really a luxurious, high security transport craft. The centrepiece of the episode is a huge, futuristic airliner, which becomes a guided missile in the hands of the Mysterons.

This is a clever way in which the series fires the imagination of its young viewers. There could be an SPV hidden in next door's garage, or the school bus might have been 'Mysteronised' and be on its way to destroy the aliens' latest target—your hated maths teacher could be a Mysteron.

The most effective sequence in 'Winged Assassin' is the destruction of DT-19. There is a real sense of creeping horror as each of the plane's engines cut out in turn, followed by its electrical systems. The way this scene is handled by director David Lane and the voice artists is fascinating—the action is handled entirely deadpan as the pilots approach certain death. The dialogue is played entirely straight and, in a period when Century 21 was experimenting with puppet expressions (the opening scene of *Thunderbird 6*, with its grotesquely laughing board members of the New World Aircraft Corporation, was filmed while *Captain Scarlet and the Mysterons* was in production), the only sign of strain is the sweat on the pilot's brows.

The plot demonstrates the true nature of the Mysterons war strategy. It is often described during the series as a war of nerves and the overly complex nature of their scheme, to destroy an airliner and aim its duplicate at the Director General's personal jet as it takes off, is revealing. If the Mysterons know which plane their target is to take-off in (and it is the Director General's personal jet, which is a major clue), then why bother destroying DT-19? It would be easier and more effective to just blow up the plane he is actually on. The answer is that the Mysterons are not fighting for all-out victory, but instead to cause a state of terror among the people of Earth.

The payoff to 'Winged Assassin' is an absolutely spectacular ending, the best the series has to offer. As DT-19 heads for the Director General's jet, Scarlet rams its landing gear with his SPV. The airliner crashes into the runway, where the jet clips its tailfin and crashes, killing the Director General.

Yes, for those of you who have not seen 'Winged Assassin' (and I am afraid spoilers are in the nature of a book like this), the Mysterons do exactly what they set out to do—they win. This does not happen often in the thirty-two-episode run of the series, but often enough to establish this invisible enemy as a truly formidable opponent. Previous recurring villains in Supermarionation series, such as Masterspy, Titan, and The Hood, were undermined by the fact that their schemes always failed and that eventually they tended to become figures of fun. Even when Spectrum foils their latest plot, the Mysterons prove that they can strike anywhere, causing chaos at will.

The Stirling Road studios of the Century 21 Organisation, used for all the company's series from *Stingray* until *UFO*. It is seen here in the summer of 2015, shortly after the forthcoming demolition of the building was announced.

Devil Girl From Mars: This 1954 romp from B-movie producers the Danzigers gave Gerry Anderson his first brush with SF filmmaking. The film was granted immortality via leading lady Patricia Laffan's patent leather outfit and a robot apparently made from cardboard, looking nothing like the representation on the poster.

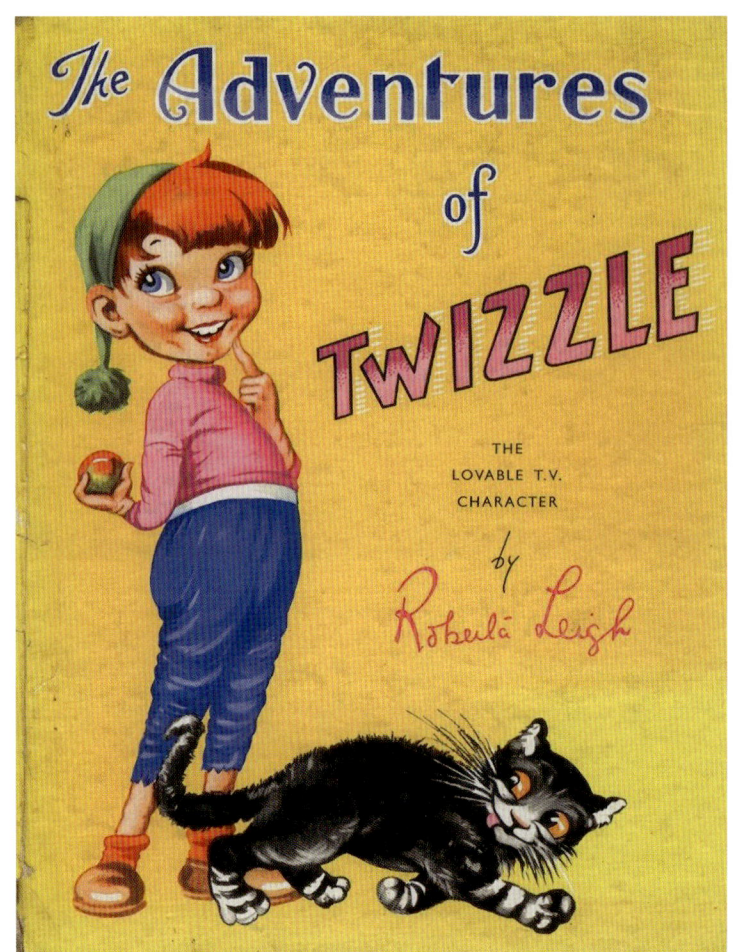

The Adventures of Twizzle: Roberta Leigh's winsome puppet character gave AP Films their first television series and put the company on an unlikely route to fame and fortune.

The Ipswich Road, Slough, building that became AP Films' new home in June 1959, pictured here in 2015.

Above left: Ever the prolific author, *Torchy the Battery Boy*'s creator Roberta Leigh produced a series of books about the character, and was keen to have AP Films make another series for Associated-Rediffusion. APF had other plans, however.

Above right: Sheriff Tex Tucker himself, Nicholas Parsons, reliving old times during an in-depth interview with the author for *FAB Magazine* in 2012.

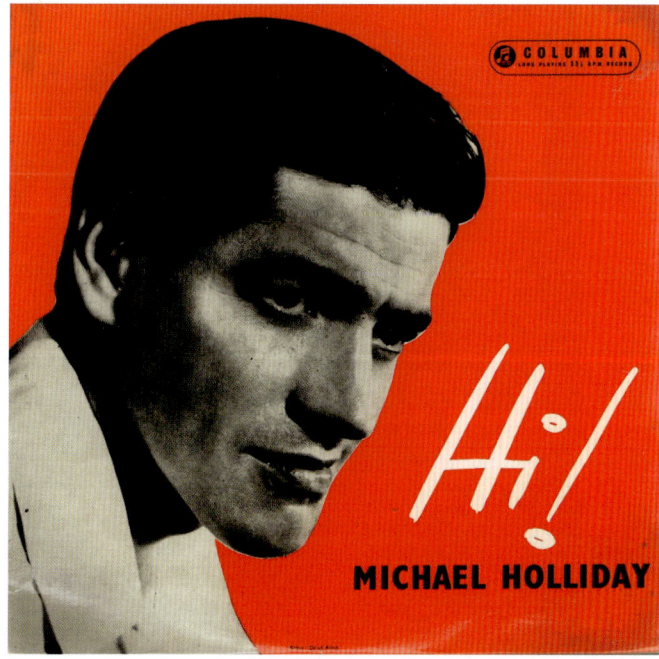

Michael Holliday's 1958 album *Hi!* saw the Liverpool-born singer at the peak of his success. The years after the making of *Four Feather Falls* were a sad story of decline and depression.

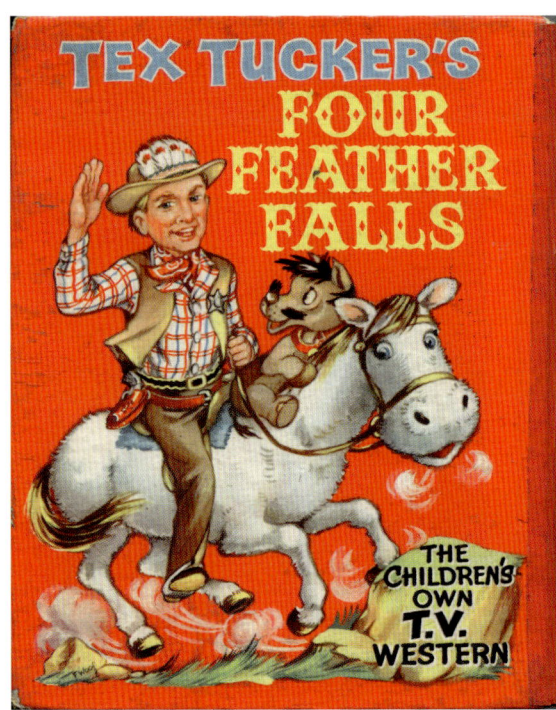

Left: Tex Tucker's *Four Feather Falls* was published by Collins in 1961 and featured stories by Sylvia Anderson. The cover art looks rather more like Nicholas Parsons on horseback than Tex Tucker.

Below: The *Supercar* family, featured on the cover of a Long Playing record featuring the original voice artists, first issued by Golden Guinea in 1961 and reissued on CD in 2012.

![Supercar LP cover]

SUPERCAR

Original Recording

AN ORIGINAL TV CAST RECORDING

This fascinating *Supercar Annual*, published in 1962 and written by Sylvia Anderson and Eric Eden, introduced Super-R, a space rocket invented by Beaker and Popkiss that was clearly based on *Fireball XL5*, which would have been in production at the time.

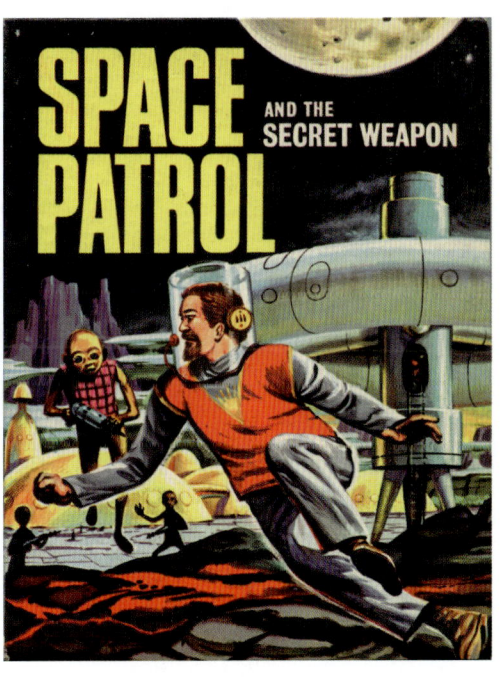

Above left: *Space Patrol and the Secret Weapon* saw Roberta Leigh transfer the quirky approach and charm of her and Arthur Provis's *Space Patrol* onto the printed page.

Above right: Barry Gray's end theme 'Fireball' was aided in its rise up the pop charts by an up-to-the-minute arrangement by Charles Blackwell—top producer Robert Stigwood was also credited.

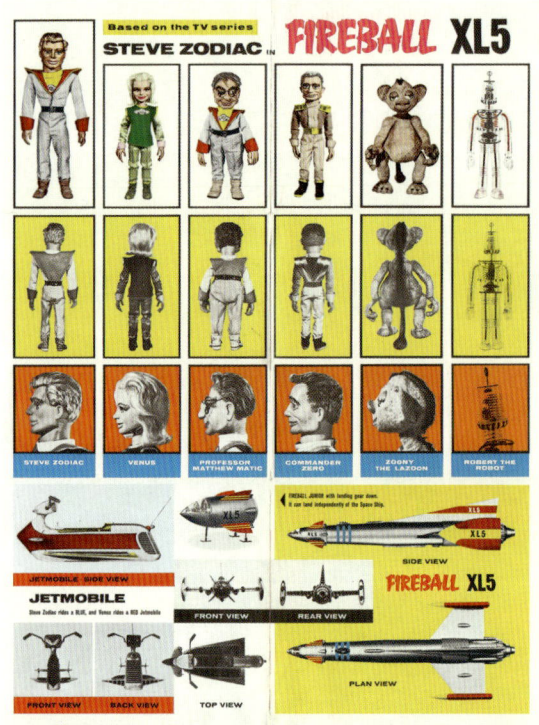

The puppet characters and craft of Fireball XL5 seen on a specification sheet prepared as a guide to companies issuing licensed merchandise.

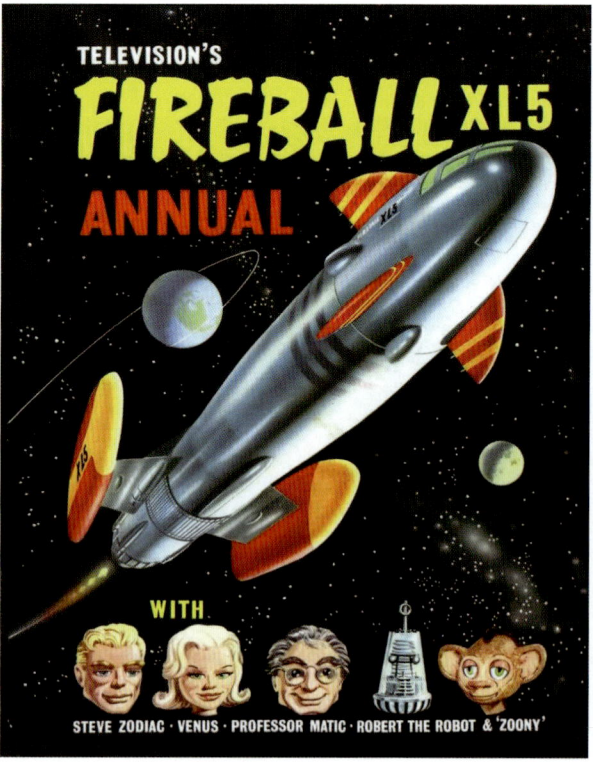

Above left: Like *Supercar*, *Fireball XL5* was picked up by American comics' publisher Gold Key, noted for their superb painted cover artwork, here by George Wilson.

Above right: This British *Fireball XL5 Annual* from 1963 features a very well-designed cover, with Fireball seeming to leap out at the reader.

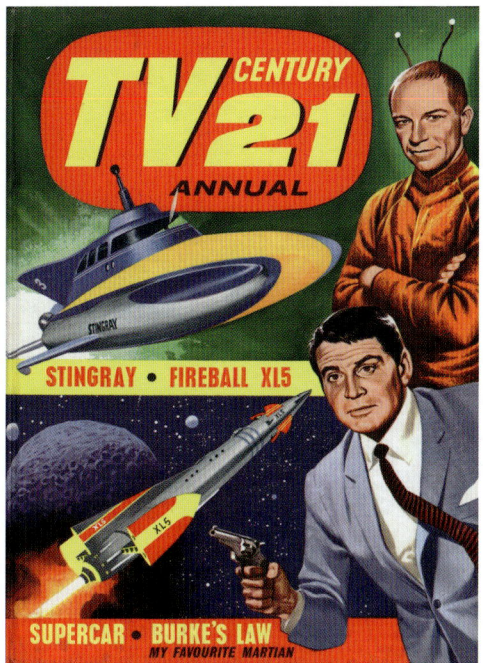

Above left: *TV Century 21 Annual* 1966, published in late 1965, demonstrates on its cover the comic's winning mix of Supermarionation series and American shows such as *My Favorite Martian* and *Burke's Law*.

Above right: *Stingray* was the subject of two novelisations by John Theydon, a pen-name used by the prolific John W. Jennison, who was to write novels based on future Supermarionation series.

Below: British poster artwork for *Thunderbirds Are Go*. The warning that 'Adults over 16 should be accompanied by children' was perhaps not helpful for the film's box office fate.

Above: This *Thunderbirds Are Go* Front of House still features Alan Tracy and Lady Penelope in FAB 1 from the extended 'Swinging Star' sequence that formed the movie's centrepiece.

Below: Zero X takes off for Mars in another Front of House still from *Thunderbirds Are Go*.

Interesting and modern-looking poster art did not help *Thunderbird 6* become any more successful at the box office than its predecessor.

The Spectrum SPV was a big selling point for the series, and a major success for Dinky Toys. Advertising for the Dinky models took place in publications such as *Meccano Magazine*.

The Airfix Angel Interceptor model kit was a huge success—it remains in production almost fifty years after the series was made.

Above left: Pop band The Spectrum were recruited to provide *Captain Scarlet and the Mysterons'* end theme. The nearest they came to a chart hit was this cover of The Beatles' 'Ob-La-Di Ob-La-Da'.

Above right: Joe 90's Mac's car was another popular seller for Dinky, despite the series itself being noticeably less popular than previous Supermarionation series.

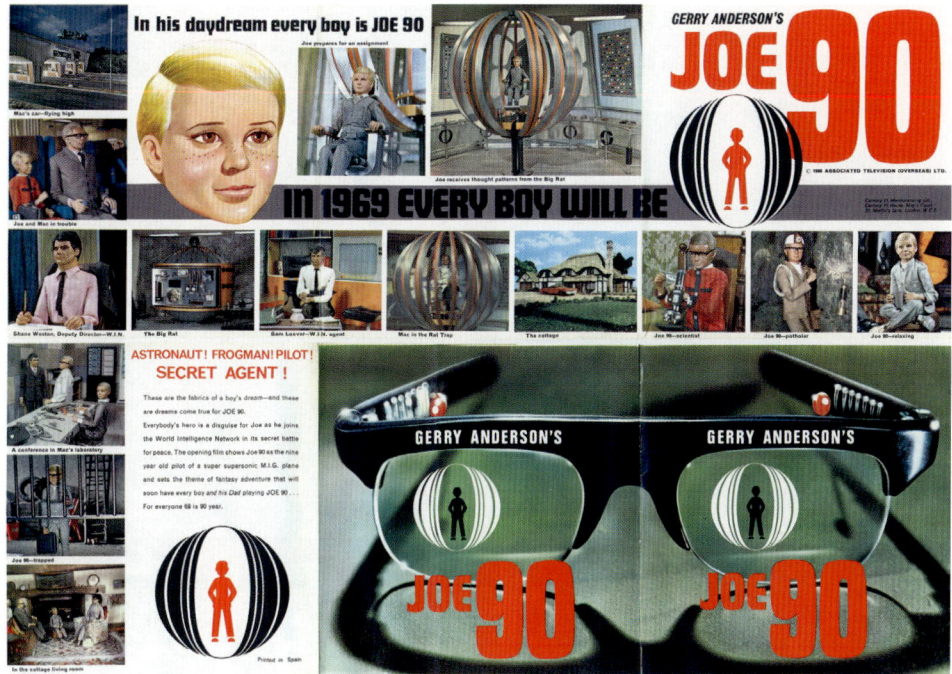

'In 1969 every boy will be Joe 90'. It didn't work out that way, but there was a lot of pleasure to be had out of the attempt for the by now declining Supermarionation audience.

Above left: The flood of merchandise, which was released for *Thunderbirds* and *Captain Scarlet and the Mysterons*, slowed down to a trickle for *Joe 90*, including Howard Elson's novel *Revenge*.

Above right: After disappointing sales of *The Secret Service*'s Model T Ford, *UFO* gave Dinky Toys a huge hit with its Moonbase Interceptor model, unaccountably painted green instead of the original's white.

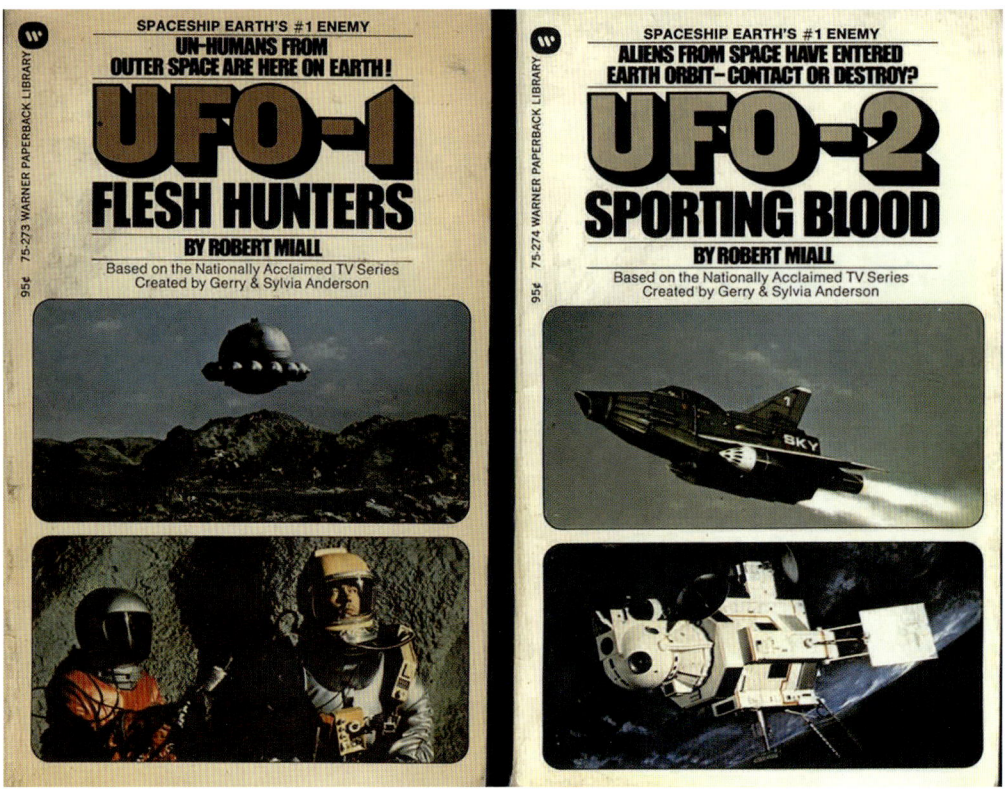

UFO eventually achieved popularity in the important US market, as evidenced by these two paperback releases. A revamped second series came agonisingly close to fruition.

The Protectors saw the Andersons and Reg Hill's new company, Group 3, unexpectedly make a glossy adventure series with location filming all over Europe.

METRO-GOLDWYN-MAYER presents **ROBERT VAUGHN** · **DAVID McCALLUM** THE MEN FROM U.N.C.L.E.
in **THE SPY IN THE GREEN HAT** Ⓐ METROCOLOR
This copyright advertising material is leased and not sold and the Property of National Screen Service Ltd. and upon completion of the exhibition for which it has been leased it should be returned to National Screen Service Ltd.
Printed in England

The Protectors star Robert Vaughn had seen *The Man from U.N.C.L.E.* become a campy shadow of its former self, an experience that informed his attitude towards *The Protectors'* producers.

Below left: *Space: 1999* was the most expensive drama ever produced for television. Episodes were often screened as cinema versions in some countries, especially when *Star Wars* made SF hugely popular.

Below right: *The Investigator*'s pilot film was never shown publicly until this 2014 DVD release by Fanderson: The Official Gerry Anderson Appreciation Society.

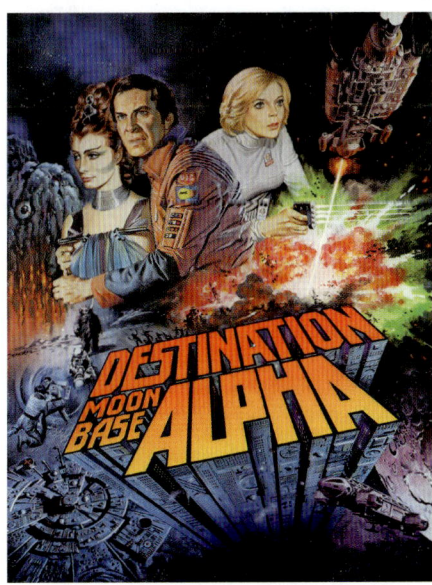

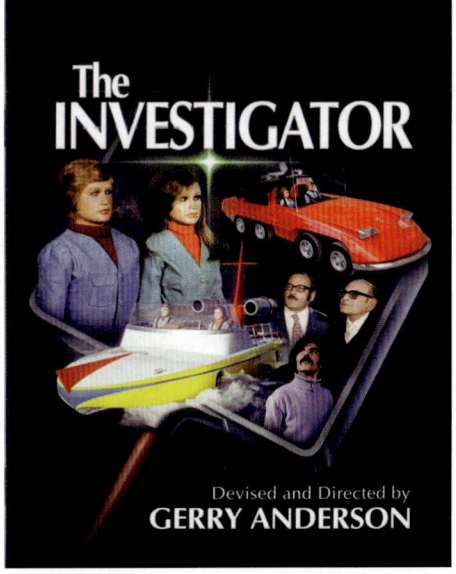

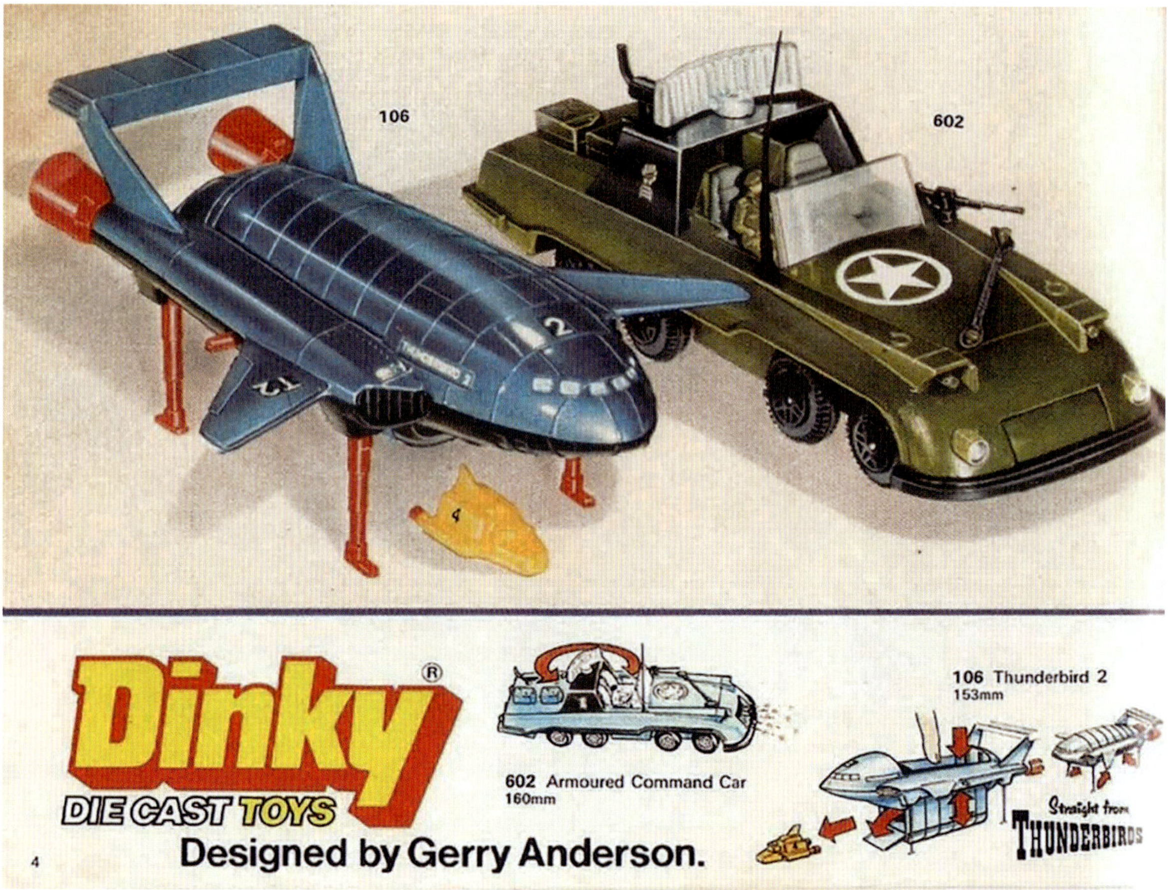

Above: Dinky tried to salvage some of their investment in *The Investigator* by revamping the show's car as an Armoured Command Car. Meanwhile, Thunderbird 2 still sold healthily.

Below: Stanley Unwin's contract for appearing in *The Secret Service* reveals that the series was originally meant to last for twenty-six episodes, instead of the thirteen eventually produced.

July - Dec '68

CENTURY 21 PRODUCTIONS
Stirling Road
Slough
Bucks.
Slough 27141

Chitty (end)
(Premiere)

Stanley Unwin, Esq.,
c/o Riscoe Film & Television
Agency Limited
137 Ballards Lane
LONDON, N.3.

20th August, 1968.

Dear Mr. Unwin,

"THE SECRET SERVICE"

This is to confirm that we have engaged and you have agreed to render your services to us in connection with the production of the above series of 26 Supermarionation television films ("the series") upon and subject to the following terms and conditions.

1. You agree that we shall have first call on your services for the period from 15th July to 23rd December, 1968. During such period you agree:-

(A) to render such services in such studios as may be required of you in accordance with the provisions of the two attached engagement forms ("the Equity Engagements") by way of recording dialogue for sound tracks and appearing before the cameras to perform the part of Father Unwin all in respect of the Series;

(B) to attend such sittings and to assist in such processes as we may reasonably require to enable a puppet with a facsimile of your face in the make-up and pose of Father Unwin as portrayed by you to be made for use in the Series.

2. You hereby confirm your consent to the making and use in the Series of the said puppet but acknowledge that any copyright and all other rights in both the said puppet and the character Father Unwin (including your portrayal of the character) belong to us absolutely.

Continued........

3. Accordingly it is further mutually agreed between us that you will not perform, portray or otherwise make use of your portrayal of the character of Father Unwin or any likeness thereof in any medium for the benefit of any third party without our prior consent which shall not unreasonably be witheld in respect of any such use which will not be contrary to the provisions of the Television Act 1964 or the requirements of the Independent Television Authority with respect to the use of programme material in any advertising context and for which a suitable fee payable to us shall have first been agreed.

4. By way of remuneration for all services rendered by you in accordance with this agreement we agree that you shall receive not less than £250 in respect of each film in the Series which shall include the salary and Exploitation Fee payable under each of the two Equity Engagements but shall not include the various percentages of the said Exploitation Fee for additional transmissions. The payment of £250 shall be made up upon and subject to the completion of your services in connection with each film. In the event of the payment of salary or Exploitation Fees being suspended under the provisions of either of the Equity Engagements you shall be entitled to such proportion of the remainder of the said £250 in respect of those films in the Series affected as shall fairly be attributed to the services already rendered by you in connection with those films.

5. We shall have an exclusive option exercisable by written notice to you on or before 1st November, 1968 to extend your engagement hereunder (including the Equity Engagements) to a further thirteen films in the Series during a further period of first call of thirteen weeks otherwise upon and subject to all the same terms. Thereafter we shall be entitled, subject in each case to the exercise of the preceding option, to similar successive options in respect of thirteen films and an additional period of first call of thirteen weeks each exercisable by written notice on or before the date two months before the expiry of the first call period under the previous option.

Yours sincerely,

Gerry Anderson

I agree and confirm the above:-

.... Date ....

STANLEY UNWIN

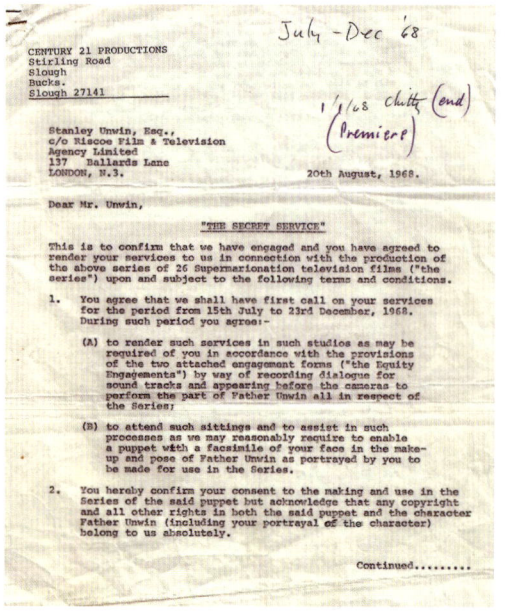

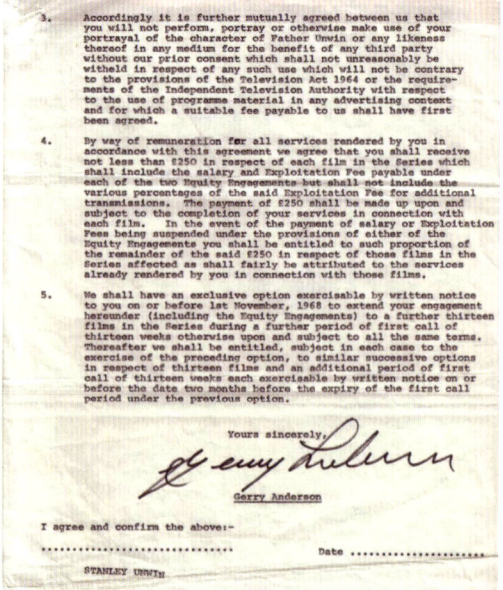

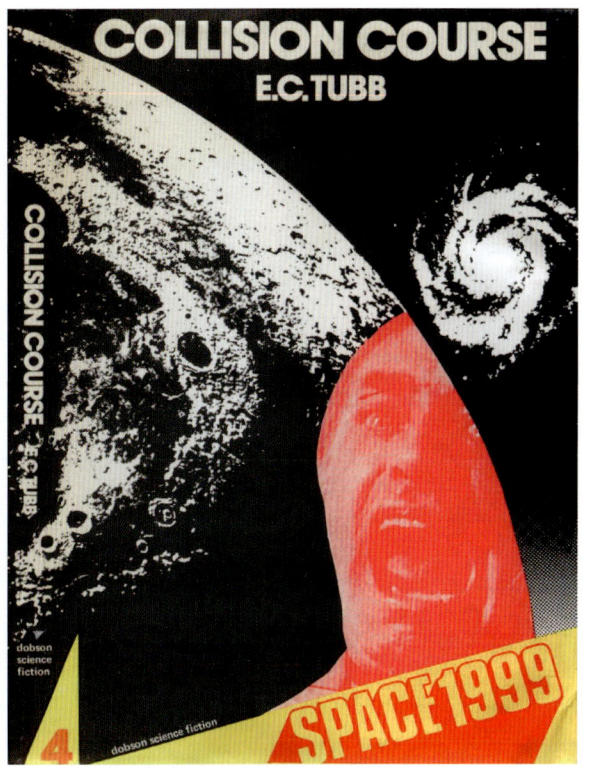

Above left: Ten novelisations were released of *Space: 1999* episodes in English-speaking countries. This rare hardback version of *Collision Course* blends the stories 'Collision Course', 'Full Circle', and 'Death's Other Dominion' into a single narrative.

Above right: This *Space: 1999* annual, released as late as 1979, features not only lovely cover art, but also strips from Charlton Comics' lively adaptation of the series.

Starcruiser was a series idea from Gerry Anderson and Fred Freiberger, which was rejected by the American TV networks, but still generated a comic strip and a model kit from Airfix.

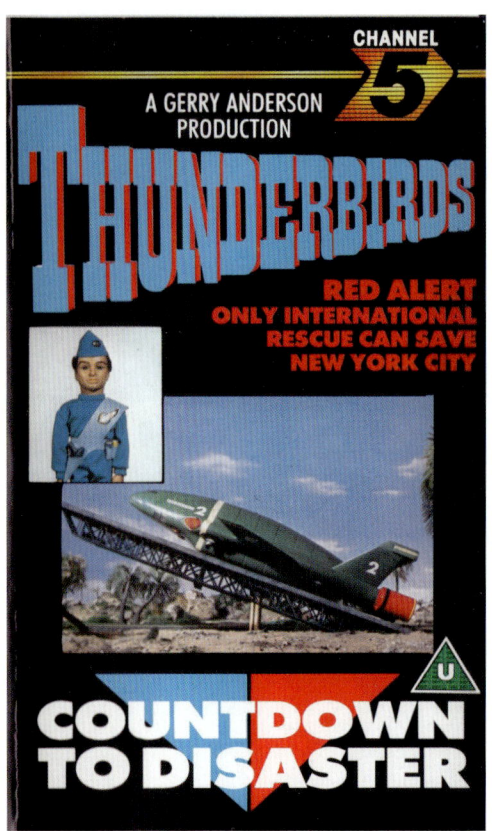

Thunderbirds lived on for future generations thanks to VHS releases in the 1980s, initially in compilation films such as 'Countdown to Disaster'.

The author on stage with Gerry Anderson for one of his final interviews, at the Fanderson *TV21* convention in October 2010.

17

Joe 90

'You are trying to tell me that a nine year-old boy climbed into the cockpit of the world's most advanced aircraft and flew it away?'

Executive producer Reg Hill
Produced by David Lane
Format by Gerry and Sylvia Anderson
Music composed and directed by Barry Gray
A Gerry Anderson Century 21 Television Production
An ITC World Wide Distribution
30 × twenty-five-minute episodes
First broadcast Sunday 29 September 1968 (ATV)

It is the year 2012, and Professor Ian 'Mac' McClaine has invented a machine, BIGRAT, which allows him to record people's brain patterns and transfer their skills and experiences to his nine year-old adopted son Joe. Mac's close friend, World Intelligence Network's London Deputy Head Sam Loover and his boss Shane Weston convince him to use the machine on their behalf and use Joe on dangerous secret missions for which being a small boy is the perfect cover story.

By the time the final episodes of *Captain Scarlet and the Mysterons* were being filmed it had become clear that the series had not attained a level of popularity, which would make it economic for Lew Grade to commission more episodes. We never did get to find out how the war of nerves between Earth and the Mysterons was resolved, as Century 21's television production effort was already concentrating on its next project, which began production with barely a pause following the completion of *Captain Scarlet and the Mysterons*.

In its own way, *Joe 90* is an absolutely key series in the history of Supermarionation. Each series from *Supercar* onwards had been a development from the last, different in important ways, but after five series it was no longer tenable for Century 21 to produce yet another show about a military-style organisation with a fleet of futuristic vehicles. If Supermarionation was going to have a long-term future the range of what the form could be and do had to be explored and tested.

Thus a more character-led format was devised, set in the slightly nearer future of 2012. This set the production the task of designing a realistic-looking televisual world that looked, for the most part, like the real world of 1968. This is reflected in the home bases of the series—instead of a fabulous Pacific island or a flying aircraft carrier, Joe and Professor McClaine lived in a beautifully detailed country cottage, complete with thatched roof, while WIN's London base was a fairly anonymous office building.

Joe 90 saw Supermarionation attain technical perfection. It cannot be overemphasised just how beautifully made the series is. The sets achieve an incredible standard of reality and both direction and editing are razor sharp. Although many of the puppets are reused or revamped from *Captain Scarlet and the Mysterons*, the new puppets created for the series have subtly larger heads, and the sculptors learned how to create more distinctive faces while keeping the puppets in realistic proportions. Similarly, the puppeteering had been adapted to make the characters seem more animated within the limited range of movements possible while keeping within the bounds of realism.

Joe 90 also sees the welcome return to Supermarionation of a sense of playfulness. This is not only seen in characters and dialogue—World Intelligence Network Deputy Head Shane Weston is written to have the love of a (usually terrible) joke—but also in its design. The BIGRAT is visually stunning in a way that no other piece of Anderson equipment before or since managed. Freed from any responsibility to look like it might serve its actual purpose—after all, who knows what a machine to transfer brain patterns is supposed to look like?—the apparatus was designed to be as bright, colourful, and visually striking as possible. This machine was the visual touchstone of the whole series, representing Supermarionation's return to a more light-hearted approach.

Century 21's film production unit was busy during the production of *Joe 90*, from November 1967 to August 1968, as the post-production phase of *Thunderbird 6* was still being completed, followed by the start of production on *Doppelgänger*. This meant that some familiar names were missing from the crew list of *Joe 90*, not least of which being Gerry Anderson. As was traditional on the Supermarionation series, Gerry and Sylvia Anderson created the format and Sylvia developed the characters. Besides co-writing credits on two episodes (the series pilot 'The Most Special Agent' (with Sylvia Anderson) and the fourth episode in production, 'Operation McClaine' (with David Lane), Gerry took no credit at all for the series other than on the Century 21 logo that opened each episode.

With Reg Hill, who had been credited as producer on *Captain Scarlet and the Mysterons*, acting as *Joe 90*'s executive producer, David Lane was given the job of producing the new series. He set about putting his own stamp on the show and correcting some of the faults he saw in *Captain Scarlet*. Therefore *Joe 90* has a noticeably lighter touch than *Scarlet* did. It was also more character-based than both *Thunderbirds* and *Captain Scarlet*, something built into the format by Gerry and Sylvia Anderson in an attempt to vary the formula from the shows they had produced since *Fireball XL5*.

Bob Bell was designing the sets for both *Thunderbird 6* and *Doppelgänger*, leaving him unavailable for *Joe 90*, for which art direction was put into the hands of Gren Knott (who had been art director on *Captain Scarlet* under Bell's supervision) and Keith Wilson.

Derek Meddings' main contribution to the series was the design of Professor McClain's flying car, his duties on the two Century 21 films leaving him no time to contribute to *Joe 90*. His design role was largely filled by Mike Trim, while Jimmy Elliott took the role of senior visual effects director. As before, there were three model units, Shaun Whittacker-Cooke and Bill Camp directing one each, while Peter Wragg directed the visual effects second unit up to episode thirteen, at which point Alan Berry took over direction of the unit.

Tony Barwick remained as script editor for *Joe 90*, writing seventeen of the thirty episodes himself. By now, though, he had developed a regularly utilised group of writers familiar with the needs of a Supermationation script. Shane Rimmer wrote six episodes, while experienced television writer Pat Dunlop contributed the script for 'Mission X-41'. Dunlop, the father of actress Lesley Dunlop, had written for *Doctor Who*, *Doctor Finlay's Casebook* (on which had had also been story editor), and *Z Cars*, as well as the BBCs 1965–67 football-based soap opera *United*. He would also write episodes of *The Secret Service* for Century 21 before going on to have a successful career writing for American television.

Donald James, who had co-written the script of *Doppelgänger*, was drafted in to provide two episodes late in *Joe 90*'s run. He was a highly experienced film and television writer who had previously provided scripts for Associated-Rediffusion's detective series *No Hiding Place*, and was reaching a peak of productivity around this period—he wrote three scripts for the final season of ITC adventure series *The Saint* in 1967–68, and eight stories for the same company's *The Champions* (1967). He would later write for *The Secret Service*, *UFO*, and *Space: 1999*, James' scripts being his final writing directly for television before taking up a career as an author. This included a series of novels co-written with Tony Barwick.

A single script, 'Child of the Sun God', came from the pen of the prolific John Lucarotti. The English writer began his career in Canada, where he wrote over 200 scripts for television and radio. Returning to England, he wrote three serials for William Hartnell's *Doctor Who* and six episodes of *The Avengers*, mostly for the pairing of Patrick Macnee and Honor Blackman. At the time he wrote 'Child of the Sun God', Lucarotti was in the midst of a long stint as one of the main writers of the BBC's *The Troubleshooters*, starring former Anderson voice artist Ray Barrett. Although he never wrote again for an Anderson series, Lucarotti did contribute two scripts to *Star Maidens*, the 1976 Anglo-German SF series that employed many crew members from *Space: 1999*.

Besides two scripts from Gerry and Sylvia Anderson, the other scriptwriting duo to work on *Joe 90* were Desmond Saunders and Keith Wilson, the show's production controller and co-art director respectively. From this source came 'Lone Handed 90', in which Joe falls asleep watching a Western on television, then dreams about the regular cast of the series in a Wild West adventure. This particular episode could serve as an example of how the production team of a series often had more fun than the audience, but it provides an opportunity for the viewers to witness how skilled the staff had become in making realistic settings. Instead of futuristic vehicles, the model builders were tasked with building a steam train, designed by Mike Trim.

Episodes were directed by a core team of four—Alan Perry, Leo Eaton, and Ken Turner returned from *Captain Scarlet and the Mysterons*, but Robert Lynn was busy directing two feature films for producer Harry Alan Towers: *The Face of Eve* in Spain and Brazil and *Sandy the Seal* in South Africa. Peter Anderson (no relation to Gerry and Sylvia) was recruited in his place, and was promoted from assistant director. Brian Heard was another assistant director for *Joe 90*, and he directed episode twenty-seven, 'Trial at Sea'; he remained as one of the episode directors for *The Secret Service*.

Only three entirely new puppets were created for the series—Professor McClaine, Joe, and their housekeeper, Mrs Harris (small boys and middle-aged women being notably absent from the narratives of the previous series). Mrs Harris made very few appearances in *Joe 90*; she was the series only female regular character, which is representative of the growing tendency for later Supermarionation series to become more male-focused environments. The puppet was used more memorably in the final episode of the following series, 'More Haste, Less Speed', as the monstrously greedy minor aristocrat Lady Martha Hazlewell.

The rest of the cast was adapted from the new, correctly proportioned puppets created for *Captain Scarlet and the Mysterons*. The Sam Loover puppet was first seen in the *Scarlet*'s fourth episode, 'Point 783', as the Supreme Commander of Earth Forces. Shane Weston's puppet generally had blonde hair for its appearances in *Scarlet*, in which it appeared right from the first episode. For *Joe 90*, the puppet was given dark hair, changing the entire look of the character. For these puppets' elevation to main character status, duplicate heads were made, which not only allowed them to smile or frown as required, but also to appear in scenes being shot simultaneously on both puppet stages.

Advances had been made in puppetry techniques working with the correctly proportioned puppets. Despite *Captain Scarlet and the Mysterons* being a far more action-oriented series than *Joe 90*, it often appears slow and a little flat compared to *Joe*. Walking was out of the question with correctly proportioned puppets, leading to many scenes of characters standing still or sitting, or excuses being found for them to stand on moving walkways. For *Joe 90*, the puppeteers (led by puppet coordinator Mary Turner and puppetry supervisor Christine Glanville) and the directors had devised subtle and clever ways to add movement and realism to the characters. This made a huge difference to the pacing and overall tone of the series.

The other major items reused from *Captain Scarlet and the Mysterons* were the Angel Interceptor models, and their expensively produced puppet-sized cockpit. The fighter jet models themselves were reworked for *Joe 90*'s opening episode, the 'Most Special Agent', as Russian MIG-242 fighters. Mike Trim found himself having to create distinctive plane designs while reusing the Angel cockpit shape, so the puppet set—with its Perspex canopy and special adaptation for the puppets to be controlled from underneath—could be reused. Examples of designs that had to work around this restriction included the F116 Experimental Jet from the episode 'Talkdown' and the VG 104 fighter bomber from 'Attack of the Tiger'.

Two major recurring vehicles were made for *Joe 90*. Professor McClaine's flying jet car was designed by Derek Meddings, with Mike Trim designing a spacecraft hangar for *Doppelgänger* as Meddings disliked designing buildings. It is symptomatic of the more character-led direction the series took that the major vehicle designed for the series is hardly used in most episodes. As a piece of design it is quite interesting as, unlike almost every other vehicle designed for the Anderson shows, Mac's car is designed for utility rather than looks— the inner workings of the vehicle can be clearly seen. It is an example of what might be termed anti-design—it looks like it has been hand built by Mac in his garage and has never been through any formal design process to make it acceptable for commercial sales.

The second vehicle featured in the series was Mike Trim's design for Sam Loover's car. This is a silver-grey two door saloon, which the series format claims is powered by gas turbines and is capable of travelling at 200 mph. The shark-like front-end design is somewhat reminiscent of Trim's design for the Spectrum Patrol Car, but it takes design cues from sports car models of the 1960s, extrapolated forwards to the year 2012. The car's only special feature is its ability to go very quickly, which is one reason why it has a huge rear spoiler, an uncommon sight on commercially produced cars of the 1960s.

The star piece of hardware featured in *Joe 90* is the BIGRAT—Brain Impulse Galvanometer, Record and Transfer. This is the machine that the entire concept of the series revolves around, allowing Professor McClaine to record the brain patterns of individuals (a procedure generally done 'in the field', remotely from BIGRAT) and transfer them to Joe. BIGRAT is nothing short of beautiful. It is madly impractical in design: Joe's chair is raised into a circular cage that begins to spin around him while lights blink and a psychedelic oil lamp effect is seen in the background, and Barry Gray's wonderfully cheerful theme music plays in the background. The whole process resembles nothing so much as a 1960s mobile disco, its use in most episodes being a fun, exciting highlight.

Much was also made of Joe's special equipment case, which is featured in the closing credits of each episode. To the outside world, this contains Joe McClain's schoolwork, but it has special hidden compartments in the back containing his World Intelligence Network identity card and badge, an automatic pistol with ammunition and silencer, a radio transmitter allowing him to stay in contact with WIN during missions, and his special glasses. Without Joe's famous glasses, the brain patterns implanted into his consciousness are not activated and he is merely a very brave little boy.

Joe 90 was announced with great fanfare, complete with an excellent tie-in comic. The series was an excellent production that in many ways represented the very best that Supermarionation could produce. The brutal fact was that *Joe 90* was considerably less popular than the shows that preceded it. Several ITV regions decided that there were quite enough Anderson puppet series already in the market, and opted against buying another.

The series was also less popular among many of those who actually got to see it. The fact was that nine-year-old (and perhaps slightly older) viewers did not dream of being a nine-year-old boy, no matter what special abilities he had, in anything like the same numbers that they dreamed of being a Tracy brother. The reputation of the series remained poor—even among many hardcore Anderson fans—for many years, which was quite an unfair verdict on what remains today a highly enjoyable show.

Fair or not, the public had spoken. *Joe 90* was less successful as a saleable product than both *Captain Scarlet and the Mysterons* and especially *Thunderbirds*. Nevertheless, Lew Grade gave the go-ahead for a new puppet series to go into production on the completion of *Joe 90*. The search for yet another new Supermarionation format was about to lead to probably the strangest series format Gerry and Sylvia Anderson would ever invent.

Voice Artists

The casting of Rupert Davies as Professor Ian McClaine was a masterstroke by Gerry and Sylvia Anderson, signifying instantly the aim of making *Joe 90* a more human, emotional series than *Captain Scarlet and the Mysterons* was. The clipped, disciplined, purposefully emotionless tones of the *Scarlet* cast— who were, after all, playing either representatives of a military organisation or, in effect, zombies—could not have stood in greater contrast to the lovely, warm, fatherly performance given by Davies.

The career of Rupert Davies is a fascinating example of how actors are sometimes not remembered for the roles that originally made them famous. From 1960 to 1963 Davies became one of the most famous actors in Britain, playing George Simenon's Parisian detective Inspector Maigret for a BBC television series. His casting in the role even gained the enthusiastic approval of Simenon himself. When the popular series ended after fifty-two episodes, Davies struggled to find work for a time due to typecasting, and certainly was never featured in such a prominent role again. While the BBC's *Maigret* series fell into obscurity, however, Davies had an especially interesting career in horror films. In 1968 alone he appeared in Hammer's *Dracula Has Risen from the Grave*, Michael Reeves' cult horror *Witchfinder General*, and the last film Boris Karloff completed before his death, *Curse of the Crimson Altar*. In 1974, two years before his death at the age of sixty, Rupert Davies appeared in Peter Walker's highly regarded tale of suburban cannibalism *Frightmare*.

David Healy, returning from the *Captain Scarlet and the Mysterons* voice cast, was this time cast in one of the main recurring roles in the series—WIN London office commander Shane Weston. Born in New York, Healy was aged thirty-nine when *Joe 90* was being produced. He was blessed with a warm, expressive voice and had an acting range that allowed him to play everything from cold-hearted villains to the hero's best friend. Having majored in drama at the University of Texas, he was stationed in England during service in the United States Air Force, along with his close friend Larry Hagman. On leaving the USAF in 1964, he decided to base himself in England and pursue an acting career. Healy soon established himself as a popular stage and television actor with a very useful side line in voice-overs, both for the Supermarionation series and on countless adverts.

Keith Alexander provided the voice of Sam Loover, and was the latest in a line of Australian actors to join the voice casts of Supermarionation productions. Moving to England in 1965, he proved highly skilled in different accents, able to play English, American, and Australian with equal skill. He was also the voice of the famous puppet mouse of the era, Topo Gigio, which brought Alexander one of his earliest contacts with the Century 21 organisation, recording the mini-album *Topo Gigio in London* for the company. He also provided voices for the film *Thunderbird 6*, including replacing Ray Barrett as the voice of John Tracy. *Joe 90* saw Keith Alexander firmly established as a key part of the Century 21 repertory company, staying on for *The Secret Service* (for which he provided numerous character voices). He also appeared regularly in the live-action series *UFO*, in which he played SHADO HQ Communications Officer Keith Ford for the first seventeen episodes filmed at MGM-British Borehamwood.

In an attempt at greater realism, the voice of young Joe McClaine was not provided by an actress, as was traditional on cartoons and previous Anderson puppet series, but by a young male actor. Len Jones was a sixteen-year-old actor who had been appearing in films and television productions since 1964, an early role being in ITC's filmed action series *Espionage*. While *Joe 90* was in production, Jones was also appearing in the Thames Television comedy drama *The Queen Street Gang*. His acting career continued for some years after *Joe 90*, and he appeared in episodes of popular series such as *Hadleigh* (1971), *Follyfoot* (1971) and *The Adventures of Black Beauty* (1972), plus films including *Straw Dogs* (1971) and *Made* (1972). Jones' final screen roles came in 1975 when he appeared in small roles in episodes of *Survivors* and *Dixon of Dock Green*.

Key Episode

Episode 2: 'Hi-Jacked'
Written by Tony Barwick
Directed by Alan Perry
First UK broadcast: 20 October 1968 (ATV)

When Johnson, one of WIN's best agents is seriously injured, his brain patterns are recorded and transferred to Joe 90, who is assigned to complete the agent's mission: to find the secret base of dangerous gun runner Mario Colletti and bring him and his gang to justice.

'Hi-Jacked' represents the *Joe 90* format at its most basic. This is a very straightforward adventure story in which Joe gets the brain patterns of a highly-skilled spy and completes his mission, which is not to denigrate the episode in any way. In fact, 'Hi-Jacked' sees all aspects of the *Joe 90* production working at their absolute peak and it all works splendidly well. A story like this—which does not try to be too clever with the format, but uses it to its full potential—is needed in any series as a benchmark. It gives audiences a point at which to orient themselves so that when the writers start to vary and play with the format—something they need the freedom to do over a thirty episode season—everyone knows where they are coming from.

Some of the variations on the basic theme the series manages are interesting and intelligent. The episode 'Double Agent', for instance, takes basically the same plot as 'Hi-Jacked' and gives it a twist—the WIN agent whose brain patterns Joe receives is a traitor, so as soon as Joe puts his glasses on, he deviates from his mission and does what the double agent would have done. In another of the more spy-themed episodes of the series, 'Project 90', an international spy ring decides to look into exactly what WIN's relationship with Professor McClaine is. Although the episode ends up being light-hearted fun, the original idea remains serious and clever.

The plot of 'Hi-Jacked' also makes intelligent use of Joe being a nine-year-old boy—the standard plot gag of the series is that nobody ever believes that Joe could possibly be a highly skilled agent. In 'Hi-Jacked' a second factor is added—Joe gets into Colletti's hideout by hiding in a 4-foot-long case that is supposed to contain rifles. Colletti really is a nasty piece of work, which gives the story some edge; even though he does not believe Joe is the WIN agent he claims to be, he orders him to be killed anyway, as he's seen too much of his operation.

This sense of danger continues with the climactic shoot-out between Joe and Colletti, which takes place in the villain's arms warehouse, with the two characters surrounded by high explosives. Joe, operating with his brain patterns of Agent Johnson, is quite literally taking no prisoners and eventually kills Colletti with a hand grenade. The resulting explosion is absolutely huge and we clearly see the villain engulfed by it. This aspect of *Joe 90*, of a nine year-old boy committing acts of violence, would result in the series having censorship problems by the time it was repeated during the less forgiving 1990s.

The opening sequence, in which Sam Loover meets Agent Johnson at a nighttime rendezvous only to find him unconscious and badly injured, is a masterclass on how to direct for Supermarionation. The puppet characters air of realism fully depended on them sticking to a limited range of actions that they could perform convincingly. Sam's distinctive car, seen parked in an alley, announces his presence. We cut straight to Sam cradling the badly injured Johnson, movement created by the slow zooming in of the camera. Loover tries to question Johnson, subtle movements of his head bringing the character and the shot to life. The camera cuts to a shot of real hands, as Sam takes Johnson's voice recorder out of his coat. We hear, then see an ambulance arriving, and when the shot returns to the alley Sam is gone, the puppet's rapid movement implied, but not seen. The camera slowly zooms in on Johnson while we hear the medics approaching from the ambulance, so we have movement in the frame, but the ears and imagination of the audience do part of the job of animating the scene.

The atmosphere of the episode is helped enormously by featuring highly impressive art design, both on the puppets sets and for the model sequences. Colletti's secret base is simply beautiful, one of many sets in the last three Supermarionation shows that looks completely realistic until puppet characters appear. At Colletti's desk is one of this author's personal favourite miniature props—a perfectly reproduced Charles and Ray Eames chair. The model unit sets are equally as well-filmed and convincing as those on the puppet sets. The gun-runner's underground lair is superbly designed and lit, and the scenes where Colletti's trucks arrive at the base were approaching the standards of model work achieved on *UFO*, on which the models were made on a larger scale.

The voice artists also put in some excellent work to bring Tony Barwick's script to life. Rupert Davies, as always, humanises the dialogue, especially in a scene near the episode's climax where he discovers Joe unconscious in a burning building. The note of concern in his voice is a marvellous touch.

With *Joe 90* a fine balance was achieved between action and a human touch, which was missing for the most part from *Captain Scarlet and the Mysterons*. 'Hi-Jacked' demonstrates just how good a series *Joe 90* was at its peak—it is a genuine shame that by this point Supermarionation was starting to wane in popularity. The series deserved a better reception than the muted one it received.

18

Doppelgänger

Doppelgänger (aka *Journey to the Far Side of the Sun*)
Directed by Robert Parrish
Written by Gerry & Sylvia Anderson and Donald James
Produced by Gerry & Sylvia Anderson
A Gerry Anderson Production for Universal Pictures Limited
World premiere 27 August 1969 (USA)

Britain was undergoing a filmmaking boom in the mid-1960s, largely fuelled
by American money. While the James Bond films were the most obvious
example of this, rather more important were hit movies such as *Alfie* (1966).
Not only was this a major box office attraction in both the US and Britain, it
was made for what was, by the standards of a major American studio, peanuts.

This was the background to Universal Pictures executive Jay Kanter arriving
in Britain with a view to backing European productions. As a result, Universal's
release slate for the next few years had a distinctly European flavour, British
films being partly financed and distributed by the company included *Charlie
Bubbles*, the 1967 directorial debut of actor Albert Finney, *Work is a Four
Letter Word* (1968), which featured the only acting appearance of singer
Cilla Black, and two films by émigré American director Joseph Losey starring
Elizabeth Taylor, *Boom!* and *Secret Ceremony* (both released in 1968).

Gerry Anderson read of Kanter's arrival and arranged a meeting to pitch an
idea for what would become Century 21 Productions' first live-action feature
film. Kanter agreed on principle, if a suitable script could be agreed on. Gerry
came up with the idea of Earth having a twin planet, which he and Sylvia
Anderson worked into a full-length script. This was then worked on by Donald
James, an experienced television scriptwriter who had already contributed

three scripts to the as-yet unscreened *Joe 90*. James was to maintain a long professional association with the Andersons, continuing right up to the mid-'80s and *Terrahawks*. The Donald James adaptation of the script led to Universal commissioning the film.

Gerry Anderson's first instinct was to keep his choice of the film's director in the Century 21 family. His initial choice was David Lane, who had just directed the two *Thunderbirds* feature films. Final approval of the director of *Doppelgänger*, as the film was titled from its earliest stages, lay with Jay Kanter, who wanted someone with more experience on major productions. The only problem was that every major feature film director based in the UK was busy, such was the healthy state of film production in Britain at the time. Gerry Anderson reported what happened next when interviewed about the film for his official fan club, Fanderson:

> ...we waited eleven long weeks. We came into the studio every day waiting to hear of a director who might become available, but nothing. At the end of the eleventh week we heard that a picture being made over here had collapsed for some reason or another and the director, Bob Parrish, was probably free. So we contacted Bob and invited him to our home in Gerrards Cross and he was very excited, or so he said. He told us that it would be an absolute honour to work with us, that he knew of all our programmes and couldn't wait to get started. There were lots of handshakes and it was all very warm and lovely, so we signed him up. That was mistake number one.

This gives some clue as to the direction the relationship between Parrish and his producers went. American former actor and film editor Robert Parrish had long been based in Europe as a film director. His experience of working on a large-scale special-effects-driven movie was largely restricted to being one of the five credited directors on the previous year's expensive disaster *Casino Royale*. While that film blighted Peter Sellers' American film career for years after, Parrish escaped blame and remained in regular employment.

Filming began on 1 July 1968 and relations between Parrish and his producers did not remain cordial for long. As both the producers and writers of the original script, Gerry and Sylvia must have felt more than usually attached to their original concept. The feeling in the Century 21 boardroom was that Parrish was not communicating with them and that they were unhappy with the direction that the film was taking.

It may be that a clash between Gerry Anderson and almost any outside director was inevitable. Gerry was used to calling the shots on the productions that bore his name. His methods and attitudes as studio boss were formed by the exceptional circumstances by which his company had grown to prominence and by the unique products they made. He was, in effect, an old-style studio boss in the Jack Warner or Sam Goldwyn mould, who was used to having ultimate control of his productions.

American film directors, on the other hand, were in the midst of a long-running struggle with the major film studios to gain the same sorts of artistic freedoms their counterparts in countries such as France and Sweden took for granted. Save for an elite few, Hollywood directors were traditionally allowed little say in the editing process of their own films. This caused many to direct in as simple a visual style as possible, so their footage could only edit together in one way, thus limiting the ability of producers to interfere with their work. By the mid-1960s, American films were beginning to look increasingly old-fashioned compared to European and Scandinavian films from directors such as Ingmar Bergman and Sergio Leone. When Dennis Hopper's maverick road movie *Easy Rider* became the major box office hit of 1969 while mega productions such as the musical *Star!* lost fortunes, the director replaced the producer as the major creative force in American films for most of the 1970s. For Gerry Anderson, who had had the final say on all his productions since *Four Feather Falls*, this was new territory.

Unfortunately, this effected Gerry's relationship with John Read, who had been chief cinematographer on the Anderson productions ever since Arthur Provis had left early in the production of *Four Feather Falls*. As lighting cameraman on *Doppelgänger*, he felt that he was in the service of the director and could not take sides in the various disputes between Parrish and the Century 21 board, of which Read was a member. Gerry and the other board members felt that that Read should be at least reporting back to them what was happening on set. This unhappy situation resulted eventually in John Read resigning from the Century 21 board and he worked on no further productions for the company.

Roy Thinnes, meanwhile, clashed with both Gerry and Robert Parrish. In a fascinating article in the October 1978 edition of *Science Fantasy Film Classics* magazine, Thinnes reported that Parrish walked off set until Thinnes (who had already undergone three different hairstyles until a symmetrical look vital to the film's plot could be achieved) would get a crew cut. Not surprisingly Thinnes refused and a studio executive had to be called in to mediate in a Sunday morning meeting, which ended in an acrimonious row between actor and director.

Relations between director and star thawed considerably under the heat of the Portuguese sun of the film's location shoot. Parrish, it transpired, had earlier received a letter from a mutual acquaintance who had worked on Thinnes' television series *The Invaders*, saying he was difficult to work with. The argument about the haircut, Thinnes concluded, was the director's way of keeping a potentially argumentative star in line. Gerry Anderson later recalled that he and Thinnes also did not get along, though he admired the performance his star actor gave on-screen.

Two other major cast members, Ian Hendry and Patrick Wymark, were notoriously heavy drinkers. Interviewed by Fanderson, Gerry Anderson reported that Hendry was very well behaved throughout the production, save for a scene, shot at night, in which the EUROSEC landing craft, the *Dove*, had crash-landed on the new planet and Hendy must pull Roy Thinnes from the wreckage. Gerry recalled:

By the time he was called to play his part, he could hardly stand up. They had to help him into the capsule, set fire to the whole thing and then shout 'Action!' Of course, he walked out and stumbled down the rocks like a man who was in deep shock and had been injured. But as a matter of fact, he'd had one over the eight and the performance was absolutely fantastic!

The film's production problems extended beyond squabbles between the director, actors and producers. A full-size model of the *Dove* landing craft had been built at Century 21 Studios, in Slough, for scenes in which the actors had to enter it in zero gravity. Unfortunately, the producers failed to take into account that Pinewood Studios agreement with the film technicians unions meant that any props used on a film shot at Pinewood had to be made there. The fabulously detailed Century 21 model was burned and the Pinewood crew made a replica, less detailed than the original. This did nothing to alleviate Gerry Anderson's life-long dislike of having to deal with the film unions.

The finished film also had some censorship trouble, as the BBFC insisted that a close up of a packet of contraceptive pills be removed from the film if it were to be awarded an 'A' certificate. The only alternative certification at the time was an 'X', which would have prevented under-eighteens from seeing the film at all. It is indicative of the lack of confidence in the finished film that its UK distributor, Rank, even asked the BBFC if there was any possibility that the film could be cut to achieve a 'U' certificate. Fortunately, the certifications board was able to convince Rank that any such effort would reduce the film to incomprehensibility.

Public interest in space was intense in the late 1960s, with America working towards a manned flight to the moon and the 1968 release of Stanley Kubrick's hugely influential *2001: A Space Odyssey*. Strangely, this did not lead to a boom in SF film production. In Hollywood, John Sturges directed *Marooned* (1969), which was about the rescue of three American astronauts stranded in space. Meanwhile, over at Elstree and Bray studios, Hammer Films were spending £500,000—a massive sum of money by the famously frugal standards of the horror specialists—on what was described as 'the first moon "Western"'. Both Hammer's effort, *Moon Zero Two* (with future *Space: 1999* star Catherina von Schell) and *Doppelgänger*, received UK releases in October 1969.

All three films performed badly at the box office. Universal had only ever appeared lukewarm about the *Doppelgänger* script and appeared underwhelmed by the finished product. This must have proved almost fatal for the film's chances of financial success as, apart from some rather odd poster art for the American release (the main image of which was artwork of the dullest space vehicle imaginable, as opposed to Derek Meddings' wonderful vehicle designs) and an excellent trailer, Universal offered the film very little support.

In the UK, film fans had to be quick if they wanted to catch *Doppelgänger* at their local cinema. In most places, and on a double bill with the Western *Death of a Gunfighter*, the film ran for less than a week on the Odeon circuit.

This latter film has a small place in film history as the first production to bear the pseudonymous director's credit Allen Smithee.

What the film was even called depended on where in the world you happened to live—Universal and Century 21 disagreed over the title of the film once it was completed. The eventual result was that the film was released under Universal's preferred title, *Journey to the Far Side of the Sun* in the US and Australia. *Doppelgänger* remained the title of the film's UK release where Ian Hendry was top billed, Roy Thinnes getting first billing in the rest of the world. *Journey to the Far Side of the Sun* has become the film's de facto title over the years thanks to subsequent television screenings and home video releases. None of the above made an awful lot of difference to the film's box office results once Universal actually released the film, which remained on the shelf for a year between its completion and release.

The Power Game had turned actor Patrick Wymark into a major star of British television and a popular character actor in big budget films, such as *Where Eagles Dare* (1968) and *The Battle of Britain* (1969). The role of EUROSEC Chief Jason Webb was quite blatantly trading on his *The Power Game* persona of ruthless businessman Sir John Wilder, transposing the character into a SF setting. Even the press materials for the film describe Webb as 'John Wilder (2069 model)'. So good was Wymark that for much of the film he acts as the engine that keeps the film moving along rather than top-billed stars Roy Thinnes and Ian Hendry.

Other *The Power Game* cast members pepper the *Doppelgänger* cast, including George Sewell, Philip Madoc, and, perhaps most notably, Norma Ronald. Ronald played Patrick Wymark's secretary in *The Power Game*, filled the same role in *Doppelgänger*, and then was rehired to play Ed Straker's secretary Miss Ealand in *UFO*.

Sewell, seen in *Doppelgänger* as the tough security chief Neuman, was, of course, brought into the *UFO* cast as genial ladies' man Alec Freeman. This might seem odd casting given Sewell's normal casting as coppers and gangsters over a forty-five-year career. His recurring *The Power Game* character of construction engineer Frank Hagadan gives some clue as to the thinking of the Andersons in casting him in *UFO*. In *The Power Game* Hagadan spends most of the first two series romancing John Wilder's wife, Lady Pamela (played with great aplomb by Barbara Murray).

The Power Game inspired Gerry Anderson to attempt adult drama set in environments such as politics and business in his productions that followed. With this in mind, once *Doppelgänger* was completed, he worked with *The Power Game*'s creator and editor, Wildred Greatorex, on a new project entitled *Youth is Wasted on the Young*. This was about an ageing dictator who arranges to have his brain transplanted into a younger body in order to become his own successor. Although the project never progressed beyond the script stage, it is interesting to note that the theme of prolonging life through transplant surgery reappeared in *UFO*.

19

The Secret Service

'Ah yes. Writey scribbly in your bookery. All uttery words speed of your pencilode must exceed my eyebold.'

Executive producer Reg Hill
Produced by David Lane
Format by Gerry and Sylvia Anderson
Music composed and directed by Barry Gray
A Gerry Anderson Century 21 Television Production
An ITC World Wide Distribution
13 × twenty-five-minute episodes
First broadcast Sunday 21 September 1969 (ATV)

It is the year 1969. Father Unwin, an elderly country priest, is also a secret agent working for a department of MI5 called BISHOP (British Intelligence Service, Headquarters Operation Priest). His gardener, a simple yokel called Matthew, is really a highly skilled MI5 officer whom Father Unwin shrinks with a device called the Minimiser before going on missions, and is carried about in a specially adapted suitcase. Father Unwin drives a yellow Model T Ford named *Gabriel* and bamboozles opponents by reverting to his own gobbledegook language that is almost, but not quite, English.

The Secret Service is a definite oddity in the career of the Andersons—although, it would have been an oddity in anyone's career. The really surprising thing about *The Secret Service* is that—despite its own wilfully strange format—on-screen, taken on its own terms, it all works very well. There is a real sense of all concerned actually having fun. The model department builds on their work on *Joe 90*, which presented a more realistic near-future setting than the SF fantasy worlds of previous series, to recreate the contemporary reality of 1969. It was especially important that this aspect of the series worked, as their work would often be intercut with live-action footage.

The writing, meanwhile, retreats further from the grimness and horror of *Captain Scarlet and the Mysterons* to head towards outright comedy at times. The basic idea was so outlandish that a serious treatment would not have worked at all, but the overall impression is of two conflicting ideas competing within the same series. The idea of an eccentric elderly priest who is really a spy is quite sound, being both an inversion of the *Joe 90* format and a variation on G. K. Chesterton's Roman Catholic priest detective Father Brown. The second strand of the format—that of a miniature character interacting with a full size world—does not always seem like a natural fit with the rest of the series. No onscreen explanation is given as to how Father Unwin came to have the Minimiser—apparently he was given it by his friend, the inventor Professor Humbolt, on his death. The only place in which this part of the story was publically told was in the pages of *Countdown* comic, in which *The Secret Service* had a short-lived strip. This was an idea deserving of a series of its own, and indeed the Andersons attempted a variation on it in 1973, with the failed pilot film *The Investigator*.

In many ways, the driving force behind *The Secret Service* can be seen as a desire to take Supermarionation to its next stage of development. This manifested itself in two ways. Firstly, in order to make the new series visually distinctive from what had gone before, puppet scenes would be intercut with live-action footage. The puppet sculptors had often based their creations on real actors, such as Sean Connery and Robert Mitchum, but for the first time the actual performer would play the character alongside his puppet likeness.

The puppet and live-action mix was, in theory, a good idea. Century 21 was beginning to struggle with market saturation of puppet series in both the British and international markets, with both the Supermarionation series and the lower budget work of the erstwhile Roberta Leigh and Arthur Provis still being distributed. If Century 21 was to make further puppet series it was vital that they be made distinctive from what had come before.

So outlandish was the concept of *The Secret Service* that the Andersons and their script editor Tony Barwick gave themselves licence to create eccentric plots to match. This made a degree of sense, as there had been a trend in the mid-'60s towards comic-strip action and a far less serious approach to drama. This was led by *Batman*, which was the American ratings sensation of 1966. Existing series soon took the Caped Crusader's example, most notably *The Man from U.N.C.L.E.* and *The Avengers*, which became far more extreme in their camp humour. The trouble was that *Batman* was cancelled in 1968, audiences tiring of the comic book approach, while *U.N.C.L.E.*'s adoption of the approach was a disaster for the series, contributing to its cancellation in January 1968. *The Avengers* had grown ever wilder with its story-telling, but its ratings eventually dipped in the US and it ended its run in May 1969. It is perhaps significant that the great survivor of the spy shows of this period was *Mission: Impossible*, which was in the middle of its third season as 1969 began. This utterly serious spy series outlasted both the spy boom and the fad for camp humour, running from 1966 until 1973, in the process seeing off ITC's expensive and none-too-serious *The Persuaders*, which aired in the same time slot as *Mission: Impossible* in 1971.

The plots of the individual *The Secret Service* episodes are of interest, as they often key into the fears of post-war Britain and its industrial decline. The accession of Queen Elizabeth II to the British throne in 1953, along with the conquering of Mount Everest—news of which reached a rapturous Britain on the very morning of the coronation on 2 June—led to a great deal of talk of a 'new Elizabethan age' and a resurgent Britain capable of recapturing its former glories. This carefully skirted round the fact that the two climbers involved were a New Zealander and a Nepalese respectively, as well as a few more pertinent facts. Britain remained burdened by the responsibilities of an empire it could no longer afford to defend after being involved in total war twice in thirty years, besides the moral questions of whether the empire should exist at all. As the decade wore on, Britain's decline as a world power continued, in contrast to the popular narrative of a country triumphant in war. This was especially punctured by Britain being forced to back down after it and France took military action to gain control of the Suez Canal in 1956.

In popular fiction this resulted in a number of stories in which British industry, with world-beating products, was being done down by industrial spies and saboteurs from other countries. Even many of the later James Bond novels of Ian Fleming were ultimately about Britain coming under economic threat from abroad. These included *Goldfinger*'s large-scale gold smuggling, *Thunderball*'s nuclear blackmail, and *On Her Majesty's Secret Service*'s attempt to destroy the country's economy by spreading diseases to its farming sector.

The Secret Service enthusiastically joined in this skewed analysis of Britain's industrial decline—let's face it, stories about poor management and labour disputes were probably not going to be very popular. Thus 'A Case for the Bishop' sees a new miniature computer being stolen by a foreign power, and 'A Question of Miracles' has British-designed desalinisation plants being sabotaged by overseas competitors who need time to catch up technologically. 'The Feathered Spies' features a revolutionary British jet fighter being spied upon, them bombed by a foreign power, while 'The Cure' has a freelance spy trying to sabotage an additive that was making high octane fuel from water.

Even more so than *Joe 90*, *The Secret Service* represents an attempt to make character-based drama in a Supermarionation format. Taken on its own terms, it works very well; however, the overall impression is that no one involved particularly wanted to make a series with appeal to children. *The Secret Service* is a dialogue-heavy spy comedy largely populated by characters in their fifties. The one younger regular character, Agent Blake, is an ineffectual junior grade agent who is never told what is really going on, not only regarding Father Unwin and Matthew, but also any case he's asked to help with. One can see now the point of putting Jimmy Gibson in the *Supercar* cast—he acts as a point of identification for younger viewers, and saves the cast from being entirely made up of older men. It must be noted that the cast of *The Secret Service* is largely made up of men, with the exception of Mrs Appleby, who is not a character who drives the plot along. The secondary cast is also largely male, the first female character was Jackie in episode five, 'Last Train to Bufflers Halt'. What is striking about this character is that there is no particular reason for her to be female (which, by extension, means that there could have been a female character in any of the previous stories).

The semi-classical theme tune, complete with views of a church yard, hardly made for the promise of thrilling viewing to audiences who might have been attracted by the crisply edited *Thunderbirds* opening, the eerie beginning to *Captain Scarlet and the Mysterons*, or the cheerful *Joe 90* theme. This was not to bode well for the future of the series.

The origin of *The Secret Service* came when Gerry Anderson happened across Stanley Unwin at Pinewood Studios in 1968. As it transpired, Gerry was a big fan of Unwin's many 1950s radio appearances, and he set about creating a format around the performer for Century 21's next series. A new idea was needed as it seemed unlikely that more episodes of *Joe 90* would be ordered by Lew Grade. Unwin was signed up to a contract for a twenty-six-episode series, and production began in August 1968, following directly on from *Joe 90*.

Stanley Unwin was born in Pretoria, South Africa, on 7 June 1911. His family returned to their native England when Stanley was four years old on the death of his father. The adolescent Unwin's imagination was fired by a chance encounter in Manchester with an early BBC Outside Broadcast Unit in the 1920s. This set him on a career path not towards a future in entertainment, but as a technician, and he immediately began saving to buy a crystal radio set. Graduating from Nautical Training School with a postmaster's certificate in Wireless Telegraphy, by 1940 Stanley was working for the BBC, travelling across Europe as a recording engineer for one of the corporation's War Reporting Units.

After the war, he was redeployed as an Outside Broadcast Engineer, which accidentally led to a career in entertainment. As part of an equipment test, Stanley and a colleague performed an ad-libbed comedy skit, which included the first recorded example of the nonsense language that became known as 'Unwinese'. The recording was so well received that it was broadcast, and a parallel career as an entertainer developed. The highly popular radio comedian Ted Ray loved Stanley's work, and insisted on including him in the *Spice of Life* series. His humorous monologues were a hugely popular part of 1950's radio listening, and in 1961 he finally became a full-time entertainer, ending his twenty-year career as a BBC engineer.

By this time Unwin was seen in film roles, and during the 1960s he produced best-selling books and LPs. By the late 1960s, he changed from nationally to internationally famous, being featured as The Chancellor in the 1968 film version of Ian Flemings' *Chitty Chitty Bang Bang*, and narrating the Small Faces classic psychedelic rock album *Ogden's Nut Gone Flake*. By the time *The Secret Service* was made, Stanley Unwin was at the height of his fame.

The other voice artists working on *The Secret Service* came from the established cast of actors who had worked on *Joe 90*. Sylvia Anderson handled the vocals for the Vicarage's housekeeper, Mrs Appleby, and the few other female roles that were written for the series. Matthew Harding, Father Unwin's gardener and 'man in a suitcase' spy, had two voices—Standard English for when he was on spying duties and a country yokel voice for when undercover as Matthew the gardener—and both voices came from Gary Files. Also showing great vocal dexterity was Jeremy Wilkin who played The Bishop, a man much older than himself. These actors played other parts as required, as did Keith Alexander and David Healy, who rounded out the credited voice cast. Uncredited was old Anderson favourite David Graham, who returned to provide voices for the last two episodes produced, 'May-Day, May-Day' and 'More Haste Less Speed'— David Healy was unavailable for the recording sessions.

The directors were largely the same as those who had helmed episodes of *Joe 90*; they were Alan Perry, Leo Eaton Ken Turner, Peter Anderson, and Brian Heard, and they were joined by Ian Spurrier, who directed a single episode, 'The Feathered Spies'. He had been one of the main assistant directors on *Joe 90*, and returned in this capacity for the 'School for Spies' and 'More Haste, Less Speed' episodes of the show.

In addition to directing the aforementioned episodes, Ken Turner directed the live-action sequences, which were shot before the puppet scenes with the rationale that it would far easier to match studio-shot scenes to existing footage filmed outdoors than vice versa. Turner's crew included lighting cameraman Ted Wooldridge, who had previously photographed effects units on the Supermarionation series. With him came his regular camera operator from *Captain Scarlet and the Mysterons* and *Joe 90*, Noel Rowlands. In an interesting example of Century 21 crew being asked to carry out a variety of roles, the location unit was managed by Gren Nott, who had previously been art director. This would have also had advantages when it came to matching the live-action footage with puppet scenes, as both the live action and puppet units would have had a trained art director on hand. Keith Wilson had now been promoted to the sole credited art director for *The Secret Service*.

Among the locations visited by Ken Turner's crew was St Michael and All Angels Church, Hughenden, Buckinghamshire, which served as Father Unwin's church and was seen in every episode as part of the opening credits sequence. BISHOP was based at Horse Guards Parade, the famous location in London's Whitehall where the annual Trooping of the Colour ceremony takes place. British Intelligence itself (in the series, at least) was based in the visually striking Centre Point tower. This thirty-three-storey Brutalist office block on New Oxford Street and St Giles High Street was built between 1961 and 1966 and was one of London's first skyscrapers. By the time *The Secret Service* was filmed, the building was mainly famous for remaining completely empty. It was built by speculative property developer Harry Hyams, who insisted that it be let by a single tenant, and was wealthy enough to wait for an extended period until one turned up. By the time Hyams finally relaxed his conditions in 1975, Centre Point had become regarded as something of a national scandal, a byword for greed and wastefulness in property speculation. What better explanation for the building remaining empty for so long, however, than it being a base for Britain's spy organisation?

Keith Wilson's art direction is exemplary, each episode featuring extraordinarily detailed sets, most impressively The Bishop's office. This large room with columns, and dominated by a large globe, which many visual compositions in scenes set there are built around, fits in perfectly with its Whitehall setting. The design of the room is really rather splendid, but one cannot help but wonder if it is the wrong sort of splendid. Would it have hurt so much to have given The Bishop a huge map of the world on one wall and some kind of computer console to add visual interest for younger viewers?

When a more modern design is used the resulting sets look excellent. The desalinisation plant control room in 'A Question of Miracles' is a lovely set on two levels (not unlike the Main Mission set Wilson would later design for *Space: 1999*), and filled with visual interest and detail. 'Recall to Service' features a similarly well-executed control room set for a high-tech remote control tank, while 'The Deadly Whisper' features a clever and memorable triple target for the prototype of a new sonic rifle.

As ever, Tony Barwick was script editor, and was by now was calling upon a group of experienced writers to script Supemarionation series. As was traditional, Gerry and Sylvia Anderson wrote the first episode, 'A Case for the Bishop', themselves, setting the style they wanted for the series.

Barwick himself wrote four episodes of the series, but the load was spread more evenly among other writers this time, mainly among the core of experienced professionals he had gathered for *Joe 90*. Donald James returned to write three scripts, as did Pat Dunlop, while Shane Rimmer was engaged to write 'A Hole in One', inspired by both men's love of golf. The story 'May-Day, May-Day' was written by Bob Keston, a new writer to Supermarionation, but, like the others Barwick had recruited, hardly new to writing. Keston was a Canadian scientific journalist and broadcaster who had begun writing professionally for comics, his early experience being with *Rick Random: Space Detective*, memorably drawn for the *Super Detective Library* series by Ron Turner. Turner went on to become one of the key artists for *TV Century 21* comic, his work including the *Stingray* and *The Daleks* strips.

Keston then went on to write for various television series, including the 1960 Armchair Theatre production *The Innocent*, which featured the unlikely screen pairing of Diana Dors and Patrick Macnee, plus episodes of the BBC's long-running Scottish medical series *Dr. Finlay's Casebook*. He also wrote the 1962 B-movie *K.I.L. 1*, which starred Ronald Howard, son of the famous screen star Leslie Howard, and also featured none other than David Graham.

Following, as it did, immediately on from *Joe 90* with barely a pause, *The Secret Service* shared most of the same directors with that series. This time there was no need felt to have one of the producers such as David Lane or production controller Desmond Saunders direct the first episode, with Alan Perry taking on the first episode, he and Leo Eaton were the two directors responsible for the most episodes. Ken Turner, Brian Heard, and Peter Anderson from the *Joe 90* pool of directors also worked on *The Secret Service*, with one episode, 'The Feathered Spies', being directed by Ian Spurrier. This was another example of Century 21 promoting from within. Spurrier was first credited for his work on *Thunderbird 6*, on which he worked on the lip sync, moving on to the *Captain Scarlet and the Mysterons* crew to do the same job for four episodes. By the later episodes of that series he had been promoted to assistant director, and he was one of the main assistant directors throughout the production of *Joe 90*. 'The Feathered Spies' would be Ian Spurrier's only credit as director, but he returned as assistant director for two later episodes of the series, including the final Supermarionation production of all, 'More Haste, Less Speed'.

Barry Gray's incidental music was generally in the style he had set for previous series, which allowed, where necessary, for the use of cues originally recorded for earlier series. The theme tune, which was repeated in different variations during the episodes themselves, was a radical departure for Supermarionation, and reportedly Barry Gray's favourite. The inspiration for the complex choral piece that introduced each episode came from the 1960s vogue for jazz interpretations of the work of classical composer Johann Sebastian Bach. Several arrangers made this a speciality in this period, most notably the French musician Jacques Loussier, whose jazz trio of piano, percussion, and bass became highly popular with their Play Jazz series of albums, beginning in 1959. The Jaqcues Loussier Trio's version of 'Air on the G String' became very well-known via its use over many years on television adverts for Hamlet cigars.

Also based in France was the American-born Ward Swingle, who formed The Swingle Singers in Paris in 1962. This vocal octet achieved great popularity with their first album, *Jazz Sebastian Bach*, sung largely a cappella with minimal accompaniment from drum and bass. Barry Gray was clearly a fan; his *The Secret Service* theme and its associated variations are strikingly similar to the performances on this album. The Swingle Singers were asked to perform *The Secret Service* theme, but the successful touring and recording outfit proved too expensive for the show's budget. Instead the erstwhile Mike Sammes Singers were hired, having previously recorded the theme songs for *Supercar* and *Stingray*.

As with *Joe 90*, very few new puppets were needed for *The Secret Service* voice cast, the other characters being portrayed by the cast of puppets made for *Captain Scarlet and the Mysterons*, often revamped by the use of different hair or slight remodelling of facial features. The major new puppet was, of course, Father Unwin, who had to look as much like the real Stanley Unwin as possible as a part of the series format of showing the real Unwin in long shots. It has to be said that the puppet that emerged was a remarkably good likeness.

Father Unwin's MI5 controller, The Bishop, also had a specially constructed new puppet, and was an interesting example of how puppet design had evolved in the era of correctly proportioned puppets. The puppet designers had become better at designing more characterful puppets, but these tended to be puppets of older characters, which were not necessarily the type of characters that would have kept young audiences riveted to the screen. Similarly, the Unwin Vicarage gained a housekeeper, the homely Mrs Appleby (sculpted by Christine Glanville to resemble her own mother). As with *Joe 90*'s Mrs Harris, Mrs Appleby was the only female regular character in the series.

With some time having passed since the production of *Captain Scarlet and the Mysterons*, the production felt able to reuse the main character puppets from that series in *The Secret Service*. The Captain Scarlet puppet had its raven black locks replaced by light brown hair, and with the addition of glasses became Secret Service Agent Blake. One cannot help but wonder if this was a light-hearted reference to George Blake, the British double agent who escaped from prison to the Soviet Union in 1966.

Colonel White, re-wigged with dark hair, turns up in two episodes, 'A Question of Miracles' and 'To Catch a Spy', Captain Blue makes two appearances, and even Captain Black gets an airing in 'The Deadly Whisper'. To complete the Spectrum repertory company, Captain Magenta is seen four times and Captain Grey is in three episodes. The Angel Interceptors are reused once again in the episode 'Recall to Service', while other reused props include the Tiger Moth biplane used in *Thunderbird 6*, featured in the final episode of the series ('More Haste Less Speed') and Sam Loover's car from *Joe 90* is driven by Agent Blake in 'A Question of Miracles'.

This last reuse of a model is especially interesting, as Sam's car was a prominent feature of the previous Supermarionation series and is reused in only episode two of *The Secret Service*, at which point it was envisaged that the series would run for a full twenty-six episodes. Even though the puppet series were becoming increasingly expensive to make, they were produced with great economy. By the end of the series run, when the series was doomed, the series began to reuse models from earlier episodes, for instance the Mach 3 aircraft from 'The Deadly Whisper' (episode eleven) is the same as the XK4 fighter seen in 'The Feathered Spies'.

The Secret Service was to be the last of the Supermarionation series, receiving a disastrous reception from Lew Grade when he saw the first episode. Famously, in a nightmare reversion of his reaction to seeing the *Thunderbirds* pilot episode, Grade ordered the whole series cancelled as soon as he heard Stanley Unwin speak in his gobbledegook language. By this point, ten episodes had been filmed and another three were ready to film. This at least meant that there was a saleable number of episodes, television series traditionally being made in multiples of thirteen.

Grade's explanation was that the Americans would never understand Unwin, which has tended to be regarded as him missing the point—but what if he got the point completely? As someone who had spent a lifetime in the entertainment industry, it is reasonable to assume that Lew Grade knew who Stanley Unwin was and what his act consisted of. His Unwinese language had become ingrained into British culture and audiences would have known what to expect from him.

Would audiences not knowing who Stanley Unwin was have known how to react when he suddenly starts talking in this strange way for no apparent reason? It is likely that there were other things about *The Secret Service* Lew Grade did not like, but the Unwin double-talk was the final straw.

Ultimately, a series made for television is a commercial product—a means by which audiences are delivered to advertisers. On those terms *The Secret Service* undoubtedly failed and the era of Supermarionation ended on a sour note. Thirteen episodes was a perfectly saleable number of episodes for the UK market, but the series was only screened in three ITV regions. ATV, by now only broadcasting to the English Midlands, naturally showed a production that came from its own stable. The only two other regions to sign up for *The Secret Service* were Granada (ironically always an enthusiastic consumer of Anderson product, despite having turned down the opportunity to make further series with AP Films after *Four Feather Falls*) and Southern Television, which served the south and south-east of England.

The flood of merchandising that had accompanied previous series had slowed down to a trickle; Dinky Toys produced a die-cast model of Father Unwin's Model-T Ford, now a highly valuable collectable, two novelisations were published, plus a set of sweet cigarette cards.

Even though it is probable that ITC were not wildly enthusiastic about promoting *The Secret Service*, it is hard to imagine that many more regions would have taken the series even if it had run to its planned twenty-six-episode length. Many ITV regions had already turned down the opportunity to screen the rather livelier and child-friendly *Joe 90* the previous year—it was time for a change. Gerry Anderson had taken increasingly less personal control of the puppet series as he pursued the feature films and live-action productions that had been his ambition ever since he had co-founded AP Films.

Doppelgänger was already in the can awaiting a release date from Universal, which was showing signs of having cold feet about the film. The project had already proved to Lew Grade, however, that the Century 21 team could deliver a good-looking production aimed at an adult audience on time and on budget. Even while *The Secret Service* was in production in late 1968, Gerry and Sylvia Anderson and Reg Hill were hard at work developing the format of the company's first live-action television series. *UFO* was coming.

Key Episode

Episode 8: 'Hole in One'
Written by Shane Rimmer
Directed by Brian Heard
First UK broadcast Sunday 26 October 1969 (ATV)

BISHOP is called in when it is discovered that an intelligence leak, which is endangering a crucial early warning satellite, has occurred. This leak has originated from discussions that General Brompton has had on the golf course. Father Unwin is put on the case and discovers that enemy agents have developed an ingenious method of bugging golfing conversations.

There is an expression popularised by CGI films and the games industry—'the uncanny valley'. This is where a simulation of a human is so close to reality that the part of the brain that recognises other humans is slightly stimulated, causing a sense of unease. The opening scenes of 'Hole in One' shows two characters playing golf portrayed by both humans and puppets, dependent on the requirements of the individual shot. On a technical level the scene works well, but it just seems a little odd.

Make no mistake, 'Hole in One' is a fun episode with a lot to recommend it, but it just adds to the overall impression that the Century 21 team were not that interested in making a series with appeal to younger viewers. After viewers see an opening sequence, which might as well be from *Songs of Praise* with a theme tune based on a Bach cantata, they see a lovingly crafted scene in which two middle-aged men play golf (not a sport traditionally seen as popular among pre-teens).

Like the series itself, so much about 'Hole in One' works, but the overall impression is of a series that simply does not play to the strengths of Supermarionation. With live actors, this is a series that would play very effectively to adults. With puppets, it was only ever going to get slotted into the children's television ghetto.

The plot is gloriously silly: the villains have found a method of hiding recording devices into golf balls, which are collected by a special mechanism in the cup of the fifteenth hole. This sends the balls to the villains' hideout and substitutes a real ball. It is based around the phenomenon, popular at the time, that a lot of major business discussions were taking place not in the boardroom, but on the less pressured environment of the golf course.

The villain's scheme is quite ludicrous, but we go along with it because the episode is generally good fun. The effects work is excellent. This might sound rather obvious as observations about Anderson series go, but the two major model sequences are really very well done, showing that, in the two years since *Captain Scarlet and the Mysterons*, the Century 21 organisation had continued to develop and perfect their methods. The early warning satellite and a sequence in which a petrol tanker being used to transport vital components for the satellite project is blown up are almost up to the standards Derek Meddings and his team would display later that year when *UFO* began filming.

20

UFO

'A long finger of tragic coincidence, stretching across a billion miles of space.'

Produced by Reg Hill and Gerry Anderson
Format by Gerry and Sylvia Anderson with Reg Hill
Music composed and directed by Barry Gray
A Gerry Anderson Century 21 Television Production
An ITC World Wide Distribution
26 × fifty-minute episodes
First broadcast Wednesday 16 September 1970 (ATV/Tyne Tees/Border Television)

The mid-1980s. Earth is engaged in a secret war with a dying alien race. The planet is defended by SHADO—Supreme Headquarters Alien Defence Organisation—run by Commander Ed Straker from a secret base underneath Harlington-Straker—a film studio in southern England. To the outside world Straker is a high-powered film executive, but in reality he commands a fleet of submarines, aircraft, ground stations, and vehicles, and a base on the moon with interceptor craft. If the people of Earth were to find out about the alien threat there would be mass panic, so SHADO's existence must remain a closely guarded secret.

The change from puppets to live action, and the aiming of *UFO* at a slightly older audience, gave the Andersons and their collaborators on the series format—Reg Hill, Tony Barwick, and Donald James (though only Gerry and Sylvia Anderson and Reg Hill would be credited)—the chance to put a new spin on some old ideas. Freed from the treadmill of having to devise a new Supermarionation series format every year, they returned to the basic idea behind *Captain Scarlet and the Mysterons*, the company's darkest series format up to this time. Earth would once again be under attack from an alien foe and defended by an organisation with fantastic vehicles.

This time, however, the alien threat would not be from an invisible enemy, but instead one with a real physical presence who required spaceships to travel to Earth. This alters the mood of *UFO* in important ways from its thematic predecessor. *Captain Scarlet and the Mysterons* had an atmosphere akin to *Invasion of the Body Snatchers* or, perhaps even more pertinently, William Cameron Menzies' cult 1953 SF film *Invaders from Mars*, in which a small boy learns that aliens are taking over the minds of adults. *UFO*, on the other hand, works on some levels as a SF variation on Britain's experience in the Battle of Britain and the Blitz on London. By 1968, this was passing from the realm of lived experience and into something experienced via the many films on the subject. The British film industry in the 1950s seemed to make almost nothing but war movies, and the sight of Moonbase Interceptor pilots scrambling to their vehicles as early warning systems announced the arrival of incoming craft had a familiar ring to it.

The motivation behind the alien threat also changed. Instead of the Mysterons launching a war on Earth in revenge of an attack by humans making first contact who are nervous and trigger-happy, a different irony is behind the conflict in *UFO*. The alien invaders are highly advanced technologically, in ways that we can barely comprehend, but are dying physically. Hereditarily sterile and in poor physical condition, they are travelling across the universe in order to use human bodies to prolong their lives.

With *UFO*, it was vital that the highly expensive series, budgeted at £100,000 per episode, reach an older audience. In addition to being an action-adventure series, *UFO* attempted to be a series that covered adult issues, the politics of running a large and complex organisation, and the emotional lives of its main characters.

Writer Ian Scott Stewart's 'Flight Path' sees SHADO technician Paul Roper, played by George Cole, blackmailed into giving the aliens some mysterious computer information, or they will kill his much younger wife. Alan Pattillo's 'The Square Triangle' sees an adulterous couple (again with an age difference, played by Patrick Mower and Adrienne Corri) plot the murder of the woman's husband, only to accidentally kill an alien instead. 'Close Up' makes very heavy weather of a Tony Barwick story that hinges around a technician trying to get SHADO funding for a macro photography project, which has precisely nothing to do with saving the Earth from aliens. The episodes 'Computer Affair' and 'Ordeal' also touched upon issues of racism, quite a brave move in an era when the southern states of America could still refuse to screen episodes of series that did not fit with their attitudes towards race.

Most notable in this trend of *UFO*'s stories was a matched pair of Tony Barwick scripts, which delve deeper into the background of the most magnetic character of the series—Ed Straker. 'A Question of Priorities' introduces

Straker's ex-wife Mary (Suzanne Neve) and their ill-fated son John, who was critically injured after getting hit by a car in the episode's opening sequence. 'Confetti Check A-OK' looks back to the Straker's marriage and how it buckled under the weight of Ed Straker's unexpected elevation to Commander of SHADO, an organisation Mary can know nothing about. To fans of the series, this was fascinating stuff, taking the series back to the very formation of SHADO. To ITC's powerful New York office, this was a soap opera, and not the direction in which *UFO* should be going.

The more action-oriented episodes tended to showcase the *UFO* series format better. 'Conflict' is thrilling, as the aliens hit upon the idea of hiding their version of limpet mines in space junk orbiting the Earth. The story is given added spice by the reintroduction of the character of General James Henderson, seen briefly in 'Identified'. He is now the combative head of the International Astrophysical Commission, which oversees the work of SHADO. Actors Ed Bishop and Grant Taylor really tear into Ruric Powell's script, striking sparks off each other and ensuring that Henderson would return in future episodes.

Other highlights included Tony Barwick's 'Ordeal', in which Paul Foster, hungover on arrival at his annual SHADO fitness check, is apparently kidnapped by aliens, and 'Court Martial', in which Foster is convicted of selling SHADO secrets to the press by a military court and sentenced to death. Michael Billington's best performance is probably in Donald James' 'Kill Straker!', in which Foster and his Lunar Module co-pilot are hypnotised into wanting to kill Ed Straker. The climactic scene, in which Straker pushes Foster to his limits in order to test that he is free of alien influence, is riveting. Billington stays in character and on script as Ed Bishop slaps him hard around the face.

'Sub-Smash', the final episode of the first seventeen stories to be shot at MGM-British Borehamwood, shows just how far the series had come since its dramatically shaky beginnings. Alan Fennell's story sees Straker, Foster, and Nina Barry, plus Paul Maxwell (formerly *Fireball XL5*'s Steve Zodiac), and Anthony Chinn (soon to become a regular in *The Protectors*) trapped in Skydiver when it is attacked by an alien craft. Director David Lane achieves a high degree of tension as the surviving crew escape one by one until, with both time and air running out, only Straker and Barry remain. Ed Bishop and Dolores Mantez work well together and it is hinted that the two characters are somewhat closer emotionally than had previously been revealed.

With the sudden and unexpected demise of *The Secret Service*, it became possible for Century 21 to redeploy some of the crew from the company's now-closed puppet operation to its first live-action television series. Gerry Anderson directed the first episode, 'Identified', himself, his first directorial work since 'Planet 46'—the pilot episode of *Fireball XL5* made in spring 1962—and his first direction of on-screen actors since *Crossroads to Crime* two years before that.

A core of three directors handled most of the episodes for *UFO*'s first production block, all taken from the roster of Supermarionation directors. David Lane finally got the chance to direct live action, having been denied the chance to direct *Doppelgänger* by Universal the previous year. Lane alternated episodes with Ken Turner and Alan Perry, though Turner was unavailable for the episode, 'Court Martial', with the assistant director Ron Appleton stepping up to helm the story. Appleton was highly experienced, having just finished a year-long stint as assistant director on the final season of *The Avengers*.

Tony Barwick remained as script editor with the intention that he was to write the lion's share of the episodes—he was to write nine of the first production block of seventeen episodes, and co-wrote *UFO*'s opening episode, 'Identified', with Gerry and Sylvia Anderson. Working with Gerry and Sylvia, Reg Hill, and Tony Barwick on the series format and the script for 'Identified' was Donald James, who had become a close friend of the Andersons and Barwick. The intention was that James would contribute four scripts—the stories that would eventually be titled 'Flight Path', 'Conflict', 'The Dalotek Affair', and 'Kill Straker!'.

James had to reduce his involvement with *UFO* when he commissioned to write multiple scripts for *Randall and Hopkirk (Deceased)* and *Department S* for Monty Berman and Dennis Spooner and also for the American espionage drama *Mission: Impossible*. Instead, he arranged for two new writers to work on three of these stories, Ian Scott Stewart writing 'Flight Path' (originally titled 'The Sun Always Rises') and Ruric Powell writing 'Conflict' and 'The Dalotek Affair'. James acted as script editor for Stewart and Powell while writing 'Kill Straker!' himself.

Other writers for the first group of episodes were familiar names. The multi-talented Alan Pattillo wrote 'The Square Triangle', his first work for Century 21 since the *Captain Scarlet and the Mysterons* episode 'The Trap'. Alan Fennell, having left the editorship of the Anderson-themed *TV21* comic, returned to scriptwriting duties for the first time since the second series *Thunderbirds* episode 'Atlantic Inferno'. His contributions were the episodes 'ESP' and 'Sub-Smash'.

Leo Eaton, on the *UFO* crew as one of the assistant directors, also had a story idea, the African-set 'The Patriot', accepted by Tony Barwick for development into a full script. Unfortunately, Eaton left *UFO* for unknown reasons after working on the Alan Perry-directed 'Close Up' and the script was never filmed. It is possible that 'The Patriot' was deemed unsuited with the more action-oriented tone of the series second production block.

After the departure of John Read, following *Doppelgänger*, a new director of photography was needed for *UFO* and Brendan J. Stafford was drafted in. Stafford had worked on many of ITC's filmed adventure series. In the years leading up to the production of *UFO*, he had worked extensively with Patrick McGoohan on both the half-hour and one-hour version of *Danger Man*, moving on to photograph *The Prisoner*, then the final series of *The Saint*. After

UFO, Stafford went on to photograph *The Protectors*, plus four episodes of the second series of *Space: 1999*, which were shot in tandem with episodes shot by Frank Watts—the regular lighting cameraman for that series.

Returning to Century 21's television production crew was art director Bob Bell, assisted by Keith Wilson, who was now freed up from his responsibilities on *The Secret Service* to work on *UFO* as assistant art director. Wilson got to work on some sets on his own, and also worked uncredited on costume design—Sylvia Anderson was credited for 'Century 21 Fashions'. The sets for the series were superb, the SHADO headquarters and Moonbase sets, plus the interiors of vehicles (such as Skydiver and the Moonbase Interceptors) set new standards in realistic detail on SF productions. Bell felt able to use a more subtle colour palate than he had on his puppet sets for series such as *Stingray* and *Thunderbirds*, while his Moonbase set was in a clever circular design, which Bell claimed never quite came across how he meant it to on-screen.

The fashions were possibly less successful at first than the sets. This is always a difficult area for SF productions. The SHADO headquarters uniforms were simple unisex jumpsuits, while the female crew running Moonbase were give skin-tight silver uniforms and purple wigs. The latter were visually very effective, but their practical use was never explained. Where *UFO* got into some difficulty at first was in the design of civilian outfits in the series predictions of mid-1980s fashions. Some use was made of costumes from *Doppelgänger*, the double-breasted men's suits in particular reflecting the fashions of 1968 rather more than they did the 1980s.

Earlier episodes also featured men's suits in very bright colours with no lapels and a central stripe, which was not a flattering look for the actors having to wear them. Civilian costumes for the actresses were no more flattering— the use of heavy make-up and hairstyles using masses of hairspray gave the performers a curiously doll-like appearance. This situation improved as the series progressed, especially during the second production block, when Straker, in particular, looked very stylish in a black, collarless suit, which set off the character's blond hair.

One beneficiary of the ending of the puppet series was the model unit, once again under the supervision of Derek Meddings, with Jim Elliott as his senior director and effects units being directed by Shaun Whittacker-Cook and Bill Camp. With the puppet stages gone, they were able to expand to fill the whole of Century 21's Sterling Road studios. The added space allowed the scale of the effects shots to increase, enabling the effects shots to reach new heights of believability—a necessary step if they were to adequately match the live-action footage.

UFO featured a highly memorable array of equipment and vehicles. Some of these were in the form of full-sized vehicles that had been constructed for the film *Doppelgänger* by Derek Meddings—most famous of which were the futuristic cars driven by Ed Straker and Paul Foster throughout the series. These featured large new body shells on Ford Zodiac running gear and were apparently very difficult to drive and hard for the driver to see through the windshield—they were not road legal and scenes featuring them being driven had to be shot on private roads. The personnel-carrying SHADO Jeeps, built around Mini Mokes, were also seen in many episodes and were also adapted from vehicles created for *Doppelgänger*.

The highly impressive vehicles and craft made in miniature for *UFO* were designed by Derek Meddings and Mike Trim. Possibly the best-remembered vehicle used in the series were the Moonbase Interceptors, which emerged from their sub-lunar hangar through craters on the Moon's surface. The original design for the Interceptor, by Mike Trim, was based on a one-line description in the script of 'Identified'; it had a tough, utilitarian look with a large single missile mounted at the craft's front. This was one of the very few Mike Trim designs to be largely rejected by Derek Meddings, whose alternative, a slightly more polished-looking take on the design, became one of the best-known of all the vehicles used on Gerry Anderson series.

Another Meddings design, which looked wonderful on-screen, was Skydiver. This was an extremely clever concept of a submarine, the entire front section of which was a detachable fighter aircraft. It was never explained quite how Skydiver managed to achieve the 45-degree angle undersea in order for the front section, known as Sky 1, to launch, but this hardly mattered. The launch sequence for Sky 1, like that of the Moonbase Interceptors, was a highlight of any episode it appeared in, aided immensely by Barry Gray's pulsating score.

SHADO's ground attack vehicles and personnel transporters were their fleet of SHADO mobiles. These large, tracked vehicles were designed by Mike Trim, and were so well conceived and realised that many viewers did not realise at the time that they were not real, full-sized vehicles. Their air of reality was aided by the model unit's mastery of creating realistic outdoor settings for the vehicles to appear in. By this point they were particularly skilled at producing forest settings, including the use of real greenery and ferns made to look like much larger fauna.

The series, of course, required some actual UFOs for SHADO to detect. The term 'UFO' was actually redundant in this context, as the alien craft were not unidentified at all. Derek Meddings' design for the alien spaceships intelligently suggested a craft that operated on a completely different principal to human technology. Held aloft on wires, the UFOs had a see-through Perspex dome revealing an inner section, plus outer paddles that spun thanks to an internal motor.

The exterior of SHADO's Moonbase was largely designed by Mike Trim, always far keener on visualising buildings than Meddings. It was made up of a linked series of four domes and a central section, which gave the impression of a structure that had been transported to the Moon in modular sections and assembled on the lunar surface. Meddings added the detail of a landing and launch platform for the lunar module used to transport personnel to and from the complex, which looked rather uncomfortably close to the rest of the building.

Barry Gray's *UFO* score was right up there with the very best of his work, his theme tune for the series employing a pulsating backdrop with a relatively simple melody, creating an absolutely thrilling one-minute theme. For the score, the two main elements were often split off and used separately, the melody orchestrated and re-orchestrated into a myriad of different styles, from light and airy to heavily dramatic. The backbeat, matching the rhythm of the human heartbeat, was often used on its own, particularly during the Interceptor launch sequences, adding a real sense of urgency and danger to these scenes. As well as traditional orchestration, the score made use of the Hammond organ as a lead instrument for many of the cues Gray wrote for the series, and his favourite electronic instrument—the ondes Martenot—was also used, particularly during scenes set in outer space.

UFO had a very large regular cast—probably too large and unwieldy at first for audiences to strongly identify strongly with any particular character, especially as many of the performers chosen had limited acting experience. Ed Bishop was a familiar face to the Century 21 crew, having provided the voice for Captain Blue in the puppet series *Captain Scarlet and the Mysterons* and played the part of NASA liaison David Poulson in the film *Doppelgänger*. His casting in the lead role of Ed Straker in *UFO* was not a forgone conclusion though, and he had to audition with other actors for the part. As soon as they saw his audition performance, the Andersons and the other Century 21 executives knew they had their man.

Second in Command at SHADO was Alec Freeman, an old friend and confident of Straker. This role was filled by George Sewell, one of several *UFO* cast members to have appeared in the television series *The Power Game*, as well as *Doppelgänger*. Sewell and Bishop worked exceptionally well together; however, it was believed that a younger man would be necessary to handle the more action-oriented scenes. Here the casting process failed, Sylvia Anderson's choice was Italian actor Franco DeRosa, who had already had virtually his entire part cut from *Doppelgänger* due to the sub-plot he appeared in being excised. DeRosa was fired from his role as Franco Desica during the shooting of 'Identified', which resulted in some last-minute rewriting. His role as Moonbase commander was filled by Gabrielle Drake, who had already been cast as Gaye Ellis and had particularly impressed Gerry Anderson while he was directing the episode.

A new actor was required for the role of the young action lead, a character who was quickly developed and named Paul Foster. Michael Billington, a twenty-seven-year-old actor born in Blackburn, Lancashire, was cast for this role. He had previously gained some stage experience and had appeared in thirteen episodes of the BBC's football-based soap opera *United!* in 1965, plus he had a small role in an episode of *The Prisoner* in 1967, which was noticed by Sylvia Anderson. Handsome and well-built, he was a serious student of acting, and, despite having no formal training at this stage, he proved a boon to the production. Paul Foster debuted in the episode 'Survival', in which his character had to walk a huge distance across the moon to safety accompanied by an alien.

However, as Foster would have appeared seemingly from nowhere as a senior member of SHADO, an introductory episode was required to expand on his character's significance. Thus Tony Barwick wrote 'Exposed', a script giving Foster the backstory of being a test pilot whose craft was damaged during a UFO attack. His frustrations at not being believed and investigations into what had really happened led him to discover SHADO, in what was ultimately a test to see if he was worthy of recruitment into the organisation. The episode was slotted into the approved screening order of the series as episode two, and is actually one of the very best of the show's earlier stories.

Featured heavily in 'Identified' was Skydiver Captain John Carlin, played by Peter Gordeno, who was not an actor at all, but a dancer and singer well-known to British audiences. Born in Rangoon, in what was then Burma, Gordeno was closely associated with *UFO*, appearing in the opening credit sequence of every episode and in much of the merchandise associated with the series. In fact, he appeared in five of the first six episodes, then his character disappeared entirely. Although he was never told in his lifetime, Gordeno's agent had upset Lew Grade's brother, theatrical impresario Lord Delfont. This resulted in an order that he be pulled from the series, it being explained to Gordeno by the agent that he had gained some acting experience, but now should avoid typecasting.

His role as Skydiver captain was filled by the absurdly handsome Australian model Gary Myers, whose character, Lew Waterman, was promoted from Moonbase Interceptor pilot. Although well-known to audiences from his continuing series of James Bond-esque Milk Tray adverts, *UFO* represented Myers first screen-acting experience. Rather more experienced was Harry Baird, who played Interceptor pilot Mark Bradley. Born in British Guyana, Baird had been acting since 1955, appearing in films such as Basil Deaden and Michael Relph's *Sapphire* (1959), and had spent some time acting in Italian peplum dramas, popular worldwide after the success of Steve Reeves in *Hercules* in 1957. He also had a notable role in the Michael Caine comedy-thriller *The Italian Job* (1969). Baird was given two very strong episodes to showcase his abilities, 'Computer Affair' and 'Ordeal', both of which raised the subject of racial prejudice. Unfortunately, and despite giving excellent performances elsewhere, Baird comes across as somewhat stiff and uncomfortable in *UFO* and his character only appeared in six episodes, spread across the first fifteen stories filmed.

As the series progressed, the focus of the stories was narrowed from the rather unwieldy cast the series began with. Ed Straker was rightly seen as *UFO*'s strongest character, and while early stories featured him largely in SHADO HQ, Ed Bishop's performance was magnetic and more stories were written to feature him. The focus was firmly now on Bishop, Sewell, and Billington, with the Moonbase crew, particularly Gabrielle Drake and Dolores Mantez, also being featured strongly.

Episode seventeen of *UFO*, 'Sub-Smash', was the last ever production to be made at the MGM-British Borehamwood studios, which were closing down. Legend has it that the production of Stanley Kubrick's *2001: A Space Odyssey* took so long—using huge amounts of studio space, but paying no rent as it was an MGM production—that it had made the studio uneconomical to run. In the 1969–70 period, British film and television production was undergoing a short-lived boom, which meant that there was no suitable studio space available to house the production. Production on *UFO* closed down for five months.

This was a source of intense frustration to Century 21, as the production had really started to find its feet by this point. It also represented an opportunity for the producers to assess the direction the series was taking and make a few changes. The final nine episodes of the series, shot at Pinewood when studio space could finally be booked, have a different look and feel to the Borehamwood stories.

In addition to various changes of minor cast members and background artists, there was one major change in the series acting line-up. George Sewell was dropped from the series at the insistence of ITC's powerful New York office, who told Gerry Anderson bluntly to 'get rid of the ugly guy'. Sewell was never told of the real reason why he left the series and it certainly did his career no harm. By 1973 he had landed the lead role in his own filmed series, Euston Films' *Special Branch*.

It was decided to replace the Alec Freeman with a character who had appeared briefly in 'Identified'—Virginia Lake, played by Wanda Ventham. Aged thirty-four when she began work as a regular cast member on *UFO* in April 1970, she would probably have been best known to *UFO* viewers for two parts she played on television in 1967—as Jean Rock in the *Doctor Who* serial 'The Faceless Ones' and as the computer attendant in *The Prisoner* episode 'It's Your Funeral'.

Also drafted in were some different directors—experienced old hands from ITC's other live-action filmed adventure series, who could be relied upon to deliver a stylish end product and still work quickly. With the production having gone on an expensive five-month hiatus through no fault of its own, production efficiency was now vital.

Most notable among the new recruits was David Tomblin, who wrote and directed two episodes, 'The Cat with Ten Lives' and 'Reflections in the Water', and wrote a third, the final episode of the series, 'The Long Sleep'. The thirty-nine-year-old Tomblin was a native of Borehamwood and had been working in the film industry since the age of fourteen, remaining in the industry for his entire working life, save for time spent performing National Service, which led to him becoming a Royal Marine. It is estimated that he worked in total on some 500 films and television productions.

It was while working on the original half-hour formatted *Danger Man* in 1959–60 that Tomblin first met Patrick McGoohan, and the two remained professionally associated for most of the 1960s. When *Danger Man* returned with a one-hour format a few years later, Tomblin was tempted back from work on feature films to act as an assistant director. The two men got on well and when McGoohan began work on his pet project *The Prisoner*, Tomblin was made producer. He also wrote and directed episodes of the series and was a partner in McGoohan's production company, Everyman Films. It was clear from Tomblin's work on *The Prisoner* that he was a major talent, so he was specifically recruited to help push *UFO* in a slightly different direction when production started up again.

Jeremy Summers, director of Tony Barwick's script 'The Psychobombs' and David Tomblin's 'The Long Sleep', was the son of Walter Summers, a British writer and director who had begun in the film industry in 1913, directing films throughout the silent era and up until 1940. His son Jeremy, born in 1931, worked his way up the filmmaking ranks from third assistant director to second assistant director on major films such as *The Dam Busters* (1955). Later in the '50s, he moved to work in the booming television sector to work on series such as *Overseas Press Club-Exclusive!* in 1957. One such series, *International Detective* (1959) gave Summers his long-awaited start as director and he never looked back.

He next got his break in films, directing Tony Hancock (then at the height of his fame) in the 1963 film *The Punch and Judy Man*. The film was not a financial success, but established Summers as a director. In between film assignments, including four for British-based international exploitation film producer Harry Alan Towers, he became one of ITC's most in-demand directors for their filmed adventure series. Before starting work on *UFO*, he had been working on ITC's *Randall and Hopkirk (Deceased)*.

Cyril Frankel was one of ITC's most experienced directors, called in to direct a single episode of *UFO*—the Terence Feeley story 'Timelash'. He had begun directing with documentary shorts in the early 1950s before moving on to direct feature films for Group 3, a company formed at the urging of the National Film Finance Corporation in 1951 to give opportunities to new talent. Frankel's film-directing career never developed to the extent that he directed big-budget features, but he directed two lesser-known, but still notable, films for Hammer, *Never Take Sweets from a Stranger* (1960) and *The Witches* (1966).

For ITC he directed episodes of *The Baron*, *Gideon's Way*, and *The Champions* before both directing and acting as creative consultant on Monty Berman's series *Department S* and *Randall and Hopkirk (Deceased)*—filming on which finished shortly before *UFO* began shooting its second production block at Pinewood. Frankel's episode of the series, 'Timelash', was one of the most experimental and controversial of the series.

The first episode of *UFO*'s second batch of stories, 'The Sound of Silence', came from an unusual source, being written by David Lane and Bob Bell. Tony Barwick wrote two episodes of the new, slightly reworked *UFO*, with the aforementioned David Tomblin contributing three stories. Dennis Spooner came back to the Anderson series to provide his first script since his work on *Thunderbirds*, while Terence Feeley contributed two very strong stories, 'The Man Who Came Back' and 'Timelash'. Feeley had been story editor for ITV's famous drama anthology series *Armchair Theatre*, where he helped turn James Mitchell's 1967 story 'A Magnum for Schneider' into the hit spy series *Callan*. Feeley then became one of Patrick McGoohan's partners in Everyman Films, along with David Tomblin, writing two episodes of *The Prisoner*, and around the same time became foreign story editor for Paramount Pictures. After *UFO*, he went on to write two stories for the second season of *Space: 1999*.

David Tomblin's 'The Cat with Ten Lives' was boldly experimental in both its storytelling and its filmmaking style, throwing down the gauntlet to the rest of the series that this is the standard that has to be met in future. It also starts a process in which the motives of the aliens is questioned—here, instead of taking humans for spare-part surgery, which has been the aliens assumed motive ever since the beginning of the series, it is speculated that they are able to transfer their entire consciousness into another body, even that of a cat.

This is one of several episodes during this part of the series in which aliens take over the actions of humans. It was followed into production by Dennis Spooner's 'Destruction', in which the secretary of a Royal Navy Admiral (played by Stephanie Beacham) is hypnotised via her home telescope to give the aliens information about the movements of a ship. The ship the aliens want to attack is disposing at sea a deadly nerve gas, which, if exposed to the air, could destroy all human life on Earth. Although the point is not raised in the episode, this might lead alert viewers to wonder what the aliens motives might be in doing this if their aim is really to use human bodies to prolong the life of their own race.

Terence Feeley's 'The Man Who Came Back' introduces an element of sexual tension and gender politics. Colonel Craig Collins is found stranded on a desert island after being presumed dead after his spacecraft is crippled in flight. One of Ed Straker's oldest friends, there is something different about Collins, and his former girlfriend Virginia Lake suddenly finds him repulsive. Derren Nesbitt, as Collins, gives a towering performance, managing to appear funny, charming, and creepy at the same time. The episode ends with Collins having managed to manoeuvre Straker into accompanying him on a vital space mission to repair S.I.D. This is the start of a process in which Straker's role in the series is changed utterly from the deskbound boss of early episodes to an action hero.

Tony Barwick's epic 'The Psychobombs' sees the aliens take over the consciousness of three humans, imbuing them with super strength that allows them to penetrate SHADO's defences. This is the closest *UFO* came to emulating the format of *Captain Scarlet and the Mysterons*. The main difference is that the humans do not act under alien influence until they are 'activated', which means that they appear convincingly innocent until they spring into devastating action. 'The Psychobombs' is so packed with plot and incident that the decision was made to drop the series' opening credits sequence to prevent it from running over-length. As tightly written and directed (by Jeremy Summers) as anything seen on the series so far, it is hard to imagine what might have been cut instead.

Davis Tomblin's next story, 'Reflections in the Water', sees Straker thrust into the role of an action hero like never before. It somewhat stretches the bounds of believability to have SHADO's commander go out on a highly dangerous mission to investigate an underwater alien base. The plot is quite clever though, as the aliens set up a duplicate of SHADO HQ and its key personnel in order to give false instructions to Moonbase and the Skydiver submarines during a major UFO attack.

'Timelash' is almost entirely a vehicle for Straker and Colonel Lake, as they return to Harlington-Straker Studios to find that the whole area has been frozen in time by a traitorous SHADO operative whom the aliens have given control of time itself. The result is one of the series' most memorable episodes, and one that attracted controversy at the time due to Straker and Lake's having to inject themselves with drugs to stave off the influence of the time field.

'Mindbender' takes the idea of altered states even further, Tony Barwick's script giving director Ken Turner the chance to create his masterpiece with his final episode of *UFO*. The story was written as a cost-saving exercise with no budget left to create new effects and only existing sets available to use. Once again the film studio setting was called upon, along with the attractive and very handy location of Pinewood's Heatherden Hall and its surrounding gardens. The plot involves a crystal being found on the Moon, which causes anyone touching it to live out their deepest fears as if they are reality. In Straker's case, he suddenly finds that the two parts of his life—that of the film executive and the Commander of SHADO—come together as one. His whole life appears to him as being a part he's playing in a film.

Finally came 'The Long Sleep,' another David Tomblin script this time directed by Jeremy Summers. This takes the 1960s hippie subculture head on in a far more intelligent manner than had some other SF series of the era. The episode revolves around a young woman who wakes up from a ten-year coma, which she suffered after stepping in front of Ed Straker's car. It transpires that she and a newly-found hippie friend, under the influence of what appears to be LSD, disturb a group of aliens who are planting a huge bomb. She removes a section of the bomb and is running away from aliens who are chasing her to learn its location when Straker's car hits her. When she awakes, the attention of the aliens is attracted once more. In 'Timelash', the use of drugs can be explained as instrumental to the plot, but 'The Long Sleep' shows the effects of recreational drugs use. This ensured that the episode would be regarded as highly controversial, and in the UK it was screened in late-night slots sometime after the rest of the series.

This final group of nine *UFO* episodes represents an enormous achievement—a body of work of a truly exceptional standard, which includes several episodes that remain acknowledged classics of television SF. At the very end of the company's existence, Century 21 reached the very apogee of its achievement.

The way in which *UFO* was screened ensured the end of Century 21 Studios. Unusually, almost the entire series had been produced before a single episode was ever shown publicly. The last day of principal photography on the series took place on 11 September 1970 (post-production continued until November) with the first UK episode screenings taking place five days later in the ATV, Tyne Tees, and Border Television regions.

UFO was not seen in America until 1972, by which time most of the *UFO* production crew was busy on *The Protectors*; the sets had been struck and the props had begun their second life as the mainstay of British series such as *Doctor Who* (as late as 1985), *Blake's 7*, and even *The Muppet Show*. The series did well enough in the American ratings to be seriously considered for renewal for a second series, which would have played on the popularity of the episodes set on Moonbase.

Lew Grade had made the decision at the end of *UFO*'s production to close down Century 21 Studios. It was simply too expensive to keep an entire filmmaking operation running when it might be several years until their next project received the green light. The Stirling Road studios were sold off, the models and sets, some of which had been there since the production of *Stingray*, were deemed worthless and destroyed, save for what crew members could save from the skips they had been dumped in.

While Gerry and Sylvia Anderson and Reg Hill quickly formed a new company, Group Three, the era of Anderson SF productions was at an end—at least for now.

Key Episode

Episode 19: 'The Cat with Ten Lives'
Written and directed by David Tomblin
First UK broadcast 30 September 1970 8.00 p.m.

After a UFO attack on Moonbase is repulsed, Interceptor pilot Jim Regan returns the Earth on leave. Regan and his wife Jean visit relatives and play with a Ouija board that was delivered anonymously that day. Jim appears to go into a trance, which he puts down to tiredness. Driving home, they stop to avoid a Siamese cat in the road, at which point the Regans are abducted by aliens. Jim is returned to his car, but Jean is taken. Jim reports the incident to Straker, who orders him back to duty as SHADO is short of pilots. The cat has followed Regan to SHADO headquarters and it eventually becomes clear that Regan is under alien influence.

Unlike the attempt a few years later to make *Space: 1999* more palatable for the American market, what might be termed *UFO* version 1.2 retained its intellect and basic identity. More than this, the series produced stories as thoughtful and intelligent as anything coming out of British studios in 1970. Of these, one of the very best is 'The Cat with Ten Lives', which bears the stamp of David Tomblin. A newcomer to the Anderson series, Tomblin's maverick sensibilities brought a fascinating new slant to the *UFO* format, which can also be seen a later episode of the show he was to write, but not direct, 'The Long Sleep'.

It was on *The Prisoner* that Tomblin first encountered Alexis Kanner, and he constructed his story largely as a showcase for the Canadian actor. Kanner made a big impression on the detective series *Softly, Softly* in 1966 before leaving the series in murky circumstances. Although Kanner was well-known at the time, his appearance here represents more than opportunistic casting of a currently popular actor. Instead, 'The Cat with Ten Lives' sees *UFO* being used as a vehicle for the intelligent use of different acting styles with fascinating results.

The preeminent figure in the *UFO* cast is, of course, Ed Straker, played with great skill and care by Ed Bishop. Bishop was a master of the internalised performance, not displaying a great many emotional fireworks, but with a great deal going on behind the eyes. With the second batch of *UFO* episodes, the producers had clearly come to the realisation that Bishop was the show's greatest asset and the casting began to offer contrasts to Bishop and the other regular cast members. Consequently, we start to see guest actors such as Derren Nesbitt ('The Man Who Came Back'), Mike Pratt ('The Psychobombs'), and James Cosmo (Reflections in the Water').

Kanner's Jim Regan goes through a variety of emotional states from near catatonia to domestic normality to the edge of madness. In less-skilled hands the results could have been mannered and laughable, but Kanner gives a brilliant, highly detailed performance. The small details he inserts stay in the memory; Regan is given a routine before and after firing his Interceptor missile—he touches a panel behind his head with his right hand, kisses the hand, then gives the firing button on his steering column a little flick. There is also an interesting little detail that director Tomblin highlights—after the UFO carrying Jean gets away, thanks to his being under alien influence, Regan moves his wedding ring from his left to his right hand.

In contrast to the wild emotional mood swings of Regan, Straker manages to be more of a tough and demanding a character than we see during the entire series. He coldly sends the traumatised Regan back to duty on Moonbase because the needs of SHADO and the protection of Earth are more important to him than one man's well-being. This is grown-up drama and we see that Straker is not infallible; he later admits that sending the unstable Regan back on duty was a terrible mistake. The episode ends with Straker returning to his office with the door closing behind him, alone and as always bearing a terrible responsibility.

'The Cat with Ten Lives' also gives a good role to the Polish actor Vladek Sheybal, a regular in later episodes as SHADO's doctor Doug Jackson.

Sheybal has a knack of putting an unusual spin on a line of dialogue to reveal a layer of his character's personality. We hear a good example here—when told of the kidnapping of Regan's wife, he replies, 'Poor man. A tragedy.' The lines, however, are delivered in an expressionless monotone. He is saying the words because they are expected of him, not because he feels any of the emotions the words imply. Later in the story we learn what really stirs Jackson's emotions. The autopsy of the alien's body reveals that the body is completely human—previously we had thought that the aliens used humans for spare part surgery. Jackson's eyes are ablaze as he exclaims that 'it could shatter all our past theories'.

This episode also gives us the most realistic view of life on Moonbase. The constant threat of UFO attacks brings with it a constant undertone of strain and weariness. This is clear from the first exchange of dialogue, as an incoming flight of UFOs is not greeted as a cue for cardboard heroics, but a weary 'here we go again'. We see the Interceptor pilots operating close to exhaustion, but as a closely bonded team. Tomblin gives us a quick visual metaphor for their team spirit—all three make a point of going down their launch tubes in unison. When Regan returns, in shock and possibly under alien influence, we can immediately see that he is out of step with his comrades.

'The Cat with Ten Lives' is also an episode in which we can learn that the alien menace may ultimately be unknowable. From an entity that we think we know the motives of, suddenly we suspect that everything we think we know about them may be wrong—now that is a scary thought.

21

The Collapse of the UK Film Industry

Despite the boom in production that had made it difficult for *UFO* to find a new home, film production in Britain was in a parlous state. Already drifting down from their 1946 peak, UK cinema attendances plummeted from 1.275 billion in 1954 to 395 million in 1962, as commercial television transformed the entertainment habits of the country. The decline continued throughout the '60s, and by 1970 attendances dropped below 200 million for the first time since figures were first recorded in 1935 (for the record, the nadir of British film going was finally reached in 1984, when a mere 54 million people visited the cinema).

This meant that the home market was no longer big enough to fund bigger films—the boom in production was largely fuelled by American money of the type that *Doppelgänger* had been made with. In 1968, some 88 per cent of British film production was backed by American money, and with most Hollywood studios losing money by the end of the decade, this situation was clearly unsustainable. Within a couple of years, the majority of this finance had been withdrawn and chilly economic winds were blowing down the film company offices of Wardour Street.

The American economy was suffering a balance of payments crisis, causing President Lyndon B. Johnson to call for a curtailment of US investment in Europe. Perhaps a more serious consideration than this was that the run of British hit movies had started to dry up. Major UK-based productions, such as MGM's *Alfred the Great* (1969) starring David Hemmings (and with future *UFO* star Michael Billington in a small role), were huge flops. The $3 million *The Adventures of Gerard*, based on Sir Arthur Conan Doyle's Brigadier Gerard stories, struggled to even be released, staggering into London cinemas in November 1970 and making its New York debut as late as 1978, almost ten years after it was made. The roll call of expensive, under-performing films produced in Britain continued—*The Battle of Britain*, *Goodbye Mr. Chips* (both 1969 releases), and *Cromwell* (1970), each with big name stars such as Richard Harris, Michael Caine, and Peter O'Toole, failed to find an audience.

The immense cost of these films is a vital consideration—*Goodbye Mr. Chips* was the hardly epic tale of the life of a schoolmaster, yet cost an estimated $9 million. Britain was a profitable place to make films when the films looked good and were relatively cheap to make, thus representing a low risk to studio balance sheets. Hit films from earlier in the decade, such as *A Kind of Loving* (1962), *Tom Jones* (1963), and *Alfie* (1966) all fell into this category and encouraged the influx of American money into British film. When Hollywood's inflationary economics was imported to the UK, meaning that British productions were costing as much as American films and were regularly losing money, the game was up.

Aside from the economics of production in a time of revolt and uncertainty, American audiences had become interested in their own country once more. The popular hits at the US box office in 1967 were films such as *The Graduate*, *Bonnie and Clyde*, and *In the Heat of the Night*, which spoke about America's relationship with itself. England had, as both a place to make films and as a setting, fallen out of fashion. This was the background of declining confidence in British production that *Doppelgänger* found itself caught up in, despite its subject matter and setting being not especially parochially British and the film being made with Century 21's customary financial efficiency. Gerry Anderson was to find future movie products in the years following *Space: 1999* extremely difficult to finance, as the withdrawal of most American funding from British production came at a time when native sources of funding were becoming even more difficult to find.

Just when it was most needed, political changes threatened a vital source of alternative funding for British films. The general election, held on 18 June 1970, was widely believed to have been leading to a comfortable victory for Prime Minister Harold Wilson's Labour Party, which had been in power since 1964. Instead, the Conservative Party, led by Edward Heath, won a majority of thirty-one seats. One casualty of the resulting change of policies was the Films Act 1970, which had already been voted through parliament before the election. One of the terms of the act would have refinanced the National Film Finance Corporation, a government body to which film producers could apply for finance, to the tune of £5 million. The new government refused to put the promised finance into place and it looked for a time as if the NFFC might go bankrupt, before its head, John Terry, managed to make alternative arrangements. The NFFC lived on in much reduced circumstances.

A round of contractions and mergers had been taking place in what remained of the British film studios. Rank, who had owned Gerry Anderson's old employers at Gainsborough Pictures, had shrunk its filmmaking activities considerably from its days in the 1940s as Britain's biggest film producer and cinema chain.

Gerry had left Gainsborough as a result of Rank's first round of cost-cutting, and the company set about diversifying during the 1950s and '60s. As well as its 1956 formation of Rank Xerox photocopiers—formed almost by chance when the company was looking for ways to use a small camera lens business it owned (this was to make Rank untold millions over the years)—Rank moved into other entertainment fields. They moved into radio manufacturing, buying Bush and Murphy, and entered the recording industry with their Top Rank label, and had an audio visual arm making televisions, music centres, and cameras (the latter under the Bell and Howell name). As well as making televisions, Rank also expanded into broadcasting, being a major shareholder in Southern Television, the ITV contractor for the south and south-east of England, which began broadcasting on 30 August 1958.

All of this activity caused Rank's original major concern of filmmaking to take something of a backseat. Rank's slate of films had a tendency to coast along with easy, audience-pleasing productions. These included the massively popular Norman Wisdom comedies, the Doctor film series (which generally starred Dirk Bogarde, Rank's biggest male star), and the *Carry On* films (which they took over from Anglo-Amalgamated with 1967's *Don't Lose Your Head*). By the end of the decade all that was left were the *Carry On* films, Morecambe and Wise not proving a popular replacement for Norman Wisdom when his popularity dipped. While Rank continued to invest in others films, it largely stopped making films itself at the turn of the '70s.

An attempt was made to return to film production later in the decade, prompted by the unexpected success of the children's film *Bugsy Malone* in 1976. The box office failure of films such as a second remake of *The 39 Steps* in 1978 and the 1980's *Silver Dream Racer* (from an original story by *UFO*'s Michael Billington) caused Rank's management to finally pull the plug on a film-making tradition that had begun in 1937.

Nat Cohen and Stuart Levy's Anglo-Amalgamated, which in 1959 had pointed *Four Feather Falls* in the direction of Granada Television and in 1960 had given AP Films the assignment to make *Crossroads to Crime*, was considerably changed by the end of the '60s. The company's traditional market of low-budget features, B-movies, and film series began to disappear as the decade wore on. Anglo had a very good run in this field, making the *Scotland Yard* and *Scales of Justice* series of short crime dramas via the Merton Park Studios and introduced by the noted criminologist Edgar Lustgarten.

The longer Edgar Wallace mysteries were remembered to a much greater degree—forty-seven of these were produced by Merton Park, each of just over an hour's length. This series of films ended in 1965, as the traditional B-film began to disappear from cinema schedules. The Wallace films quickly became a television staple, so much so that other films, including *Crossroads to Crime*, were retitled with the distinctive Edgar Wallace opening titles and 'Man of Mystery' theme tune to make more saleable package for international television sales.

Associated British Picture Corporation, the owners of Elstree Studios, where the final nine episodes of *UFO* would eventually by filmed, bought a 50 per cent stake in Anglo-Amalgamated in 1962, putting B-movie producers Cohen and Levy at the heart of the British filmmaking establishment. Stuart Levy died suddenly in 1966 and Nat Cohen, seeing the way that the film business was going, tried to take Anglo upmarket. His first step was to stop making the highly profitable *Carry On* films, which moved across to Rank, initially losing the *Carry On* name for the first two films, *Don't Lose Your Head* and *Follow That Camel*. By 1969, ABPC bought out Anglo-Amalgamated with Cohen as a director of the new company.

When EMI (not often called by its full name of Electrical and Musical Industries), whose chief executive was Lew Grade's brother Bernard Delfont, took over the new company later that year, Cohen was given his own filmmaking unit. The head of EMI Films was Bryan Forbes and when he left the company in 1971, Nat Cohen found himself in the unlikely position of being the most powerful person in the British film industry. By 1973, this was because there was nobody else left—EMI were the only company still backing large-scale film production in Britain until Lew Grade's Associated Communications Company made its ill-fated move into international filmmaking.

Gerry Anderson was to largely avoid the vicissitudes of the British film industry while Lew Grade was backing his productions, but this would eventually have consequences on his career. The extended and very expensive production of *Raise the Titanic* (which eventually premiered in August 1980) took funds away from ITC's television productions, ending any chance of a third series of *Space: 1999* and causing the 1979 series *Return of the Saint* to end after a single season. There were very few sources of funding for productions of the size Gerry Anderson was used to making by the late 1970s, and he was forced to look further afield in a long search for money to make new television and film productions.

22

The Protectors

'In the avenues and alleyways...'

Produced by Gerry Anderson and Reg Hill
Script editor Tony Barwick
Music composed and directed by John Cameron
A Group Three Production for ITC Worldwide Distribution
52 × twenty-five-minute episodes
First broadcast Friday 7 July 1972 (Granada)

Harry Rule leads a team of private investigators based in London whose cases take them all over Europe. He works with talented amateur sleuth Caroline, Contessa di Contini, and young French detective Paul Bouchet.

The Protectors is a real oddity in the Anderson canon. It was a project handed to Gerry Anderson by Lew Grade, the first format not self-generated by the AP Films/Century 21 team since *Torchy the Battery Boy* in 1958. That's actually not quite fair, as a brief was handed to Gerry Anderson by Grade, which read as follows: 'There is a small group of private investigators who are able to work more efficiently since they are working outside the constraints of the law'.

This allowed the new company formed by Gerry and Sylvia Anderson with Reg Hill, Group Three, to make almost any series they wanted, so work began on *The Protectors* with something of a tight deadline. Like many of ITC's series of the '70s, *The Protectors* was a co-production, this time with Fabergé. This jewellery maker, formed in St Petersburg in 1842 by Gustav Fabergé, remains world famous for its jewelled eggs made for the Russian Tsars. The brand name was sold several times from 1964 onwards, the name becoming most famous to the general public for its Brut men's cologne. Film stars Cary Grant and Roger Moore became board members and, in 1970, a filmmaking division was formed—Brut Productions.

ITC's re-entry into the production of half-hour adventure series such as *The Adventurer* (1972) and *The Protectors* was inspired by the emergence of a new market in such shows. This was due to a piece of legislation introduced in America by the Federal Communications Commission (popularly known as the FCC) called the Prime Time Access Rule. This was designed to prevent smaller, local stations in the fifty largest US television markets from filling their prime-time slots with material from whichever of the major networks they were affiliated to. The rule came into effect from September 1971 and attempted to break the domination of the major networks and introduce more diversity into prime-time television scheduling. Thus, for the first hour of prime time, which was either 6.00 p.m. until 7.00 p.m. or 7.00 p.m. until 8.00 p.m. (depending on which time zone you lived in), local stations had to find original programming. A market had been opened up for half-hour programming if it could be made for the right price. With Lew Grade's access to the UK and world markets he could still afford to produce something for this market with decent production values.

Thus, for the first time, Gerry Anderson found himself making a series using the 16-mm format as opposed to the higher quality 35-mm film he had used ever since *The Adventures of Twizzle*. The most common format in world television was 16 mm—while there were three major video formats in use in different parts of the world, the smallest television station in the smallest country in the world could run 16-mm film prints. The normal practice up until this point had been to make reductions from the original 35-mm negatives for export purposes, but now film technology had advanced to the stage that what had been originally designed as an amateur format could now produce results, which, if lacking the sharpness and depth of 35 mm, were acceptable for television drama. Production costs were reduced as 16-mm film was cheaper to buy, process, and strike prints from while the smaller, lighter cameras were far more convenient than 35 mm for location filming.

Once again, Gerry had a tight production deadline and this time was producing the series with Reg Hill—Sylvia Anderson had no official role on the series. This arrangement was in part an attempt to save the Anderson's marriage, the stresses of both living and working together having proved too much. Although Sylvia was there at the location shooting and wrote one of the scripts, she was bringing up Gerry Jr and trying to establish a career of her own outside of her husband's work.

Casting of two of the main characters was organised by Lew Grade himself and the ITC chief soon announced that he had signed Robert Vaughn to play the lead role. Sometime later with the writing process well advanced, Gerry learned with some surprise that Nyree Dawn Porter had been signed to play the second lead. As the initial scripts had already been written with a male second lead in mind, this called for some fast rewriting—*The Protectors* now had three leading characters, a tall order for a series of twenty-five-minute-long episodes.

Robert Vaughn and Nyree Dawn Porter are very good examples of Lew Grade's strategy of hiring actors who'd had a very big hit several years earlier, and were now willing, for the right price, to make a television series that would tie them up for several years, which for American performers meant living in a foreign country. Robert Vaughn was a New York-born actor; born into a performing family, he was a keen and lifelong student and teacher of the craft of acting.

Vaughn's career really took off when he returned from Army service, gaining a Best Supporting Actor Academy Award nomination for his role in the 1959 film *The Young Philadelphians*. This was followed in 1960 by his most famous film part as the elegantly doomed gunman Lee in director John Sturges' classic Western *The Magnificent Seven*. He went on to play the second lead in Gene Roddenberry's pre-*Star Trek* military series *The Lieutenant* (1963), opposite star Gary Lockwood. This led directly to his career-making role as secret agent Napoleon Solo in *The Man from U.N.C.L.E.*, a massive success that aired on NBC and around the world from September 1964 until January 1968. Running for three and a half seasons, *The Man from U.N.C.L.E.* rode the wave of the James Bond-inspired spy-boom that was also influential on *Thunderbirds* and *Joe 90*.

Vaughn stayed busy after *The Man from U.N.C.L.E.*'s cancellation, not only on film and stage acting, but also with political activism. He was an associate of Robert F. Kennedy and active in the anti-Vietnam war movement. While shooting *The Protectors*, Vaughn also hosted a Sunday afternoon radio talk show for station KABC Los Angeles. On this talk show he interviewed most of the candidates standing for the Democratic Party candidature for the 1972 US presidential election, and examined theories contradicting the official explanation behind Robert F. Kennedy's 1968 assassination.

Since June 1969, Robert Vaughn also had his own production company, Ferdporqui Productions, which he ran with his lifelong best friend and business partner Sherwood Price. Price was also an actor and appeared in three episodes of *The Protectors*—twice in the small role of Protectors member Carter and in the notorious episode 'It Could Be Practically Anywhere on the Island'. This episode, directed by Vaughn and written by Tony Barwick from a story by Sherwood Price, has a strong case for being the single worst episode, not only of any Anderson series, but of any ITC series.

Nyree Dawn Porter was a New Zealand-born actress, whose birth name was Ngaire, which she changed to a phonetic spelling in order that people might pronounce it correctly. She moved to Britain in 1958, at the age of twenty-two after winning a competition run by Rank Films. A film contract with Rank was not forthcoming, but she found work anyway, both on stage and in guest star television roles in series such as *Danger Man* and the 1959 BBC/20th Century Fox television series adaptation of *The Third Man*. There were also films, ranging from a part in *The Man from the Carlton Tower* (part of Anglo-Amalgamated's Edgar Wallace B-movie series) and *Live Now, Pay Later*, the 1962 film that was one of the reasons Ian Hendry left the original cast of *The Avengers*.

Porter was especially well-suited to costume drama, and briefly became a huge star of the late 1960s in the key role of Irene in the BBC's 1967 twenty-six part adaptation of John Galsworthy's *The Forsythe Saga*. A massive success, repeated three times in short succession and exported throughout the world, *The Forsythe Saga* proved something of a millstone around her reputation. Although she still worked, the parts were not as prestigious as they once had been and she was only too glad to take the role of wealthy widow Caroline, Contessa di Contini in *The Protectors*.

Producers Gerry Anderson and Reg Hill cast the third of *The Protectors* leading roles, that of stylish young French detective Paul Bouchet, themselves. The thirty-year-old actor Tony Anholt was born in Singapore, and was of Anglo-Dutch parentage; he was evacuated after the wartime fall of that country to grow up in Australia, then moving to South Africa. After finally settling on acting as a career and training at the Royal Court Theatre (while also working as a continuity announcer on the BBC World Service), he found that his dark good looks allowed him to play a wide variety of nationalities. He was regarded as something of a rising star by the time he was signed to appear in *The Protectors*, having recently appeared in the Jason King episode *A Thin Band of Air* and the major role of Eduard in ATV's eight-part historical television series *The Strauss Family*. Anholt clearly made a good impression on Anderson and Hill as they re-hired him in 1976 to play Moonbase Alpha security chief Tony Verdeschi in the second series of *Space: 1999*.

Secondary regular cast members were also chosen, with Anthony Chinn playing Chino, Caroline, Contessa di Contini's Chauffeur cum bodyguard, who is seen regularly during the first season by his employer's side and is even in the opening credits. Anthony Chinn was a Guyanan actor of Chinese and Brazilian parentage, who moved to the UK in the early 1960s and was almost never out of work for the next forty years. Although parts for actors of oriental appearance in British films were often quite stereotyped, there were still more parts than there were actors, which is why the sight of white actors in unconvincing make-up was a regular sight in the '50s and '60s. To illustrate, the 1957 war movie *Yangtse Incident*, regarding a military incident involving the Royal Navy vessel HMS *Amethyst* during the Chinese Civil War, not only cast Russian actor Akim Tamiroff in the key role of General Peng, but had to cast virtually every waiter from the Chinese restaurants of Soho to fill out smaller roles.

Harry Rule's personal assistant Suki, a Japanese martial arts expert, was played by Yasuko Nagazumi, a Tokyo-born actress who first began working in Britain in the late 1960s, appearing in the 1967-released spy movies *You Only Live Twice* and *Deadlier than the Male*, appearing regularly on British television whenever a beautiful oriental woman was needed on series such as ITC's *Shirley's World*. After *The Protectors*, Yasuko was cast in the second series of *Space: 1999* as Yasko, by which point she had married one of the show's directors, Ray Austin.

The Protectors is one of the great car shows of the early 1970s featuring a fascinating array of unusual vehicles, including Caroline di Conini's NSU Ro80, a rotary-engined car the warranty claims on which caused its manufacturer to go out of business, and her Citroen SM, a beautiful and luxurious sports saloon that was prevented from sales success by its expensive mechanical complexity. Robert Vaughn drove around southern England in a dark blue 1970 Jensen Interceptor Mk2. This was Harry Rule's regular transport throughout *The Protector*'s first series, but was seen far less often in series two.

In the second series, Harry drove a gold Volvo 1800 ES, a much slower car than the Jensen, but in its own way just as distinctive and attractive, being a sporting estate car. This was a redesign of the original P1800, first introduced in late 1960 and made famous around the world when it was chosen as Simon Templar's transport in ITC's long-running series *The Saint*.

The opening credits for *The Protectors* were shot by John Hough, who had also directed the credit sequence for ITC's previous half-hour action series, *The Adventurer*. This would be the only part of the series to be made using 35-mm film, and was a crafty mix of footage starting with a close up of Big Ben (English locations were still a major selling point of the series) and featuring Harry Rule's morning routine, including feeding half of his breakfast to his Irish wolfhound. This is intercut with action footage, none of which comes from *The Protectors*—a shot of a helicopter flying over a man is from the James Bond film *From Russia with Love* (1963), while a scene of women swimming underwater appears to be from another Bond movie, *You Only Live Twice* (1967). A spectacular shot of a yellow car overturning, seen through the back window of another car, was actually shot by John Hough when he was second unit director on *The Saint* and was a genuine accident, unused in a finished episode.

The music in *The Protectors* was, for once, not composed by Barry Gray, as John Cameron had already been signed for the series before Group Three took on producing the show. It has to be said that Cameron's score is very listenable and suits the series very well, at times going into the heavy, dramatic territory that Barry Gray was so good at, while also having many lighter moods. As with many of ITC's dramatic series, a 'name' composer was hired to write the main theme music. In this case, two composers were responsible for theme song 'Avenues and Alleyways', Mitch Murray and Peter Callender, who had been responsible for many hit records. The vocal version featured at the end of the series featured the stentorian tones of English balladeer Tony Christie. This was rather punchier than the version released as a single, which reached No. 37 in the British pop charts in 1972.

Robert Vaughn was in a powerful position in the production of the series. Although he did not have a production role on *The Protectors*, despite the crediting of his Ferdporqui Company and his friend and business partner Sherwood Price, Vaughn was the name on which the series was being sold throughout the world. This gave the actor leverage, which he was not afraid to use. Reportedly the first season's European location shooting was arranged at very short notice as Vaughn insisted on it to Lew Grade. This certainly gave the series added production values, but was a major undertaking to organise with three weeks' notice. The credited directors on the episodes did not always shoot the location footage. For example the Paris shoot for the first season's episodes was directed by John Hough, and much second unit footage was shot by David Lane.

The production was ultimately to travel from its Elstree Studios base to visit an impressive array of locations. For the first season *The Protectors* shot in the Spanish region of Catalonia, on the Costa Brava, plus shoots in Paris, Rome, and Malta. For the second series it returned to Spain, this time visiting Madrid, with episodes also being filmed in Copenhagen, Venice, and Salzburg, Austria.

It was at this location that Robert Vaughn threatened to walk off the series in a dispute over adverse comments about the production and the standard of British technicians the actor made in *The New York Times*. This time Gerry Anderson decided to call Vaughn's bluff and he turned up for work the next day. This was apparently a minor turning point in relations between the producer and his star. Reading between the lines of Robert Vaughn's autobiography, *A Fortunate Life*, his behaviour can partially be explained by the demise of his previous hit series *The Man from U.N.C.L.E.*, which went from being the biggest hit on television during its second season to cancellation within the space of eighteen months.

This he blamed on interference from the network and new producers, who insisted on *The Man from U.N.C.L.E.* changing from a light-hearted spy drama to a campy romp patterned after the new hit series on the block, *Batman*. Everyone concerned with actually making the series knew it was not working, but young stars Vaughn and David McCallum lacked the confidence to challenge the studio and network heads making the decisions. A lesson had clearly been learned and Vaughn was going to use whatever star power he had to ensure things happened his way on *The Protectors*.

Many of the *UFO* crew members were rehired for *The Protectors*, including director Jeremy Summers who was in charge of seventeen episodes across the two seasons. Summers was one of the experienced ITC directors drafted in for *UFO*'s second production block, responsible for two of the strongest episodes, 'The Psychobombs' and 'The Long Sleep'. The other director kept busiest during *The Protectors*' first series was Don Chaffey, one of Gerry Anderson's fellow graduates of Gainsborough Pictures, in his case the art department. Hugely experienced, Chaffey's credits included episodes of *The Baron* and *The Prisoner* for ITC, the Hammer movie *Creatures the World*

Forgot (1971). He was unavailable to direct episodes of the second series of *The Protectors* as he was directing Richard Rowntree and *Doppelgänger* star Roy Thinnes in Spanish-shot Western *Charlie One-Eye* (1973) for David Frost's production company.

One of the directors drafted in to replace Chaffey was Charles Crighton, the highly regarded former Ealing Studios director of classic films such as *The Lavender Hill Mob* (1951) and *The Titfield Thunderbolt* (1953). He largely stopped directing feature films after a bad experience on the 1962 Burt Lancester film *Birdman of Alcatraz*, which he quit and his footage was scrapped. Since then, he had worked on filmed television series including *Man in a Suitcase*, *The Avengers*, and *Strange Report*. After *The Protectors*, Crighton would continue working for Group Three and its successor, Gerry Anderson Productions, to become one of the main directors across both series of *Space: 1999*.

Besides the directors, other long-standing Anderson crew members returned for *The Protectors*. Tony Barwick, blessed with a 'a mind like a steel trap', as his friend Shane Rimmer once described him, was script editor, often suggesting plotlines to the writers and proving able to effectively work on a huge range of stories outside the normal Anderson range. Also proving more than able to work outside of the SF genre with great effect was art director Bob Bell, assisted by Keith Wilson. David Lane had decided he did not want to pursue a career in directing and was more than happy to work as supervising editor and second unit director on the episodes. Returning to supervise the post-production process was Desmond Saunders, whose car, a yellow 1970 MGB GT, can be seen in three different episodes of *The Protectors*. *UFO* director of photography Brendan J. Stafford was also rehired, in charge of lighting all but two episodes of the series, on which Frank Watts substituted.

For some years, *The Protectors* was a series that suffered from an image problem—the grainy prints used on television during the '70s and '80s were greatly ineffective. The production of the series was difficult, with Gerry Anderson (co-producing alongside Reg Hill) not enjoying the best of relations with his two main stars—it is tempting to speculate that the absence of Sylvia Anderson from an official role in the production was an issue. Sylvia was the member of the team that got along with the actors and smoothed things over.

The Protectors, nevertheless, does not deserve the poor reputation is has always tended to be saddled with, even from Gerry Anderson. Of ITC's early '70s 16-mm-shot series, *Jason King* and *The Adventurer* being the others, it is by far the best. These two series, products of the partnership of Monty Berman and former Anderson scriptwriter Dennis Spooner, were hamstrung by trying to maintain the production methods of more expensive earlier ITC series such as *Department S* and *The Saint* on lower budgets that simply could not take the strain. As a result, *Jason King* and *The Adventurer* exude a kind of grotty glamour, looking studio-bound despite extensive European location shooting on the latter.

The Protectors took advantage of being shot on smaller, lighter 16-mm cameras by going out on the streets far more, using one main standing set, Harry Rule's London mews house, but generally having entire episodes shot entirely on location. In this way, *The Protectors* points the way towards *Special Branch* and *The Sweeney*—tough, crime-on-the-streets police dramas made by Euston Films, an offshoot of Thames Television. Euston Films was founded in March 1971 in order to produce filmed drama for the domestic market that could also be exported to other countries. This is an inversion of the way Lew Grade worked, making series for export to the American market, their screening in the UK at times almost being an afterthought.

As Euston were producing primarily for the home market, the feel of the series was very different from anything that had been produced on film previously for British television. Sharing a title, but little else, with an earlier Thames Television series shot on video and starring Derren Nesbitt, *Special Branch* was aimed very much at the home market. Freed from the restrictions of the export market, in which anyone with a vaguely working-class accent was in effect an exotic foreigner, Euston Films presented London almost as a supporting character in their series. In the process, the look and feel of British-filmed television was revolutionised.

Key to the difference in approach between series such as *Jason King* and the Euston shows was a realisation of what '70s 16-mm film technology was good at and what it did badly. It was very bad at conveying glamour and showed up artifice such as unrealistic sets and backdrops in surprising ways that 35-mm film tended not to. *The Protectors* figured this out as it went along, early episodes such as '2,000 Ft to Die', the series pilot, and 'Brother Hood' aiming at the old ITC glamour and failing conspicuously. What 16 mm was good at, if handled correctly, was documentary-style realism. In short, anything shot on 35 mm always carried with it the slightly unrealistic air of the feature film. With the judicious use of hand-held camerawork and natural lighting, 16-mm productions could look as realistic as the nightly news.

Jason King, *The Adventurer*, and even the far more expensive ITC series *The Persuaders!*, shot in 1970 and 1971, were holdovers from the swinging '60s, despite the changing of the decade and changing tastes. The Euston Films approach has the '70s written all over it, breaking from the sanitised England for export of the ITC shows (including *The Protectors*) and *The Avengers*, which were filmed in attractive locations within easy reach of Pinewood and Elstree Studios.

This different approach also changed the nature of the protagonists of the series, and again *The Protectors* can be seen as a staging post between the old and the new. The previous ITC series of the '70s featured rich, glamorous millionaire crime-fighters (*The Persuaders!*), a rich, glamourous crime-solving author (*Jason King*) and a rich, glamourous crime-solving movie star (*The Adventurer*). While *The Protectors* gave us the rich, glamourous Contessa di Contini, it did also feature Harry Rule and Paul Bouchet, who were well-heeled and not short of a few quid, but basically working private investigators.

Watching *The Protectors*, it is surprising just how much the series improves from a shaky start. Frankly, the pilot episode, '2000 Ft to Die', is a bit of a mess, suffering from an absurd, cluttered plot involving sky diving and some nonsense about scientists creating synthetic gold. At the same time, the story has to incorporate the introduction of the main characters, which is probably why the first cut of the episode was timed at nearly forty-five minutes. Some narrative coherence seems to have been lost along with the twenty minutes of footage needed to reduce the running time to twenty-five minutes.

The stories and pacing improved considerably as the series progressed, until *The Protectors* became, at its best, a model of streamlined, efficient, and entertaining storytelling. Some characters were lost along the way—as with *UFO*, the regular cast was originally somewhat crowded. For the second series of *The Protectors*, Contessa's valet/bodyguard Chino was dropped along with Harry Rule's occasionally seen glamorous Japanese housekeeper Suki, leaving just the core regular cast of three. Also dropped was the notion, pursued somewhat half-heartedly in the first season, of *The Protectors* being some kind of international organisation of investigators—their ID cards look like they were knocked up in about ten minutes by the art department.

The most fully developed character in the series is Harry Rule, despite the fact that only a few episodes actually give us any background. The Sylvia Anderson scripted '...With A Little Help from My Friends' introduces us to Harry's former wife Laura, while 'Zeke's Blues', written by Shane Rimmer, concerns Harry's old college friend, cabaret pianist Zeke Daley (a role originally written for Tony Curtis, but eventually played by Rimmer himself as a last-minute substitute).

Most of the details regarding Harry come from the intelligent acting of Robert Vaughn, who fills in the gaps himself in ways similar to Ed Bishop in *UFO*. Even when he seems to be playing a scene or a line absolutely deadpan, there is always something going on behind the eyes to make the performance more real—he's not just remembering his lines and not walking into the furniture. Although Vaughn always gives a good account of himself and is committed to making whichever script he's performing work to the best of his ability, when he really engages with a script and director, as with the episodes 'The First Circle' and 'Shadbolt', real fireworks are produced. Interestingly, large parts of both episodes are virtually two-handers; with Nyree Dawn Porter and Tony Anholt missing, Vaughn is given the opportunity to bounce off really top-class actors—Ed Bishop in 'The First Circle' and Tom Bell in 'Shadbolt'.

The Andersons still yearned to return to the SF productions with which they had made their name. In addition to the ongoing pre-production work on what began as *UFO*'s second series and morphed into *Space: 1999*, an attempt was made to return work with marionettes once again. This was *The Investigator*, a pilot for a series that would have a mixing actors and puppets. Shot on location in Malta and directed by Gerry Anderson, it became clear when the footage was cut together that no series would result.

The Andersons future career would remain in live action, with the biggest series ever made for television.

Key Episode

Episode 22: 'Wheels'
Directed by David Tomblin
Written by Tony Barwick
First UK broadcast Friday 1 March 1974, 7.00 p.m. (ATV)

It is doubtful that anyone connected with *The Protectors* was seriously trying to make art, but occasionally it happened anyway. The conveyor-belt nature of series television in the '60s and '70s was like that—sometimes everything just works. Despite television being popularly categorised as a producer's medium (there's a reason why most of the shows examined in the book you are holding are generally known as 'Gerry Anderson series'), if there are particular episodes of a series that stand out above the rest, this is often due to an especially talented writer and/or director.

The Protectors has two widely acknowledged classic episodes—'The First Circle' and 'Shadbolt'. Neither can really be counted as a key episode of the series because both are quite atypical of *The Protectors* as a whole. These two stories are basically solo vehicles (no pun intended *The Man from U.N.C.L.E.* fans) for Robert Vaughn, so we have to look elsewhere to find out how the series worked when at its best. 'Wheels' is a story that effectively demonstrates the group dynamic between the three leading characters, which makes the finest *Protectors* stories work like finely tuned machines.

'Wheels' also shows off the work of David Tomblin, the director first employed by the Andersons on the second production block of *UFO* (helming 'The Cat with Ten Lives', among others) who proved to be one of the most talented directors to work on the Anderson live-action series. 'Wheels' was Tomblin's only episode of *The Protectors*, as he was busy for most of the production period of the series on movie projects—he was first assistant director to Sidney Poitier on *A Warm December* and second unit director for John Guillermin on *Shaft in Africa* (both films being released during 1973), which kept him bust shooting in Ethiopia, Eritrea, New York, Paris, and Spain. David Tomblin's talents were obviously recognised as he directed on three series in a row for Century 21 and its successor company, Group Three; these series were *UFO*, *The Protectors*, and *Space: 1999*.

By this stage in the life of *The Protectors*, towards the end of its second series, the show had come into its own, developing from a hurried rehash of ITC's former glories into an awesomely efficient, stripped-down adventure series in which effective storytelling was the number one priority. 'Wheels' manages the neat trick of having a plot that is at the same time utterly simple and insanely complicated. Instead of dropping two of the main characters to give the story room to breathe, as in 'Shadbolt' and 'The First Circle', the simplicity of the basic concept gives director David Tomblin time to tell Tony Barwick's story without having to rush, allowing himself a few visual flourishes along the way.

The story runs as follows: someone has stolen a sealed briefcase from a Swiss bank containing the security details of some of their private numbered accounts. Manning, representing the thieves, meets Sneider, representing the bankers, and the two men agree a deal where the case will be handed back in exchange for an amount representing 0.1 per cent of the value of the contents—$2 million. The bank, however, has called in the Protectors as they do not want the deal to go through. They think it is an inside job and believe if they pay up then the same thing will happen again.

A plan is hatched where Harry Rule and Paul Bouchet will break into Manning's safe and swap the sealed case for an exact duplicate. The contents of the real case will then be photographed, by which time Manning will be on his way to exchange the case for the $2 million. This means that Harry and the Contessa must stage an accident to delay Manning, while Paul swaps the fake case out of Manning's car for the real one.

The joy of the episode is not in the clockwork precision of its plot, but instead in the hoops our heroes have to jump through to make it all happen. The actual detail is not important in and of itself (to be honest, I have watched the episode four or five times over the years and am still hazy as to exactly how it is supposed to all work). All we really need to remember is that they have to steal a case then return it undetected in a very entertaining manner.

So what 'Wheels' is really about is not secret Swiss bank accounts, but instead staging a daring burglary and rally driving—lots and lots of fabulous rally driving. At times, 'Wheels' plays like a love letter to the rally prepared twin-cam Ford Escort that Paul throws about the muddy Hertfordshire countryside with wild abandon. In a series that is a classic for lovers of '70s cars, 'Wheels' is like *Top Gear* with detectives. The preparations for the cross-country trip to head off Manning's car are shown in great detail, which adds enormously to the episode's sense of realism.

Paul and Harry are not presented as superheroes who can drive like stink at the drop of a hat. Instead we see their first run, which looks pretty darned fast, but is nothing like good enough to make the time they need. In the course of the plot we see Paul tinkering with the car, and eventually he reports that the entire engine will need to be changed in order to shave some time off their journey. However, we never see Paul or Harry being so mechanically able in any other episode of *The Protectors*. David Tomblin really allows himself to let rip during the rallying scenes. Always a highly visual director (see *UFO*'s 'The Cat with Ten Lives' and *Space: 1999*'s 'Force of Life'), here he directs with real brio and verve, using fast editing, but also swooping camerawork and helicopter shots. These scenes do not overpower the narrative and are balanced by a more restrained approach elsewhere.

Just to finish off the motoring part of the episode, The Contessa turns up in an old clunker that she's bought for £100 for Harry to stage an accident with Manning in. This being *The Protectors*, a series in which somebody clearly had an eye for an unusual car, she's purchased a 1962 AMC Rambler Classic, possibly the ugliest car ever to be seen on a British television series.

Aside from the motoring action, 'Wheels' benefits, like many episodes of *The Protectors*, from being able to cast from the pool of highly experienced character actors available in this era. In this case, the two guest stars are played by Dinsdale Landen—wearing an overcoat, apparently borrowed from a New York pimp, with lapels that look like the flight deck of a furry aircraft carrier—as bad guy Manning, and George Pravda as Sneider, representative of the Swiss bank Manning is attempting to rip off. Both actors, but especially the Czech actor Pravda, were capable of giving big scene-stealing performances, but here they play it low key and deadpan.

This is appropriate to the material as, in a subtly well-written and directed scene, the blackmailer and victim's representative discuss the details of the handover of the sealed briefcase just as if they were talking about any normal business transaction. Despite the restrained performances of the two actors, it is clear that they both have plenty in reserve, which lends the scene a quietly powerful edge.

It does not matter that we do not get to see Manning get his comeuppance. Once the case is swapped back (and it is a good job Manning does not leave someone in the car to guard it) the story has reached its natural conclusion. At its best *The Protectors* was fast, efficient, and entertaining, telling its story and getting out quick. There is a lot to be said for such simple, hard-earned virtues.

23

The Investigator

'This is the voice of the future, from a galaxy a million light years away. We have observed your troubled planet and would like to help you. Through John and Julie, hope to make your world a better place.'

Produced and directed by Gerry Anderson
Screenplay by Sylvia Anderson; story by Shane Rimmer
A Starkits Production

The Investigator, an alien from a highly advanced civilisation many light-years from Earth, has selected young Americans John and Julie to help with his mission to understand more about Earth and to make the planet a better place. Shrunken to miniature size and given special powers and equipment, John and Julie are sent on their first mission. They are to prevent the crooked businessman Stavros Karanti from stealing a valuable painting from an island community that refuses to sell it to him. Karanti has donated a valuable icon to the art collection of the church in which the painting is kept in order to see the building's security measures.

Although *The Investigator* was not officially released until recently, poor-quality copies have been circulated among Anderson collectors for many years, first on VHS and later on the internet. This has done nothing to help the reputation of this most obscure of Supermarionation productions.

Back in 1973, despite the parlous state of most British film and television production, Gerry Anderson was contemplating a full production slate with no less than three projects at various stages of development. Production on the second season of his new company Group Three's series *The Protectors* was in its final stages, with every expectation of a third batch of episodes to follow. Meanwhile, the final Century 21 production, *UFO*, had an unusually long afterlife. The series finished production in 1970 with the last episode, 'The Long Sleep', being completed before the first had been seen anywhere in the world—*UFO*'s UK premiere came in September 1970. By 1973, the series was finally being screened in the US syndicated television market, ratings were good and Lew Grade had the studios prepare a second series. Gerry still felt the need to attract a younger audience, which had been somewhat left behind by *The Protectors* and the more soap-opera elements of *UFO*. Consequently, the Group Three trio of Gerry and Sylvia Anderson and Reg Hill hatched a plan to get a new puppet series off the ground, their first since Century 21's *The Secret Service* some four years previously. With Lew Grade unlikely to invest ITC's money in another Supermarionation series when they had so many still airing throughout the world, Gerry had the idea of approaching his friend and admirer George Heinemann, vice president of children's programming at American television network NBC. Planning to approach him with a pilot show, the trio formed a new company, Starkits, raised investment through venture capital, and set about putting a new show together. The result, *The Investigator*, was subsequently described by Gerry Anderson as 'a disaster.' Still keen on developing the Supermarionation concept, the new show kept the idea of miniaturised people from *The Secret Service*, but pushed the notion further—the pilot would be shot entirely on location with no studio sets being used. The Mediterranean island of Malta, previously used for episodes of *The Protectors*, was chosen as a backdrop for the story, which was written by Sylvia Anderson.

Gerry Anderson was producer and also chose to direct, which must have seemed a sound idea as the old team of Century 21 directors was now scattered far and wide and he knew all the unique technical problems of handling a Supermarionation production. The small crew was still largely picked from the pool of talent developed over many years, such as lighting cameraman Harry Oakes (who had shot the special effects for Anderson productions since *Thunderbirds Are Go*) and editor Len Walter, who shared duties on *The Investigator* with David Lane, whose illustrious Anderson career began as assistant editor on the second season of *Supercar*. Two new puppets were sculpted for the show, John and Julie, with *The Investigator* being represented by a flashing green light. The puppets were operated by Wanda Brown (née Webb), a puppeteer for the Andersons since *Thunderbirds*, and her husband was the puppet sculptor John Brown, who had been on the team since *Fireball XL5*. Sylvia Anderson's former son-in-law Vic Elmes is credited with *The Investigator*'s theme music, but most of the pilot is scored using tracks borrowed from John Cameron's excellent music for *The Protectors*. Two major vehicles were designed for the pilot by Reg Hill and built by Space Models Ltd—a futuristic open-topped car and a jet-powered boat. In another new departure, these vehicles were not moved by puppeteers or special effects technicians, but were radio controlled, the car being powered by a lawn mower engine. The model car and boat were operated by Plugg Shutt, who had joined the old Century 21 team as a props maker on *Thunderbirds are Go*.

Toy manufacturer Dinky was excited by the prospect of a new Anderson series as vehicles from previous shows such as Thunderbird 2 and the SHADO Interceptor were still selling well. They snapped up the rights at an early stage and set to work designing tools and moulds to produce the new vehicles. The company's enthusiasm was to prove sadly misplaced as production of the pilot episode was beset by disasters. Sylvia Anderson brought in Shane Rimmer, one of the Anderson's most trusted scriptwriters, most recently having contributed the scripts for 'Zeke's Blues' and 'Blockbuster' for *The Protectors*' second season.

In his authorised biography, *What Made Thunderbirds Go*, Gerry blames himself for the shortcomings of the pilot show, his efforts as producer to stay within budget warping his judgement as director. Technical problems did not help matters, with outdoor filming affording less light than would have been available in a traditional studio. This meant that cameras had to be placed a matter of inches from the puppets and that only a small area was in focus at any one time, severely limiting the shots the crew were able to capture. On top of this, the radio-controlled craft built for the production were caused to go haywire by radio signals from over-flying RAF Nimrod aircraft. The car gave particular problems, at one point shooting out of control and straight into a wall, causing a delay while repairs were undertaken. Gerry had further cause to miss the controlled environment of the studio, as he was unable to see rushes of what was being shot, the film being flown to England for processing and then examination by Reg Hill.

This was in contrast to previous productions, which had utilised the Add-A-Vision system that allowed instant playback of a video version of what had been shot. Hill realised immediately that the footage was not good, but did not want to add to the mounting pressure on Gerry by pointing the fact out to the producer and director. The schedule ran out with the unit unable to get all the footage they wanted, so they had to assemble the pilot as best they could, with further aerial photography taking place for scenes involving Stavros Karanti's light aircraft (the rolling English countryside not proving a good match for the Maltese footage). The consensus among the Andersons and Reg Hill was that *The Investigator* was not good enough to sell a series, and George Henemann remained blissfully unaware of the whole episode.

While *The Investigator* might not be considered an undiscovered masterpiece, it was at least made to decent professional standards—the poor-quality copies, which were all that was available for viewing up until recently, showed the production in a very poor light. Looking at the pilot, it helps to remember that it was made as a true pilot film, that is, a sales tool made to show what the potential series might be like. When Gerry and Sylvia Anderson were making the series for Lew Grade, what we think of as their pilot episodes were merely the first episode in the series, such was the confidence Grade had in AP Films. In the case of *The Investigator*, every element of the production was potentially up for negotiation, thus the sketchiness of the premise demonstrates that it was probably not meant to be the opening episode of a potential series.

Beyond the opening narration, we learn nothing about who the alien presence known as The Investigator is and why he has taken such an interest in wealthy crooks on Earth. The episode had to pack a sample story into its twenty-four-minute length, spending more time introducing John and Julie's car than telling us who these two miniaturised unfortunates actually are. John and Julie do not come across as fully developed characters. We are not told why The Investigator has chosen them, or even why (or if) they agreed to the miniaturisation in the first place. It does not help that the puppets are rather inexpressive. With the puppets supposedly being miniature people existing in the real world, any hint of caricature in their design was out of the question. We do learn a little about the powers granted to John and Julie by The Investigator, which one hopes would have been expanded upon in future episodes. John gets the very 'manly' power of being able to operate mechanical devices without looking at the instructions, while Julie gets to use a remote control and look a bit like Raquel Welch.

The low budget harms the production at times. Scenes with real actors are shot so we only see the person speaking from a distance or with their faces turned away from us in order to make post-synchronisation of dialogue simpler. It also meant that live sound did not always have to be recorded on location, which would have saved a lot of time.

Every now and then, though, there is a shot where you can see what Gerry was aiming for and the puppets work well in the full-sized, live-action setting. This is especially true in the scenes on Karanti's yacht, where John and Julie hide from Karanti after he hears a noise. Despite the technical problems, the vehicles look great on-screen, especially the boat, which makes for an impressive sight as it skips across the waves. The car, meanwhile, looks convincing travelling through the deserted Maltese streets. It is amusing, though, to hear John saying, 'We can't risk being seen,' before they zoom about in a bright red vehicle that would alert the entire neighbourhood to their presence by making a racket reminiscent of a Formula One racing car. From the evidence of the pilot episode it is interesting to speculate on how a series would have developed. We are not presented with a single villain figure, such as Titan or The Hood, Karanti was not a strong enough character to take such a role—furthermore, we are led to believe that John and Julie have made him recant his evil ways.

It is more likely that the format would have developed into a junior version of *Mission: Impossible*, with our tiny heroes sent to bring down a different villain each week who had transgressed The Investigator's code of ethics. The year 1973 was at the tail-end of the post-Bond spy craze and it is possible that the series might have gone the *Joe 90* route of having eastern-European baddies on a regular basis. Life, as the expression goes, is what happens while you are busy making other plans and none of the plans the Group Three partnership had at the start of 1973 came to fruition. The third season of *The Protectors* was cancelled when ITC's funding partners Fabergé backed out, while the second season of *UFO* Lew Grade had ordered suffered the same fate when viewing figures dropped in vital American markets. The return of Supermarionation died, unheralded, on the rain-swept streets of Malta, and it was to be ten years before Gerry was able to return to puppet adventures with *Terrahawks*.

The Investigator has only two credited cast members, the others featured on-screen were basically extras, their dialogue dubbed onto the soundtrack back in England. Ruthless businessman Stavros Karanti is played by Charles Thake, a Malta-based actor who had previously appeared in *The Protectors* episode 'Ceremony for the Dead' in the small role of a police inspector. His other major role was in the 1963 Children's Film Foundation production *Treasure in Malta*. The story of that film was adapted by none other than Mary Cathcart Borer, writer of the first two episodes of *Four Feather Falls*. Thake can also be seen in a small role in the early Jean-Claude Van Damme thriller *Black Eagle* (1988). The other credited role, that of Karanti's henchman Christof, is played by Peter Borg, whose skinny frame, droopy hair, and moustache perfectly represents the early '70s 'look'. Unfortunately, Borg has no other known credits.

Sylvia Anderson's former son-in-law, pop musician Vic Elmes, was originally chosen to provide music for *The Investigator*. Although he is credited with the opening theme to the pilot, in what would be a precursor to his problematic time on *Space: 1999*, he proved unequal to the task of writing a complete score. Instead, composer John Cameron gave Gerry permission to utilise music he had composed for *The Protectors*, which was just completing production of the second (and unexpectedly final) season. Thus, *The Investigator* was inadvertently provided with one of its most successful elements in the form of its catchy, funky score.

In the tough economic climate of 1973, Dinky Toys were overjoyed that Gerry Anderson had another series in development and immediately made a deal to produce models based on the show's vehicles. Armed with Reg Hill's two vehicle designs from *The Investigator*, the Liverpool-based die-cast toy manufacturer was more than happy to put into production scale models of the car and boat featured in the pilot episode. The production of new dyes and tools to produce the models represented a major financial commitment for Dinky at a time when the global economy was suffering due to rapidly rising oil prices. When the promised series failed to materialise, Dinky were left with a potentially large loss, a problem they addressed by releasing the models in reworked versions with no mention of *The Investigator*.

First to be released in 1976—some three years after *The Investigator* pilot film was shot—was a new version of the red eight-wheeled car John and

Julie use. The basic design remained the same, but a new military theme was adopted and the vehicle was promoted on the box as being designed by Gerry Anderson—a machine gun was now mounted on the bonnet on the passenger side, an olive green colour scheme was adopted (later variations used a metallic blue paint), and a figure of a soldier was placed in the driver's seat. Features that would presumably have featured on the original *Investigator* version of the model were a revolving scanner behind the driver's seat, which used the same clockwork mechanism that produced sparks through a hatch in the front grille. Decals were added to complete the effect, with a large US Army-style star on the bonnet and a rather sinister clenched fist logo on the side. The Armoured Command Car was only available from 1976 to 1977.

In 1977, Dinky attempted to recoup more of their losses from *The Investigator* by reworking the series motorboat, this time with a coastguard theme. Despite the Anderson name still bringing in good business for the company—*Space: 1999*'s Eagle Transporter proved to be another big seller—no mention was made of Gerry in the packaging and promotion of this model. The colour scheme of the boat was changed from red, white, and yellow to white and blue with prominent 'Coastguard' wording along both sides of the hull. The bow deck revolved to reveal a missile launcher, which was not featured in the version of the craft seen on-screen. The Coastguard Amphibious Missile Launch was only on sale for a single year.

Space: 1999

'We're sitting on the biggest bomb man's ever made.'

Produced by Sylvia Anderson
Executive producer Gerry Anderson
Created by Gerry and Sylvia Anderson
Music by Barry Gray
An ITC/RAI Co-Production
Produced by Group Three
24 × fifty-minute episodes
First UK broadcast Thursday 4 September 1976 (ATV/Yorkshire)

A huge explosion of nuclear waste blasts the Moon out of Earth's orbit and into a continuing journey through space. The occupants of Moonbase Alpha, a scientific research base on the Moon, are sent hurtling through the cosmos and search for a new planet to call home.

Space: 1999 remains the most controversial and widely discussed of all Gerry Anderson productions. For a time, a series made in an atmosphere of haste, in the teeth of the worst economic conditions since the great depression of the 1930s, achieved a remarkable combination of adventure and metaphysics mixed with a sense awe and wonder. We will probably never see anything like it again—and we were very lucky to see it at all.

The final verdict on *UFO* from audiences and the US television networks would be some time in coming as the entire series was filmed and edited before the first episode was transmitted. Although the first season of *UFO* did not achieve a network sale, it was nonetheless widely seen across America on smaller local stations through the syndication process. In those days series were, wherever possible, constructed so that they could be seen in almost any order. If a show was not to be networked, a limited number of prints would be in circulation and sent from one station to the next, known in television jargon as 'bicycling'. This was a far more expensive process than if a network had bought the series, screening one print across the country.

Despite this disadvantage, *UFO* built up a head of steam as its initial run began across America—the series was shown on 136 stations in the period between September 1972 and November 1973. The national networks were able to keep track of its popularity as the local stations were each affiliated to one of the networks—this was the process by which *The Saint* was eventually picked up by NBC for prime-time viewing. For seventeen weeks, the news on *UFO*'s ratings was good and CBS seriously considered placing an order for a second season.

Back in the UK, *UFO* was thought to be finished and with no more SF projects in the pipeline, Lew Grade closed down Century 21 Productions. The new company set up by Gerry and Sylvia Anderson and Reg Hill, Group Three, was quickly given its first commission, the internationally filmed detective series *The Protectors*. While they were busy with this project, they received the news that CBS were showing an interest in more episodes of *UFO*, this time to be screened on the full network. Most of Group Three's resources were at this point being used on the shooting of *The Protectors*, which had returned from its first season location shoot in Paris, Spain, Rome, and Malta and was, by autumn 1972, completing its UK filming.

The company was given the go-ahead by ITC to begin pre-production work on *UFO*'s second season, employing Keith Wilson to produce designs and Christopher Penfold to work on mapping out the shape of the new series— Tony Barwick being busy on *The Protectors*. This work was based at what was at this point known as EMI/MGM Studios, Elstree, where studio scenes for *The Protectors* were shot.

ITC New York had a strong voice in the direction this new series of *UFO* would take, as they were unhappy with what were viewed as soap-opera elements in episodes such as 'Confetti Check A-OK'. With a great deal of time and money spent on pre-production, disaster struck when the all-important American ratings began to fade and CBS lost interest in backing a second series of *UFO*. An American sale was vital to the continuation of such an expensive project and with that prospect gone the show was dead. The extensive and expensive pre-production work actually worked in Anderson's favour when he pitched the idea to Lew Grade to rework it into a completely new series, which might appeal to the US market. Grade approved the idea and the journey that was eventually to lead to *Space: 1999* had begun.

Events moved quickly; in early 1973, Group Three worked on getting what would be the biggest dramatic production in television history ready for broadcast for the autumn 1974 US television season. ITC's publicity department released to the industry an Advance Programme Information document, which gives a fascinating insight into the shape the series was taking at this early stage of proceedings. The document is largely based on a pilot script titled 'Zero G', written by Gerry and Sylvia Anderson in spring 1973. Even the title of the new series was up for grabs, with the working title at this point being *Menace in Space*. The main point emphasised is that the action takes place in space, with a number of other titles being listed—*The Intruders*, *Space Intruders*, *Journey into Space*, *Space Journey*, *Outer Space*, and *Space Probe*. Even at this early stage, the idea was set in stone that the cast would be wandering in space. The document is very candid about why the series format is markedly different from *UFO*, in terms that might have been dictated by the ITC New York office.

> ITC's 'everybody-in-the-pool' theory is that the best way to combine story continuity and action is to keep everybody in an action environment—*UFO* was earthbound and required a full hour for development and narrative form. Our new series is conceived as a half-hour action format and to keep it moving, all the action is far out in space.

Bearing in mind the cerebral nature of many first-season *Space:1999* episodes, this reads more like a description of year two, which saw the New York office demand radical changes. The basic idea of the Moon breaking out of Earth's orbit was established, though few details were given for how this happens:

> Earth is destroyed and the Moon, released from its orbit, wanders in space. On it are 300 men and women from all the nations of Earth, originally based there to man an early warning system and to repel invaders. Now they are Earth's sole survivors, on a quest for a new planet compatible with their needs. Ironically, they are considered the invaders by inhabitants of other planets.

What is especially interesting is just how much material can be traced back directly to *UFO*, giving some clues as to the thinking behind the aborted second season. At this stage the Moonbase was known as WANDER, which is also the name of the organisation running the base (World Association of Nations Defending Earth Rights). The complex is part of an early warning system against approaches toward Earth by alien craft. Even S.I.D. is mentioned as part of the defence system. The first section of the base to go into action in an emergency is known as First Base, a concept very similar to *UFO*'s Moonbase.

With the series' projected airdate set, and the start of principal photography looming, scripts were needed urgently, even though the show's final format had yet to be decided. Christopher Penfold brought in the Irish writer Johnny Byrne, whose work he had admired, especially his BBC Play for Today script 'Season of the Witch'. *Space: 1999*, in its first season, used many writers who were new to Anderson series, in some cases due to ITC's insistence that the series use American writers and have an American script editor. George Bellak was brought over from America to fill the latter position and, together with Gerry Anderson and Christopher Penfold, created the show's regular characters. Bellak also set to work on the opening episode, initially entitled 'The Void Ahead', though his early departure from the series meant that the script, eventually renamed 'Breakaway', was largely the work of Penfold. Bellak was replaced by English-based American Edward di Lorenzo and eventually Johnny Byrne, who had been acting as a staff writer until then.

Writers from America were sending in material, but communications technology of the time meant they were unable to get proper guidance from the team in England, rendering much of the resulting material unusable. Even Art Wallace's 'Siren Planet', which made it into production as the second episode, retitled 'Matter of Life and Death', was completely rewritten by Johnny Byrne in two weeks, a matter of some urgency as there were no completed scripts to go into production once 'Breakaway' wrapped. Eventually, the effort to recruit American-based writers was abandoned and the lion's share of the writing was taken on by Penfold and Byrne, Edward di Lorenzo leaving the production at a relatively early stage.

With an enormous financial investment in a major television series aimed squarely at the American market—with no guaranteed US network sale—Lew Grade spread the risk by making a co-production deal with the Italian state broadcaster RAI.

In 1954, RAI started the country's first regular television service. Interestingly, the two stations RAI operated in 1973, RAI Uno and RAI Due, did not start full-time colour broadcasting until 1 February 1977. This helps to explain why compilation films of popular ITC series such as *The Persuaders*, *UFO*, and *Space: 1999* were released to Italian cinemas. Since the 1950s, Italian producers had been keen on foreign co-production arrangements. The advantages of these were readily apparent when Hollywood producers used Rome's Cinecittà studios to make a series of large scale films, starting with *Quo Vadis?* (1950). The Americans not only liked the lower production costs, but were also able to spend some of their frozen financial assets, as since 1947 Italian law stipulated that a proportion of box-office receipts American films earned in Italy had to be spent there.

By 1973, RAI were not only willing to make a deal with super-salesman Lew Grade, whose shows were enormously popular on Italian television, but to reverse common Italian practice and invest in a production that did not use Italian studios and technicians. Grade's dealings with RAI worked both ways, as ITC backed *Moses the Lawgiver* (1974) at around the same time, which had a largely Italian cast and crew along with American star Burt Lancaster.

Efforts were made to find Italian actors for regular roles in *Space: 1999*. An early 1973 version of the series format indicated that two parts were earmarked for Italian performers: 'An Italian man of 28 who will be in charge of space reconnaissance' and 'a 23-year-old Italian girl who will be an expert in sensor devices'. One wonders if the last-minute casting of the dark-haired, olive-skinned Zienia Merton was a compromise to at least get a somewhat Italian-looking actress for the part. The character, originally called Sandra Sabatini, was renamed Sandra Benes.

Italian actor Giancarlo Prete was originally cast as chief Eagle pilot Captain Alfonso Catani, but (depending on which version you believe) he either could not be released from his commitment to appear in Tonino Cervi's Italian comedy *La Nottata* and was forced to withdraw, or Martin Landau objected to being cast opposite such a handsome actor with similar dark colouring to himself. The role was redrafted as Alan Carter to suit Australian actor Nick Tate, who was promoted from the minor role of Astronaut Collins in 'Breakaway' to become perhaps *Space: 1999*'s most popular character. Meanwhile, Prete would later appear in the series in *The Troubled Spirit* in a guest starring role.

Casting the role of the show's lead actor was vital, with a big-name American actor seen as essential to the series' viability. An early front-runner was Robert Culp, who came to prominence in the 1965–68 spy series *I Spy*; he also had ambitions to become a director, having recently helmed the movie *Hickey & Boggs* (1972) featuring himself and his *I Spy* co-star Bill Cosby. Culp put himself out of contention as he expressed his desire to write scripts and direct episodes as well as star in *Space: 1999*. It was felt to be out of the question for the leading man to be shouldering these additional burdens on a series of the size and complexity of *Space: 1999*.

Since their ascent to television stardom in *Mission: Impossible*, Martin Landau and Barbara Bain were keen to work together again and more than willing to work in television again, having only left the hit show because of a financial dispute that ended up in litigation. Their previous project together, a television pilot made for NBC called *Savage*, was directed by Steven Spielberg shortly before he broke into films.

Ironically, considering how much *Space: 1999* would be compared to *Star Trek*, Martin Landau had been offered and turned down the role of Mister Spock. Landau, an actor from a method school (who had also been a close friend of James Dean), felt unable to play a part where he was not required to display any emotion. However, after speaking to Gerry Anderson and ITC's New York chief (Abe Mandell), the Landaus were impressed enough with the plans for the new series that they were willing to sign on. However, they (and their agents) were not going to make a long-term commitment to relocate to Europe without being paid top dollar. Negotiations stalled when their representatives made a take-it-or-leave-it demand, which was more than Lew Grade had told Anderson and Mandell he would pay. Grade was convinced to raise his offer and the series was up and running with not one, but two leading actors—Martin Landau and Barbara Bain.

The initial idea for the series was that aliens had launched a devastating thermonuclear attack on the far side of the Moon, which redistributed critical force fields and violently thrust the Moon out of orbit. This sounds far less convincing than the eventual notion of an exploding nuclear waste dump, and is also evidence of an emerging philosophy behind the series. Instead of being victims of invading aliens, the inhabitants of Moonbase were forced to become the invading force in a universe that they cannot begin to understand and in which they do not really belong. The wider themes of the series and its technical aspects were fitting into place within the tight production deadline the show needed in order to meet its target broadcast date in the autumn 1974 television season.

The characterisations of the main characters were still quite sketchy, however, and some of the actors drew upon their training to create histories for their characters that would never be revealed on-screen, but would aid their performances. Thus Barbara Bain gave her character Dr Helena Russell some interesting family history, citing her father as being the world-renowned doctor who found the cure for cancer, causing his daughter to become an obsessive high-achiever. Barry Morse, who came from a different acting tradition to Landau and Bain, often complained that he was getting no guidance to how he should play Victor Bergman. However, the writer's guide, prepared in September 1973, does give clues as to how the Professor was to develop:

> The Professor looks upon his times with a somewhat rueful eye. He is more of a throwback—a 19th-century scientist-philosopher-humanist—and he is an intellectual counterbalance to the 21st century we are about to enter. He has a mechanical heart, which responds much more slowly to nervous stimuli than does a normal human heart. This makes him unsusceptible to panic or to emotional stress of any other kind.

The notion of the mechanical heart could be read as trying to force the character into a Mr Spock template, in an attempt to appeal to the *Star Trek* fan base. Fortunately, this route was not taken, and if the mechanical heart had any effect on his demeanour it was to give him a general air of unflappability. In any event, it is very difficult to imagine Barry Morse playing the role with suppressed emotions.

The Eagle Transporter had still not been named at this point, though its basic design had been in place for some time. In production documentation dating from both early and late 1973, the craft was known as a MTU (Multiple Transportation Unit). The exterior design of the Eagle was the work of Brian Johnson, who had left AP Films mid-way through the making of *Thunderbirds* to join the production of Stanley Kubrick's *2001: A Space Odyssey*. He also worked over the years with the ubiquitous Les Bowie on Hammer productions including *Kiss of the Vampire* (1963) and *Moon Zero Two* (1969). While work continued on the scripts and live-action aspects of the production at Elstree, Brian Johnson had assembled a model unit at Bray Studios in his quest to produce 2001-quality special effects on a television budget, albeit the largest budget spent at that point on a dramatic series. The sequences were directed by Nick Allder, who, after working on commercials, broke into feature film production with the film *A Twist of Sand (1968)*; the following year, he worked with Brian Johnson on *Moon Zero Two*. After *Space: 1999*, the two worked together extensively on productions such as *Alien* (1979) and *The Empire Strikes Back* (1980), both of which won Oscars for their effects work. Allder won a third Oscar for the special effects on *The Fifth Element* in 1997.

Johnson was inspired by the idea of the craft being designed for use outside Earth's atmosphere, thus freeing him from having to design a traditionally aerodynamic craft. He also used a modular design, with the idea that the craft's design could be reconfigured for different uses—as seen in the opening episode 'Breakaway', where Eagles are seen as personnel transport and as lifting units for nuclear waste.

The interior of the Eagle was designed by Keith Wilson (Bob Bell, who had always been the chief designer on Anderson live-action productions, was busy on *The Protectors* second season and opted to stay with that series). Unfortunately, Bell suddenly found himself unemployed when Fabergé withdrew their funding for the third season of *The Protectors*, which everyone concerned had fully expected to be filmed during 1974.

Fashion designer Rudi Gernreich (a close friend of Barbara Bain) was brought in to work on the Moonbase uniforms. Although he had no background in costume design, Gernreich was a big name who added to the air of big production values the show was aiming for. His designs were somewhat adapted by Keith Wilson, but one can clearly see Gernreich's influence in their unisex design, which was somewhat watered down when Wilson reworked them for *Space: 1999*'s second season. To his credit, Gernreich came up with a striking and practical look, which was relatively comfortable for the actors (a rarity in SF costuming) and introduced the idea of a coloured sleeve denoting the area in which the wearer worked.

Before principal photography could start, there was one remaining drama for the production team to overcome. EMI had acquired Elstree Studios in part of its 1969 buy-out of Associated British Picture Corporation and, when MGM closed down the nearby Borehamwood studios in the same year, they agreed to co-finance productions at Elstree. In 1973, MGM pulled out of the agreement and, with the future of Elstree Studios looking bleak, Group Three were being asked to commit to a year's filming at a studio that might have gone bankrupt at any time.

As a result, the entire production decamped to Pinewood over the space of a weekend after secret negotiations with that studio's management. As a result of these manoeuvres, *Space: 1999* was blacklisted by the film unions for a time. Pinewood's management were more than happy to have the business—during the majority of the time that the two seasons of *Space: 1999* were being filmed, it was the only production in residence.

Finally in early December 1973, *Space: 1999* was ready to start shooting. For the project to succeed, the series had to get off to a strong start with its opening episode, which started filming under American director Lee H. Katzin on 3 December 1973. Katzin was also heavily involved in the casting process and particularly pushed for Nick Tate to be cast as Alpha's chief Eagle pilot when Giancarlo Prete dropped out of the production. A highly experienced director of filmed television, Katzin unaccountably allowed the shoot to go wildly over its ten-day schedule, causing chaos with the show's budget and filming schedule—the episode finally wrapped on 11 January 1974. Worse news was to come when the miles of footage were edited together. Instead of producing a fifty-minute television episode, the first cut of the pilot show lasted over two hours.

Even worse, Gerry Anderson judged the film slow and dull, a view shared by Abe Mandell of ITC New York when he saw it for himself. At this stage, the entire future of the series was on the line. *Space: 1999* was set up with the intention of producing a series with similar production values to *2001: A Space Odyssey*, but made to television production schedules and a (very large for the medium) television budget. If the opening episode was going to take over double the scheduled time and still not produce a useable result, how was a full series of twenty-four episodes going to be made meeting the show's budget and screening dates?

Gerry Anderson was Lew Grade's most trusted producer, but Abe Mandell had Grade's ear and his continued support for the project was vital. At this early stage it was still possible for the series to be cancelled with perhaps a television special salvaged from the shoot that could be released to cinemas in Europe and South America. Remarkably, Anderson was able to supervise the re-editing of 'Breakaway' down to the required length, personally writing and directing twenty linking scenes to tie the by-now disjointed story together. These were filmed in a three-day shoot between the filming of the episodes 'Black Sun' (Lee Katzin's second and final *Space: 1999* episode) and 'Ring around the Moon'.

The result was a triumph—fifty minutes of television that looked better than most feature films and provided Abe Mandell with the best possible tool to sell the series to the American market. The patchwork nature of the script—Christopher Penfold's rewrite of George Bellak's 'The Void Ahead' having undergone further additions by Anderson—were as nothing. 'Breakaway' was always going to have size and scale, but now it all flowed perfectly and worked as a piece of drama. If ever Gerry Anderson proved his worth as a practical, nuts-and-bolts filmmaker it was here. The immediate future of *Space: 1999* was assured.

Barry Gray's status as Gerry Anderson's composer of SF scores was beyond question—his ability to create a huge sound from a relatively small orchestra had given the puppet series a big-screen feel way beyond their budgets. Now he would create a score where the images would be every bit as large scale as his music. Not that the size of his orchestra was a factor, with the *Space: 1999* theme and a later recording session for the episode 'Another Time, Another

Place' utilising the talents of a fifty two-piece ensemble. Other recording sessions used fewer musicians—a thirty-two-strong orchestra produced the soundtrack to 'Breakaway' and 'Matter of Life and Death'. Barry Gray's final recording session for 'The Full Circle' took place some months later on 3 December—these were to be his final compositions for Gerry Anderson.

Gray's *Space: 1999* theme was recorded almost a year earlier on 11 December 1973 and is one of his masterpieces. A real sense of awe and majesty is brought to each episode, the opening fanfare announcing to the world, 'Watch this, it's important.' The composer undercut any tendency towards pomposity by mixing this with the pop sensibility he had regularly displayed in Anderson series, from *Four Feather Falls* to *Joe 90* and *UFO*. The result was both grandiose and thrillingly catchy.

The composition of the score was effected by Musicians' Union restrictions, which dictated the length of recording sessions and meant that only five episodes in a series could be fully scored. The five episodes scored by Gray were the first three ('Breakaway', 'Matter of Life and Death', and 'Black Sun'), episode six ('Another Time, Another Place'), and the fifteenth episode ('The Full Circle'). *Space: 1999*'s requirement for more music than could be produced in the recording sessions for these episodes meant that much use was made both of tracks from previous Anderson shows and of recordings from the Chappell Recorded Music Library. 'End of Eternity' and 'The Internal Machine' in particular use a great many library tracks. It is interesting that the tracks chosen are not, on the whole, standard action-adventure recordings, but instead are unusual pieces that give the episodes in which they are used a unique feel within the body of the series.

On two occasions classical pieces were used; these were 'Adagio for Strings and Organ in G Minor' by Tomaso Albinoni, which gave 'Dragon's Domain' something of a *2001: A Space Odyssey* feel. For British audiences who were old enough to remember, the use of Gustav Holst's 'Mars, the Bringer of War' in 'Space Brain' brought back memories of *The Quatermass Experiment*.

Another potential source of music for *Space: 1999* was Vic Elmes (misspelt as 'Elms' on the credits), who initially proved useful in providing the electric guitar arrangements for the *Space: 1999* opening theme and for the 'Matter of Life and Death' score. However, he was ultimately a pop musician, whose lack of training and experience in composition and the needs of film production soon became apparent when he was put before a full orchestra. In an attempt to better use Elmes' skills, he was provided with a small group in a rock-style formation under music editor Alan Willis, and most of the resulting music was used in episode four, 'Ring around the Moon'. The experiment was not repeated and Vic Elmes took no further part in the production. Elmes, who was Sylvia Anderson's son-in-law, had previously been a guitarist with Christie, who had scored a major worldwide hit with 'Yellow River' in 1970, a recording on which Elmes had not actually performed. Though not suited to soundtrack composition, Elmes was a skilled rock musician and songwriter, and penned Christie's final hit, 'JoJo's Band', which topped the charts in Argentina and Brazil.

As with previous Anderson series, the complex needs and distinctive 'house style' of *Space: 1999* meant that a small-number of directors were employed by the production for the length of the shooting schedule. With the British film industry in apparent terminal decline, any number of experienced feature film directors would have been available. Instead, the policy was continued from the second production block of *UFO* of hiring directors that were familiar with the rigours and time constraints of filmed series television. Lee H. Katzin was already on board and slated to direct further episodes after 'Breakaway', and the plan was to have two others who were familiar with British crews and working methods.

Charles Crichton was a hugely experienced feature film director who had increasingly branched out into television work since the early '60s. He started out in the industry in the mid-'30s as a film editor for the Anglo-Hungarian movie mogul Alexander Korda. He took to directing in the mid-1940s and achieved prominence with Ealing films, for which he helmed comedies such as *The Lavender Hill Mob* (1951) and *The Titfield Thunderbolt* (1953). Crichton was happy to turn his hand to any genre, his wide experience standing him in good stead when he began taking on television work as the British film industry began to contract. Between big-screen assignments he directed episodes of the ITC shows *Man of the World* and *Danger Man*. He eventually abandoned movies altogether for television, directing episodes of *Man in a Suitcase. The Avengers, Strange Report, Shirley's World, Here Come the Double Deckers!*, and *The Adventures of Black Beauty*. At this point, Crichton began working for Group Three productions directing five episodes of *The Protectors*, impressing the production team so much that he was engaged as one of the main directors of *Space: 1999*.

Ray Austin took anything but the standard industry route into directing, with an early career including a stint as Cary Grant's chauffeur and a background in martial arts. He became a stunt man, initially with Grant on Hitchcock's 1959 classic *North by Northwest,* which led to an acting career, generally as a villainous henchman who could handle a fight scene. Austin became a stunt arranger, most famously for *The Avengers*. His interest in action scenes led to him branch out into second unit directing for the ITC series *The Champions.* After getting his start as a director on the final season of *The Avengers*, Austin became an immediate success in his new role and worked extensively on ITC-filmed series including *The Saint, Department S, Randall and Hopkirk (Deceased)*, and *Shirley's World*.

As filming progressed, these plans had to be altered as Lee H. Katzin left the production after filming wrapped on his second episode, 'Black Sun', an unacceptable five days behind schedule and still needing reshoots. The production could not run with only two directors and a replacement had to be found urgently. Ironically, the new director was both a safe pair of hands who had worked on two previous Anderson series and a boldly artistic writer-director. This role was filled by David Tomblin, who was now free from the feature film commitments, which had prevented him from directing more than a single episode of *The Protectors*.

Crichton, Austin, and Tomblin handled the episodes, which followed in the production schedule until the latter received an offer he could not refuse— Stanley Kubrick wanted him as first assistant director on his latest production, *Barry Lyndon* (1975). All people concerned realised that this was the chance of a lifetime and Tomblin was allowed leave from *Space: 1999* to work on the film. It is no exaggeration to say that this was to change the course of his career. Already growing disenchanted with what he saw as the artistic compromises of directing for television, he quickly gained the reputation as the world's best first assistant director, working on a huge number of major American productions based in the UK. After completing two more *Space: 1999* episodes on his return to the production, he left directing behind for good.

A temporary replacement for Tomblin was arranged in the form of Bob Kellett. Unlike the other three directors who had worked on the series, Kellett had no background in series television. What he did have was a solid, practical filmmaking background. Kellett had produced and written films since the '60s; these films were mainly comedies, which he had been making exclusively during the first three years of the '70s. Before joining the *Space: 1999* team, he had directed, amongst other things, the cult favourite Ronnie Barker short film *Futtocks End* (1970) and three movie spin-offs of *Up Pompeii!* in 1971 and '72—an attempt by producer Ned Sherrin to mount a rival movie series to the *Carry On* films.

Kellett attempted to bring a different approach to *Space: 1999*. The production had, up to this point, remained in the studio and even then had consistently struggled to keep to its ten-day-per-episode shooting schedule. He successfully proved that location filming was possible within the time and budget constraints of the series when he shot scenes for 'The Full Circle' on the Pinewood backlot and at nearby Black Park. Kellett even wrote his final episode as director, 'The Last Enemy', from a suggestion by Barbara Bain.

The pressures on the *Space: 1999* production team were added to by factors unique to the series and to this period—interference by the New York office, a last-minute change of studio facilities, union blacklisting, and a budget being constantly eaten away during the sixteen-month shoot by the demons of schedule overruns, raging inflation, and even power cuts, forcing the production to have its own generating equipment on site.

Despite its difficult production, *Space: 1999* proved that an intelligent, thoughtful SF series could be produced for television with cinematic production values. The episodes developed the theme that the people of Alpha represented humanity cast out from their home, with nowhere else in the universe to go. The second episode in production, and the first to be completed, 'Matter of Life and Death', sees the Alphans attempt to land on an anti-matter planet, their presence causing death and chaos. This theme is further developed in episodes such as 'The Last Sunset', in which an alien race provides the Moon with an atmosphere and food so that they do not try to populate their planet, and 'War Games', in which Alpha sees the violence of humanity reflected back on itself in apocalyptic fashion.

Another thread linking stories in *Space: 1999* is that science, as represented by the technological humanity of the Alphans, cannot explain everything. 'Black Sun', described in more detail below, is a key episode in introducing these themes, and also shows the Moon being sent to the other side of the universe, which is why Alpha is able to encounter so many inhabited planets. 'Collision Course' sees the Moon headed into a disastrous collision with a huge planet, which is part of some enormous, ancient cosmic plan. Alpha is also involved in a collision in 'Space Brain', in which it heads for a vast, god-like intelligence that untold planets in the region rely on. The final episode, Johnny Byrne's 'The Testament of Arkadia', sums up this strand of thinking in *Space: 1999*'s scripts, as two Alphans hi-jack an Eagle and take supplies so that they might populate a dead planet, which has apparently been waiting for their arrival so that it might return to life.

The writing process of *Space: 1999* had been difficult, with a great deal of rewriting needed (mainly by Christopher Penfold and Johnny Byrne). This was partially due to the difficulties of writing for the series, particularly when dealing with American-based writers with early 1970's methods of communication. Also hampering the smooth flow of the script process was a great deal of interference from Abe Mandell's New York office of ITC, which eventually led to Penfold's forcible ejection from the production. The sheer amount of work that Penfold and Byrne were forced to put into the scripts helped ensure that the series had a consistent philosophy and story arcs some two decades before such things became common in series television. It helped give this first version of *Space: 1999* its poetic soul.

This ultimately mattered little to the American television networks, who turned down the chance to screen *Space: 1999*. Abe Mandell was forced to sell the series to the syndication market. While money was probably a factor, it should be noted that the series, particularly in the form of its first season, was radically different from anything the networks were actually buying at the time.

New dramatic series for the 1973–74 season on American television fell largely into three categories: firstly, there were remakes of old properties such as *Adam's Rib* and *Shaft*, in which Richard Rowntree took his character from the 1971 'Blaxploitation' classic to a watered-down television version.

Next there were tough, gritty crime-in-the-streets dramas such as *Kojak*, which made film character actor Telly Savalas a huge star, despite largely recreating the mean streets of New York at Universal City Studios. Finally, America was in a nostalgic frame of mind—the sitcom *Happy Days*, set in the 1950s, premiered in January 1974 and ran for eleven series. Attempts were also made to appeal to nostalgic audiences by making series starring older performers. Therefore American viewers were treated to *Barnaby Jones* (Buddy

Ebsen as an elderly private investigator), *Griff* (Lorne Greene as an elderly private investigator), *Hawkins* (James Stewart as an elderly lawyer), and *The Snoop Sisters* (elderly sisters Helen Hayes and Mildred Natwick as amateur detectives). Only the first of these proved a popular hit.

Space: 1999 was swimming against the tide of what American television executives thought was popular in 1973. No matter how high the quality of the series was, it was just too tough for Lew Grade to sell. Ironically, SF made something of a comeback the following year with series including *The Six Million Dollar Man* and *Planet of the Apes*, which was an adaptation of the popular series of films that ran for only thirteen episodes. Aimed at younger audiences were *Land of the Lost* and the similar *Valley of the Dinosaurs,* made by the Australian studios of Hanna-Barbera. Also aimed at younger audiences were *Shazam!* (a live-action series, in which a teenager has the ability to turn into superhero Captain Marvel) and, strangest of all, *The Partridge Family 2200AD*. This now forgotten oddity was a bizarre attempt to reboot the 1960's SF cartoon comedy *The Jetsons* as a vehicle for the television singing family that had launched the career of David Cassidy.

Looking at this revival of SF television in the American market, despite the first series of *Space: 1999* being a more complex and interesting series than the second, its second season was genuinely closer to what was on air in the US. The retooled version of the series had a genuine chance of being picked up by one of the networks. Unfortunately, the SF series the networks chose were not space operas of the *Space: 1999* variety, which would not come back into fashion until the game-changing, global success of *Star Wars* in 1977.

Key Episode

Episode 3: 'Black Sun'
Written by David Weir
Directed by Lee H. Katzin

A meteor, then an Eagle, are destroyed by a mysterious object with a massive gravitational pull. Moonbase Alpha discovers that the Moon is being pulled unstoppably towards a Black Hole. Professor Bergman conceives a last-ditch plan that might ensure the Alphans' survival, but meanwhile they must confront their own mortality while the very nature of the universe is questioned.

Of all the episodes chosen as key in this book, 'Black Sun' probably deserves the accolade the most. The story was designed to be screened as early as possible in the series run, since it explains how the wandering Moon is able to encounter so many alien races and inhabited planets; however, typical of the luck *Space: 1999* attracted, it was screened tenth in both the US and UK, giving the show's critics further ammunition.

Unlike many stories in *Space: 1999*'s first season, 'Black Sun' is not driven by the presence of a big-name guest star. Paul Jones receives star billing, but outside of his successful music career he was a jobbing actor and his role here as the doomed Eagle pilot Mike Ryan is hardly crucial. Jones' American accent is not the best, but his look of terror as he is torn apart by extreme gravitational forces is very effective.

This is a story about the people of Moonbase Alpha, their emotions, their relationships with each other, and how they react under extreme amounts of stress as they face what seems to be certain death. Unusually for a space exploration series, the Alphans are, first and foremost, scientists rather than military men—this allows the characters to react in more 'human' ways to the events that are shown. Consequently, when Mike Ryan dies, Sandra is heartbroken having just seen her boyfriend die in front of her eyes (unlike in military-based SF organisations, the people on Moonbase Alpha must form romantic relationships in order for their race to survive).

Ryan's boss John Koenig expresses his guilt for sending him to his death, reminding us that he is a scientist and not a military leader. His order, which resulted in someone's death, is still a new experience for Koenig this early in *Space: 1999*'s run—another reason why 'Black Sun' is more effective if seen as early as possible in the series.

As an early episode, 'Black Sun' is a marvellous introduction to some of the show's regular characters, some of whom are, in other episodes, reduced to providing plot exposition. Paul Morrow is seen as careful, conscientious, and loyal (and crazy about Sandra). David Kano is very attached to Alpha's main computer, which he refers to as Computer, as if it has a personality. At times, we genuinely wonder if he thinks more about Computer than he does his fellow humans—in a later episode we discover that he is linked to Computer via a cybernetic brain implant.

Alan Carter gets one of his best scenes in the series, a magnificently staged conflict with Koenig when Alpha's chief pilot learns that an Eagle might be sent out as an emergency lifeboat without him. Carter is seen in the background during several scenes, subtly commenting on the main action—his sly grin at Kano's discomfort when he learns that Computer is to be switched off is priceless, and it is clear that he feels for Paul as he says goodbye to Sandra as she boards the survival ship.

At the heart of the story, though, is the relationship between John Koenig and his friend, mentor, and confident Victor Bergman. The deep friendship between the two is central to the climax of 'Black Sun'. Despite being the most brilliant scientist on Alpha (he has devised a force field, which might just protect Alpha from the black sun), Bergman is also wise on a human, philosophical level. His scientific knowledge is so great that he is aware of where that knowledge ends and how little we really know about the universe, which Alpha has been thrust into. In the face of certain death as Alpha approaches the black hole—and it is revealing that the writers chose to use the more poetic term black sun throughout the episode—Bergman wonders about God and the nature of the universe, saying, 'The line between science and mysticism. Just a line,' before breaking out the sixty-year-old brandy.

In a clever directorial touch, Lee Katzin pulls the camera back as the pair look around a cold and deserted Main Mission. The two men who have dominated this scene suddenly appear small and lonely, as are the Alphans in a huge, cold universe in which they may not even have a place.

As Alpha gets colder, its population becomes warmer, towards each other, at least. These people are approaching what they assume to be their doom, and they do not panic, but neither do they stay at their posts when there is nothing they can do. Some gamble, some play chess, and some play music—we see the Alphans being themselves.

Bearing in mind that *Space: 1999* was the most expensive television series ever made at this point, one might expect the series to take the easy option and go with the most spectacular climax possible. It is admirable how infrequently the series does this and 'Black Sun' is the best example of *Space: 1999*'s poetic, metaphysical leanings being maintained right until a story's close.

The force field holds and the Alphans experience the interior of the black sun—even those headed in the opposite direction in the survival ship. Existence is questioned and time itself is changed; Bergman and Koenig suddenly appear ancient and the barrier between the two men's thoughts dissolves. It is interesting to compare this sequence to Christopher Nolan's *Interstellar* (2014), which uses passing through a black hole to express dilation and contraction of the human experience of time in similar ways to 'Black Sun'.

In the finale to this sequence, Koenig and Bergman encounter, for want of a better term, God—and she is female. That is if the concept of gender has any meaning for this level of being. The Moon passes through the black sun and finds itself at the other side of the universe, as does the survival ship—the Alphans are a community, and appear to have some kind of inexplicable link with each other. Moonbase Alpha's survival is not presented as a triumph of technological mankind against the elements. They are aware that something is on their side—some force or cosmic intelligence. In a final gesture of human defiance, Bergman drops cigar ash on the floor of the antiseptically clean Moonbase.

25

Space: 1999 Year Two

'*It is better to live as your own man than as a fool in someone else's dream.*'

Produced by Fred Freiberger
Created by Gerry and Sylvia Anderson
Production executive Reg Hill
Executive producer (uncredited) Gerry Anderson
Music by Derek Wadsworth
A Gerry Anderson Production from IRC Television
24 × fifty-minute episodes
First UK broadcast Saturday 4 September 1976 (London Weekend Television)

Space: 1999 fans were lucky to get a second season of the show at all. Despite its lavish budget and the care taken in every aspect of production, the first season of the series had failed in its primary objective—to sell to one of America's national television networks. *Space: 1999*, as audiences had grown to know it, ended when the final first series episode, 'The Testament of Arkadia', was completed. This was certainly in the minds of the production team when making the episode, which ends with the people of Alpha travelling full circle to the very beginnings of life on Earth and John Koenig literally closing the book on the series at the end of the story.

Fortunately, audiences appear to have very much liked *Space: 1999*. While ratings in America's syndicated markets were healthy without being spectacular, the series was a big success throughout Europe, and there was certainly an appetite for more episodes. Changes would have to be made, both for financial reasons and due to the internal politics of ITC. Financially, the economics of the mid-1970s meant that although the second season would be made for a larger sum of money than the first, this amounted to a cut in the series budget. The £125,000 each episode was budgeted at in 1973 would by 1976 have been worth £210,000. So high was the inflation rate at this time that a Year One episode would have cost £243,000 by the end of 1977.

Despite the constant pressure from Abe Mandell's ITC New York, the first season broadly represented the series Gerry Anderson wanted to make. For the series to return, far more control had to be ceded to Mandell, which meant big changes. While a decision was awaited on the future of the series, Gerry was commissioned by NBC executive George Heinemann to make an educational SF story explaining the concepts of Einstein's theory of relativity. This became 'The Day After Tomorrow: Into Infinity', scripted by Johnny Byrne, about a family setting out on a scientific journey into outer space on the Altares. Starring Nick Tate, Joanna Dunham, and Brian Blessed, the story was structured with the wishful intention of being picked up for a series. Although no series resulted, it was screened on NBC in December 1975 and in the UK on BBC 1 almost exactly a year later.

The earliest preparation work for *Space: 1999*'s second season took place before the decision had been made to actually renew the series. The triumphs and failures of the recently completed programme were discussed, and a day-long meeting was convened; this was attended by Gerry Anderson, Brian Johnson, Martin Landau, Barbara Bain, Johnny Byrne, and Charles Crichton. Byrne was fully expected to remain as the show's script editor if the series returned, but the situation was soon to change radically.

Gerry and Sylvia Anderson's often fractious marriage finally ended irrevocably late in the production of *Space: 1999*'s first season and it was impossible for her to remain in the post of *Space: 1999*'s producer. She resigned both as producer of *Space: 1999* and from the board of Group Three, making the company name instantly redundant. A new company was formed, simply called Gerry Anderson Productions. Having gained Lew Grade's consent to produce a second season, it was insisted that an American script editor be hired to ensure that scripts were produced with appeal to audiences in the US. This made sense as it had proved impractical for American-based writers working under a British script editor to contribute a great deal to the series. A suitable American, willing to relocate to the UK, had to be found and Anderson was dispatched to the States in order to procure one.

Candidates with the right kind of experience were thin on the ground, and finding someone who was both suitable and available proved difficult. A promising contender eventually emerged in the personable form of Fred Freiberger, who had worked on series such as *The Wild, Wild West* (a sort of Western with SF trappings screened between 1965 and 69 that might now be viewed as 'steampunk') and had produced the third season of *Star Trek* in 1969.

Abe Mandell's reaction when Anderson announced that he might have found his man was to wonder why Freiberger might be available. Time was running out, though, and with no other suitable candidates to hand, Anderson went ahead and hired Freiberger. From this distance in time it can be seen that both Anderson and Mandell had a point. If Freiberger was so good, why was he able to immediately fly to England for a year? From Anderson's perspective, Mandell was insisting on an American script editor and Freiberger was the most suitable one he could find.

The first season of *Space: 1999* was the personal vision of Gerry Anderson, Christopher Penfold, and Johnny Byrne, but the series had been cancelled. In effect, this was now making a new series with the same concept and some of the same sets and cast. If the new show was going to be someone else's version of the series, Anderson decided that person should have credit as producer. Fred Freiberger was thus promoted from script editor to the vacant position of producer, Anderson taking no official credit for *Space: 1999* Year Two, despite being *de facto* executive producer. His only on-screen credit was the series credit of being a Gerry Anderson Production.

Freiberger's first action on arriving at Pinewood was to head for the screening theatre and watch eight episodes of the series. His assessment of series and views as to what needed to be done to remedy the faults were the subject of a memo to Gerry Anderson. One wonders which episodes he watched, as, aside from the production values, Freiberger had nothing good to say about the series and was particularly scathing about the writing. Characters were described as 'one-dimensional' who stand around talking instead of 'doing' and character relationships were 'plastic and meaningless'. Plot structure was described in damning terms and Freiberger was especially concerned at the lack of humour. With comments like this, damning the writing of the series on every level, it is little wonder that Johnny Byrne, despite liking Freddie Freiberger personally, did not feel able to work with him on a regular basis.

With all the changes both in front of and behind the camera, Gerry Anderson recruited an old friend to the production. Frank Sherwin Green came on board as associate producer, having served as production supervisor on the between-seasons production *The Day After Tomorrow*. Green was a hugely experienced production manager and producer whose career stretched back to the early 1930s. He had also helped introduce Anderson to Lew Grade when it looked like bankruptcy was around the corner for AP Films.

Several changes in cast were made—the characters Paul Morrow and David Kano left with no on-screen explanation, as did Victor Bergman after the producers were unable to agree with Barry Morse's management over his salary. An explanation regarding Bergman's disappearance was scripted but never used—this was that he had died due to a faulty space suit. Two new major characters were introduced in the form of Security Chief Tony Verdeschi, played by *The Protectors* regular Tony Anholt, and Maya, an alien with the power to change her form.

Anholt took on the second lead role action-man (previously occupied by Nick Tate) as Alan Carter, whose character was somewhat side-lined. Indeed,

Carter was originally not even in the shooting script of opening episode 'The Metamorph', his lines being originally assigned to a character named Mark MacInlock. As we shall see later, Tate's relationship with Freiberger remained problematic as he remained unhappy at his often much-reduced role.

Tony Verdeschi only gained his final name a couple of days before filming began, having previously been called Simon Hays, originally envisaged as an amalgam of Victor Bergman and Paul Morrow, to the extent of having a Bergman-esque artificial heart before evolving into his final characterisation.

The role of Maya was one of Freddie Freiberger's earliest additions to the series format (Gerry Anderson would later mention that the idea of having a second female lead to 'support' Barbara Bain came from Lew Grade) and developed in some interesting ways from the new producer's initial conception of 'a sensuous long-limbed, beautiful, amazingly graceful black girl who will have the ability to transform into other life forms'. That a black actress was to portray Maya appears to have remained the intention for some time, as the character's initial make-up and costume sketches fit Freiberger's initial description quite closely. In the end, however, a tortuous casting process took place for the part, despite the fact that Catherine Schell was Lew Grade's choice for the part and was always going to get the role. Barbara Bain was worried about the on-screen competition, and casting sessions were held largely so she was happy that someone's favourite was not being parachuted into the part. In the end, Bain had nothing to worry about as the character of Maya gave Dr Russell someone to play off and their on-screen chemistry contributed to the rather more relaxed, expressive performance Bain gave in the Year Two episodes.

The idea of Maya being a scientific genius was not much referred to after the first episode, avoiding the character being forced into the role of a Mr Spock-style polymath. Maya was written and played as a normal, fun-loving young woman, who just happens to be able to change her appearance at will. The fact that her father and everyone else she knows is blown to atoms at the end of 'The Metamorph' seems to have virtually no effect on her sunny disposition. A romance is quickly set up between her and Tony Verdeschi, though whatever initiates this happens off-screen. As *Space: 1999* Year Two was designed, like most filmed series of its era, to be seen in any order, the decision to have their relationship presented as a given is an intelligent one.

Budgetary and artistic considerations were to have visible effects on both the look of the series and on casting decisions. Although the huge Main Mission set was still at Pinewood ready to use, Barbara Bain claimed that its very size was time consuming to light for filming—it has to be said that this was disputed by production designer Keith Wilson, who had designed the sets to be flexible and easy to film on. The decision was nonetheless made to have a much smaller new set for the show's main setting; this was constructed by Keith Wilson using parts from Main Mission and renamed 'Command Center' (the American spelling being used).

The principal cast would be grouped together, making the pacing of the episodes faster, while encouraging writers to place fewer scenes in one set (which viewers might grow tired of seeing). Although nothing was mentioned on-screen, the official explanation was that the base of operations was taken underground to make it less vulnerable to attack. Wilson had become used to designing on lower budgets, after having worked on the low-budget SF Anglo-German co-production *Star Maidens* in the break between series of *Space: 1999*.

Even in the relatively prosperous circumstances of *Space: 1999*'s first series, Wilson had proved adept in the crafty reuse of props. For season two, he was further tested and certain sets would become very familiar sights over the next twenty-four episodes. Keith Wilson was also given the opportunity to redesign the Moonbase Alpha costumes, adding extra detailing to the basic uniforms and giving the female versions roll necks plus the option of skirts or trousers. Most notably, the jackets that Wilson had introduced wherever possible in the first season went on to become a permanent fixture for both male and female Alphans, while John Koenig was rarely seen without his commander's cardigan. This has been seen in some quarters as helping Landau and Bain relax, as they were less self-conscious now they were not being seen in figure-hugging costumes complete with a wide and tight belt.

The retooled series was upfront about its radical changes, with a pacey new title sequence explaining the series concept and on-screen text for new viewers. This was accompanied by a new theme tune composed by Derek Wadsworth. This replaced Barry Gray's majestic Year One theme with a fast-moving tune more in sync with other adventure shows of the period. The choice of Derek Wadsworth as composer for the series was an interesting one. Although he wrote a fairly conventional opening theme, his incidental music was subtly reflective of current trends in modern jazz.

Wadsworth was a renowned jazz trombonist who became a successful arranger in the 1960s, beginning his career in music by playing and conducting in the northern English brass band scene. After working as Dusty Springfield's arranger, he worked with many of the top pop acts of the period, including The Beatles, The Rolling Stones, Diana Ross, and Rod Stewart. Derek moved into stage work as the musical director of the 1968 musical *Hair*, and in 1970 was invited to orchestrate Alan Price's score for the film *Spring and Port Wine*. His growing reputation was noticed by Gerry Anderson who invited him to score his 1975 series pilot/educational television film *The Day After Tomorrow: Into Infinity*, leading to him being asked to write the music for *Space: 1999*'s second season.

Freiberger very much operated as a hands-on script editor on *Space: 1999*, often micro-managing scripts to the extent of completely rewriting them. Experienced pros, such as Terence Feeley, who wrote the two-part story 'The Bringers of Wonder', objected to what he did with their work. Scripts from Johnny Byrne and Christopher Penfold were similarly heavily rewritten by the producer, though Byrne's 'The Dorcons' survived relatively unscathed. Byrne claimed by this time to have simply given up and just gave Freiberger what he wanted in order to fulfil his contract. On the other hand, Terrance Dicks, who had a great deal of SF experience writing and script editing on *Doctor Who*, reported that his script for 'The Lambda Factor' was accepted with a minimum of fuss and filmed virtually unchanged.

One can often see good ideas struggling to emerge from bad episodes. Feeley's 'The Bringers of Wonder' and 'One Moment of Humanity', scripted by Anderson veteran Tony Barwick, are good examples of this trend with great central plots buried under absurdities. At certain points cast members rebelled against what they were being asked to perform, the episode 'All That Glisters' being particularly disliked by director Ray Austin and star Martin Landau. The latter threatened to walk off the series, as he greatly disliked the concept of the story and the way that the character of Koenig was being handled. An increasingly disenchanted Landau later wrote to Freiberger, while 'A Matter of Balance' was in production, expressing in no uncertain terms his dislike of the direction in which the series had gone.

Another performer not best pleased with his lot on the new series was Nick Tate. Having not been contacted by the producers since the end of the first series, the actor moved back to Sydney on the assumption that either the series was not being renewed or that his part had been written out. Actually the latter was closer to the truth, but Tate received a last-minute call to return to Pinewood Studios where he met with Anderson and Freiberger. The new producer did most of the talking, telling Tate that he was needed back on the series because, 'My kids think you're just great!'

While this raised the question of exactly what Freiberger himself thought of Nick Tate, the actor agreed to look at some scripts, only to find to his dismay that Alan Carter was nowhere to be found in the first five. 'Don't worry,' assured Freiberger, 'we can sort that out.' Tate was unconvinced and although Carter does indeed appear in the early episodes, he is often leaning against a desk in the background while the character of Tony Verdeschi handles dialogue and action, which would have been Carter's in first season stories.

Unlike in the first season of *Space: 1999*, when Tate's performances and charisma earned him a regular contract from the producers, he was now being paid a daily rate for his services. So minor had his appearances been that it had hardly been worth the cost of the airfare from Australia, so the disgruntled Tate quit the production. He was not the only performer to be unhappy with his reduced circumstances on *Space: 1999*, with Dr Mathias appearing in only two episodes before actor Anton Phillips sought greener pastures elsewhere. Similarly, Zienia Merton returned as Sandra Benes, but had so little to do that she walked away from the series, eventually convinced to return by Barbara Bain who had become concerned that there were no familiar faces left in the supporting cast.

Unlike Phillips, efforts were also made to convince Tate to stay with promises to write up his part in future episodes. The amount of fan mail Tate regularly received would presumably have been a factor here, but there was another important consideration—keeping a fairly large regular cast was vital to the production's plans to film certain episodes two at a time, with half the cast carrying one story while the others took centre stage for the other. Losing Alan Carter would have caused serious problems.

Tate agreed to stay and, to his credit, Freiberger was true to his word—for a while at least—giving Carter meatier roles in stories such as 'The Mark of Archanon', but there remained episodes where Tate had very little to do. His characterisation was somewhat altered at first, with Tate asked to speak in a stronger Australian accent and even sing.

Freiberger wrote three scripts himself under his *nom de plume* Charles Woodgrove. These were 'double-up' scripts, which meant that only certain cast members featured heavily in each story so that two episodes could be filmed at the same time by different units. Restrictions on available studio space meant that more location filming was sometimes written into these episodes, especially on the story 'The Rules of Luton'.

Freiberger's stories 'The Beta Cloud' and 'Space Warp' are examples of the kinds of outside pressures the scripts were sometimes being produced under. Not only did Freiberger have to think of stories, which only used certain cast members, but he also had to add more monsters to the stories during production (under order of Abe Mandell in New York). It is easy to criticise aspects of the second season, but these were not ideal circumstances in which to produce compelling drama.

Freiberger also appears to have been fairly unhappy with the leading lady and man, and his writer's guide throws up some interesting points in his descriptions of John Koenig and Helena Russell. The status of the pair's relationship is made clear in the Russell's character description where she is described as 'an attractive, vibrant woman who is as in love with Koenig as he is with her'. This seems fair enough as the status of their relationship seemed to vary somewhat during the first season. Somewhat more contentious in the character descriptions is their ages—Koenig is described as thirty-five-years old and Russell twenty-nine. Although reasonably well-preserved by 1976, Barbara Bain was forty-five and Martin Landau forty-eight. In a later interview, Freiberger stated that 'Science Fiction needs young faces', which indicates that the new producer might have had a problem with having two middle-aged leading characters.

Also feeling the pressure was Anderson. The success of the new *Space: 1999* was probably more vital to his career than any series since *Four Feather Falls*. The state of British film and television production in the mid-'70s is illustrated by the fact that *Space: 1999* (during its two seasons) was the only production filmed at Pinewood Studios.

While Anderson's career was largely televisual at this point, the long-term downturn in British film production came at a particular bad time for his future prospects. Lew Grade, Anderson's sponsor and employer since the days of *Supercar*, was retiring from television production, forced into this move by ITV rules that enforced a retirement age of sixty-five on all employees. Not ready to retire by a long chalk, Grade was moving into the movie business, but his era of glossy filmed television series made for export was coming to an end. If the new version of *Space: 1999* failed, Anderson was facing a new era as an independent producer having to find funding in a hostile environment.

A glossy new colour sales brochure for the series was prepared, stressing the new aspects of the series and bearing the slogan 'The Future is Fantastic'. Worldwide sales were relatively healthy and the series was still filming when the first episodes premiered. The reaction from ITV's regional contractors was not hopeful. While the first series episodes had failed to secure a network screening, it was at least shown in prime evening slots during its first run and given a great deal of publicity. ITV regions tended to show the episodes in Saturday morning slots, occupying the children's television slots that the Anderson series had outgrown with *UFO*. The series opening episode, 'The Metamorph', premiered in the UK on London Weekend Television in an 11.30 a.m. Saturday morning slot on 4 September 1976, ATV screening it at 5.40 p.m. on the same day. Yorkshire viewers did not get to see the series until October 1977 in a Sunday afternoon slot, and HTV covered Wales. The west of England did not screen *Space: 1999* Year 2 until July 1983, by which time many viewers probably did not realise the screenings were not repeats.

The series also failed to make as much impact as the first series in the most important territory of all—the United States. It had clearly failed to impress US programme buyers as it was scheduled poorly, if at all, generally well out of peak time and often cut to fit a shorter timeslot. This is probably the main factor that doomed *Space: 1999* to cancellation. With Lew Grade, Anderson's greatest supporter within ITC, no longer connected to the company's television interests, an expensive series that had been largely rejected both at home and in the US was not likely to be renewed for a third series.

Part of the problem with Freiberger's ideas is that they were simply out of date. The structure of the series, complete with a tension-breaking 'funny' ending back on Alpha, was how television was written in the 1960s. By 1976, when these episodes were first airing, *Space: 1999* was starting to look old-fashioned, which is deadly for a SF programme.

Filmed adventure series were becoming ever more expensive to produce, with audiences no longer accepting the studio backlot and painted backdrops as a substitute for glamorous locations. ITC had another new series ready to start production, Robert S. Baker's *Return of the Saint*. Like *Space: 1999*'s first season, it attracted co-production funds from RAI in Italy and was filmed all over Europe. Unlike *Space: 1999*, it was a fresh, new product with far more chance of attracting American buyers than a series that had already failed twice to attract the US networks. Although it was only produced for one series, any hope for a second run to be shown was swamped by the financial chaos caused by the expensive production of *Raise the Titanic*; however, *Return of the Saint* did manage to make it onto the networks, being broadcast by CBS in 1979 and 1980.

Key Episode

Episodes 17 and 18: 'The Bringers of Wonder' Parts 1 and 2
First UK Broadcast 4 and 11 August 1977 (ATV)
Written by Terence Feeley
Directed by Tom Clegg

Koenig begins to act wildly irrationally while piloting an Eagle, which he crashes, causing severe concussion. Dr Russell puts him onto an experimental brainwave feedback machine to help his recovery. While he is unconscious in Medical Center, a rescue ship arrives from Earth, containing family and friends of various Alphans. While they prepare a scout ship with three Alphans on to return to Earth Koenig awakes, but instead of humans he sees the rescuers as hideous monsters.

'The Bringers of Wonder' helps put into focus some of the problems *Space: 1999* Year 2 suffered from. In many ways it is a very entertaining story with a clever plotline, but key parts of it fail to work due to slack script editing. A key part of the plot, at the very start of the episode, has Koenig going berserk while solo piloting an Eagle on a minor survey mission. This would never have happened in the first season, in which Koenig would never have been endangered so pointlessly (and Eagles were very rarely flown without co-pilots). To be fair, *UFO* went through the same process; Straker rarely left SHADO HQ in early episodes, and by the end of the series he was completely at the centre of the action.

Also, it transpires that the aliens caused Koenig's erratic behaviour and the Eagle crash. This makes no sense as the only reason that Koenig is able to see the aliens is because of the brain machine Dr Russell uses to cure his concussion. We are never given any explanation as to why the aliens might want to bump off Koenig in the first place. Had the script simply had Koenig's Eagle crashing due to mechanical failure, the plot would have worked far better.

The basic idea of the story is a good one, though. The idea of a rescue ship filled with family and friends of key Alpha personnel works well, giving the actors some good scenes in part one. Tony Verdeschi's competitive relationship with elder brother Guido (Stuart Damon) is particularly well portrayed. Some thought is also given to the characterisation of Maya in this opening scene. Too often she is used merely as a plot contrivance with her shape-shifting abilities, while here we learn that she feels like an outsider among all these humans and wants to stay out of the celebrations.

Martin Landau tends to give a very big performance as John Koenig, especially in the second series, and here that is very effective. When he sees the alien creatures, he is overwrought, panicky, and ranting; he seems unbalanced, and there's no reason for the rest of Moonbase to believe him. Only in part two, when he's calmed down and explains rationally to Maya and Helena what he's seeing, does he start to be believed.

The aliens are a major problem—on a conceptual level they are far too simplistic. Koenig describes them as 'something hideous. Something ugly and horrendous and hostile and deadly'. In other words, they must be evil because they look so horrible. This is a simple 'ugly equals bad' correlation that would never have been made ten years earlier in *Star Trek* (see 'Devil in the Dark' for a good example) much less on *Space: 1999*'s first series. As it turns out, the aliens are a thoroughly bad lot, suffering from the same regressive attitudes as the writers—as with most scripts in this season, credited writer Terence Feeley's work was heavily rewritten by producer/script editor Fred Freiberger. The humans are of no consequence to the aliens because they find us so ugly.

Their design is, if anything, a bigger problem. The aliens are huge, cumbersome, and look ridiculous when they have to move—there is no way that they could walk as quickly as we see their human images travel. When Maya disguises herself as one of the aliens in part two, the scenes of them bobbing along the Alpha corridors (as the poor devils inside the costumes try not to bump into the walls) are the most absurd the series has to offer.

The story suffers a little in part two from being padded to fit the required length. This is a problem common with two-part stories, so it is hardly unique to *Space: 1999*. Here, a medical orderly the aliens sent to kill Koenig in part one is sent from his hospital bed again by the aliens. We are never told what for; he just picks a pointless fight with Tony and gets bashed around by Maya, who has turned into a Kendo warrior. There is also an enormously long lunar fight scene, which would surely have killed the space-suited combatants.

However, the ending is surprisingly good. Having knocked out the rest of Alpha with a special gas (now there's a plot contrivance), Koenig, Maya, and Tony must prevent the three members of Alpha's Nuclear Inspection Team, including Alan Carter, from causing an atomic explosion in one of Alpha's nuclear waste areas. The three are under the hallucination that they have returned to Earth and that Koenig is a stranger attacking them.

This is an excellent idea, supported by Keith Wilson's splendid Nuclear Waste Disposal Area set—a large-scale set of the sort not often seen in Year 2, which is very striking in red and white. Somewhat annoyingly, the best idea the story has to offer is a throwaway line at the end. The aliens tell Koenig that they could have offered the Alphans a lifetime of happy experiences on Earth in an instant, leading to one of the best lines of dialogue the series has to offer: 'It is better to live as your own man than as a fool in someone else's dream.'

26

Rebirth:
Gerry Anderson Post-*Space: 1999*

Space: 1999 was finally, indisputably, dead, and Gerry Anderson's career reached a crossroads. By 1977 Lew Grade had reached ITV's mandatory retirement age, meaning he had to relinquish control of his ATV television franchise. Sir Lew, as he was known by then, hatched plans to become a producer of major films, leaving control of ITC's television productions in other hands. This left Gerry Anderson without his main supporter within the company. Any funds that might have gone into even a shorter, thirteen-episode third series of *Space: 1999* were poured into the bottomless pit that was ITC's $40 million epic production *Raise the Titanic*. As Grade famously remarked: '…it would have been cheaper to lower the Atlantic'. Shot in 1978, the film was finally released in 1980 to a critical drubbing and widespread audience apathy.

While SF on-screen was about to reach unexpected new heights in popularity thanks to the success of *Star Wars* (1977), Supermarionation made one last appearance in a commercial for Jif Dessert Toppings. The commercial was directed by David Lane, using impressive new sets for the Intergalactic Rescue control room and the John and Julie puppets created for *The Investigator*. A new puppet was made for the character of 'The Professor'—the last Supermarionation puppet ever made. Although it retained the more realistic proportions and fibreglass construction of the post-*Thunderbirds*' puppets, it featured a return to a more caricatured design, giving it much more character than the somewhat bland John and Julie designs. As it was only required for a single, very short production there were some differences in the finish of the puppet—the clothes were glued to the body (no costume changes were required) and the shoes were simple leather covering attached to the feet.

Written by Michael Everett and Paul Smith, the commercial was filmed over six days at Elstree Studios (the puppet section) and at Bray Studios (the space sequence). Several members of the Century 21 and *Space: 1999* crews returned for this last hurrah, including special effects directors Brian Johnson and Nick Allder, and model maker Martin Bower. Bower made just one flying saucer model, which was made to appear as a whole fleet on-screen by the tried-and-trusted technique of running the film through the camera multiple times, each time exposing a different part of the frame. He also made the flying fruit-shaped dessert topping dispensers and the lunar surface set they were launched from, which contained part of the original Moonbase Alpha model. Voices were provided by Anderson regular Ed Bishop (The Man), along with David Tate (The Professor), and Angela Richards (The Woman). To complete the familiar Supermarionation effect, the advert utilises music composed by Barry Gray, taken from the *Thunderbirds'* opening sequence and the show's end theme.

The advert was very widely seen in the UK, being shown in cinemas before the original release of *Star Wars* and for several years on television. Colman Foods carried on the space theme in their promotion of the Jif range beyond the Alien Attack advert, offering a giant wall calendar made up of seven posters that would transform one's bedroom into the control panel of a giant starship. Bizarrely, their offer of a 1979 calendar was made in August of that year via popular comics such as *Starlord*. The commercial was entered into an advertising awards scheme called D&AD and was honoured with an entry in the 1978 Annual of the scheme.

For the first time since he was pitching the format of *Supercar* in 1960, Gerry had to go out and find finance for his ideas. The film business in Britain was at its lowest ebb for native productions—*Space: 1999* had kept Pinewood open, being the only production shooting there for two years. The film business had become international, with the massive success of *Star Wars* making Britain an in-demand destination for major American productions. If Gerry was to fund future productions, he would have to look overseas.

During the production of *Space: 1999*'s second series, Gerry formed a partnership with producer Fred Freiberger, working on two television formats to present to the American television network NBC—*Rescue 4* and *Starcruiser*. NBC rejected the proposals so, finding no other takers for these ideas and having tired of Freiberger's rewriting of previously agreed formats behind his back, Gerry struck out on his own.

Two film projects came close to fruition—in 1978, Anderson and Tony Barwick's contemporary thriller story *Operation Shockwave*, set in the US and Israel, underwent months of pre-production work that came to naught when the funding collapsed suddenly. In 1979, Gerry came even closer to getting the film project *Five Star Five,* from another Anderson and Barwick script, off the ground. With major feature film director John Guillermin signed to direct and Alan Hume in place as director of photography, financing for the film fell through on the eve of production at Pinewood and Bray.

Eventually Anderson's search for backers led to Japan, always a big market for his Supermarionation and live-action SF series, which had also proved hugely influential on that country's anime productions. The prospects of a Japanese co-production being distributed internationally seemed good, as several previous Japanese series had been screened in English-speaking countries, including *Astro Boy*, *Marine Boy*, and *Battle of the Planets*.

In 1977, Gerry Anderson began talks with Producer Banjiro Uemura, head of the company Tohoku Shinshua and also in charge of the Japanese arm of ITC about an animation project entitled *Thunderhawks*. The idea went through many changes from those originally proposed by Anderson, receiving a title change in the process to *Terrahawks: Order to Recapture Earth*. This was ultimately stillborn, as the Japanese network the project was being developed for decided it saw no market in SF. Soon afterwards *Star Wars* opened in Japan, causing everyone to scramble round for any SF properties they could rush into production. Back in England, with the backing of Japanese toy manufacturer Bandai and ITV contractor London Weekend Television, Gerry adapted the story material into his first new puppet series for fourteen years (save for 1973's abortive *The Investigator*)—*Terrahawks*, which successfully re-established him in television production.

Terrahawks saw Gerry form a partnership with financial expert Christopher Burr—Anderson-Burr, the combination providing ideas, filmmaking experience, and financial intelligence. Taking the *Captain Scarlet and the Mysterons/UFO* idea of Earth under threat from an alien invasion, *Terrahawks* saw marionettes replaced with highly detailed latex hand puppets. Although this hardly justified designation as a special filmmaking process, it was given a name anyway—for old times' sake—Supermacromation. Some old faces were back, including Tony Barwick (who wrote virtually all the episodes under jokey pseudonyms), Bob Bell, and Denise Bryer (who provided a memorable shrieking, cackling villainess Zelda).

The series was shot at Bray Studios, the beautiful little facility near Maidenhead that was formerly the home of Hammer Films and where *Space: 1999*'s effects had been shot. The model work, under the supervision of newcomer Steven Begg, improved in leaps and bounds as the series progressed, eventually becoming very impressive indeed. On its debut in September 1983, some old-school Anderson fans refused to forgive *Terrahawks* for not being some kind of continuation of *Space: 1999*, but the series was well-received by its young target audience and ran for thirty-nine episodes.

Banjiro Uemura, meanwhile, made an anime version of the material rather closer to its Anderson origins, seen internationally as *Thunderbirds 2086*, but released in Japan as *TechnoBoyager*. This downright odd title, which is often misquoted as *Technovoyager*, gave an excuse to have the letters 'TB' featured on the side of the show's vehicles. The March to April 1982 edition of the show business trade magazine *Variety* saw ITC promote the series as *Thunderbirds 2086*. It would appear from this that the plan was always for there to be to different versions of the series—one for Japanese consumption and one for the western market.

Terrahawks ran for two seasons, coming very close to securing American funding for an extended third run. Anderson-Burr continued with *Dick Spanner*, which began screening in May 1987 as a part of Channel 4's pioneering magazine programme *Network 7*. This was produced cheaply, using stop-motion techniques, and was written by Tony Barwick, from an original idea by Terry Adlam, as a comic take on film noir detective thrillers. Shane Rimmer narrated in the person of the titular Dick Spanner, a robotic private detective. Two serials of eleven six-minute episodes were produced.

Anderson-Burr needed a bigger production to keep the momentum they had gained from *Terrahawks* going. The company funded the one-hour live-action pilot 'Space Police', starring Shane Rimmer opposite life-size puppet alien characters. Shot at Bray in 1986, the series had a long, nine-year journey to the screen. Although this was the longest period Gerry Anderson had ever gone without seeing a new production going to air, his professional situation was far better than it had been in the wake of *Space: 1999*'s cancellation.

Despite the break-up of his partnership with Christopher Burr, Anderson underwent a creative rebirth in the 1990s, his refusal to give up on his career against the odds finally paying off after long years of struggle. *Terrahawks* and *Dick Spanner* had helped to re-establish Anderson as a working filmmaker. At the same time, the children of the '60s and '70s, who grew up loving the classic SF series that Gerry produced, had grown up and still loved the series following their release on home video.

Unlike his post-*Space: 1999* 'dry spell', which was marked by failed series formats and disappearing movie financing, Gerry remained a busy filmmaker throughout the long period in which he attempted to get new series ideas off the ground. He did this by becoming a busy director of television commercials, pop videos, and promotional videos.

Anderson-Burr had started making commercials in 1985, when the company was commissioned to produce an advert for the Royal Bank of Scotland. This was made using stop-motion animation, which was eventually to lead to the technique being used on Anderson-Burr's short comedy series *Dick Spanner* in 1986–87. The *Dick Spanner* concept span off into a series of adverts for Tennant's Pilsner lager in 1987, which featured a very similar character named Lou Tennant.

Much of Gerry Anderson's work in this field had no reference whatsoever to his previous work. Audiences who watched Gerry's 1991 commercial for Golden Wonder Ringos would have had no clue that it was directed by the producer of *Thunderbirds*. Occasionally a commission came along that traded on his previous creations, with *Thunderbirds*-themed commercials for Exchange and Mart, Swinton Insurance, and KitKat chocolate biscuits. In 1993, there was a final Anderson-directed *Stingray* commercial for Weetabix breakfast cereal. By this time, however, Anderson was working on his long-gestating *Space Police* project.

Meanwhile, his back catalogue of work, rather like their creator and producer, refused to fade away. The Anderson series of the '60s and '70s were still being screened internationally during the 1980s. ITC packaged together various episodes of *Thunderbirds, Stingray, UFO, Captain Scarlet and the Mysterons, Joe 90*, and *Space: 1999* into feature length form for the US syndicated television market under the umbrella title Super Space Theatre. New title sequences were added and various changes were made to the music, plus laser beam effects were put over missiles in some scenes. Although not ideal for purists, these compilation films allowed the series to be seen more widely decades after their original production and were to form the basis of the original home video releases of these shows in the 1980s. This helped to prove that there was still a market for these series, and paved the way for full, uncut episodes to be released.

In 1990, eight episodes of *Thunderbirds* were rebroadcast as audio dramas by BBC Radio 5, with introductions by Gerry and extra linking dialogue by Shane Rimmer. The success of these prompted BBC television's head of youth programming Janet Street Porter to buy the series for a full early evening rerun on BBC 2. This was the first time that *Thunderbirds* has ever been fully networked (shown at the same time throughout the country) in the UK, and the results were successful beyond all expectations. Quite out of the blue, *Thunderbirds*-mania had returned to the UK with new toy ranges and comics being produced to meet the demand.

The new popularity of *Thunderbirds* was sustained over several years with Christmas 1992 seeing demand for Matchbox's Tracy Island playset far outstripping supply. With parents desperate to get their hands on the elusive toy, the BBC's long-running children's magazine show *Blue Peter* demonstrated how viewers could make their own from household objects. The result was that *Blue Peter* was, in turn, overwhelmed by the demand for instruction sheets. Another spin-off from the huge popularity of *Thunderbirds* was that the BBC also began to show reruns of *Stingray, Captain Scarlet and the Mysterons*, and *Joe 90*—the latter with the unwelcome addition of an ugly new logo.

Anderson took full advantage of the promotional opportunities, his media profile soaring. Another production setback occurred when the pilot episode of his latest project GFI, produced in Russia using traditional cell-animated techniques, proved disastrously poor, causing him to immediately shelve the project.

Anderson's high profile helped him to finally make some progress on *Space Police*, which the BBC commissioned in 1992. The corporation backed out of the project the following year, but Gerry and his production partners at Mentorn films persevered, the series (retitled at the last moment *Space Precinct*) went into production in May 1994 at Pinewood Studios.

Ultimately, *Space Precinct* proved to be a disappointment. The basic idea, of a New York street cop reassigned to another planet, was solid enough and the cast was personable. Shane Rimmer, who had starred in the original pilot film, was felt to be too old to carry a series, and American star Ted Shackleford was brought in to play Lt Patrick Brogan. Budgetary problems fatally undermined the series, with the result that the CGI effects looked significantly better than the live-action work. The series reached the American syndicated market first, the financiers having to sell the rights to show the series wherever they could in order to keep money coming in to actually complete the production. The full series of twenty-four episodes was shown on Sky One in the evening slot it had been intended for, and on BBC 2 at 6.00 p.m. The series as originally produced was too violent for this time slot, which meant that the producers had to re-edit and even reshoot some material to make it suitable for pre-watershed viewing.

Gerry Anderson was undaunted by the failures of *Space Precinct* and excited by the possibilities he had seen in computer animation. Future projects would feature these techniques heavily, starting with *Lavender Castle*. The impetus for this largely forgotten gem began in 1989 when fantasy artist Rodney Matthews met Gerry, showing him samples of his unique and very distinctive style of work. The BBC agreed in 1991 to fund the series, but later withdrew their support. *Space Precinct* took priority on Gerry's time for a few years, but after production on that series ended a deal was made with ITV-owned animation producers Cosgrove Hall to make *Lavender Castle*. This was the first series Gerry had made since *Torchy the Battery Boy* that he had not at least partially created the format of. This helps give the series a unique feel within the Anderson canon, in effect steampunk for kids, with high-tech equipment and spaceships referencing various different historical styles. Rodney Matthews' rich design work mixed Victoriana, J. R. R. Tolkien, and an English pastoral feel to create a distinctive visual style for the series. Gerry both rediscovered himself as a writer on this series (writing or co-writing some nineteen of the twenty-six episodes) and reconnected with a very young audience that he had not catered for since splitting with Roberta Leigh. As with everything he attempted in life, Gerry threw himself into the project wholeheartedly.

ITV's attitude to *Lavender Castle* was somewhat curious; ITV screened the series in full, splitting the episodes into two series, screened between January 1999 and March 2000. They did not heavily promote the series, however, and never repeated it. It was even more than five years until the series was released on DVD. In a repeat of Gerry's experience with Granada and *Four Feather Falls*, he had produced ground-breaking work his employers did not attempt to capitalise on. With ITVs commitment to children's broadcasting slipping, this situation would become drastically worse with his next series.

Anderson had been attempting for many years to mount a revival of *Thunderbirds*, but Carlton (which was to all intents and purposes now ITV), who owned all rights to the series since Gerry and Sylvia sold them during a mid-'70's financial crisis, instead granted remake rights to production company Working Title. Their long-gestating feature film version was eventually released in 2004, and despite its heart being in the right place, it failed to find favour with either fans or the general audience. It was generally thought that the film aimed for too young an audience, side-lining most of the Tracy Brothers in favour of youngest brother Alan.

Anderson did gain the remake rights to another of the Supermarionation series, *Captain Scarlet and the Mysterons*, after producing an impressive test film featuring original voice artists Francis Matthews and Ed Bishop. ITV was a major investor in the series, but the majority of the investment came from private backers. Gerry Anderson's *New Captain Scarlet*, to give the series its full title, was produced on a budget of £22 million at Pinewood using CGI motion capture techniques dubbed Hypermarionation. David Lane returned as supervising director and Phil Ford was hired as the series' head writer.

The result was an artistic triumph, the best series Anderson had produced since *Space: 1999* and arguably better than the 1967 original. ITV, however, threw the series away in a Saturday morning slot, buried within the children's magazine programme *Ministry of Mayhem*. This was a particular waste as the series was aimed at precisely the same family audience as the BBC's revival of *Doctor Who*, the first series of which was being produced at around the same time. Both series reflected the huge influence Joss Weedon's *Buffy the Vampire Slayer* had on the SF and horror genres, with a knowing sense of wit and irony actually adding to the atmosphere and thrill of the narrative instead of detracting, as occurred during the mid-1960's vogue for 'camp' humour.

New Captain Scarlet was regarded as a failure, which had a ruinous effect on Anderson's career. He attempted to get further projects off the ground, especially his long-cherished dream of remaking *Thunderbirds*, but now nobody was seriously listening. Worse still, his health was now failing, a diagnosis of dementia signalling the reason behind his decline. Even in his darkest hour, supported by his wife Mary and their son Jamie, Anderson was determined to stay as busy and useful as he could by campaigning for charity with The Alzheimer's Society.

Gerry Anderson died on 26 December 2012 at the age of eighty-three. His death was the end of an incredible era in British filmmaking, but the greatest creation in the career of Gerry and Sylvia Anderson lived on as ITV announced the production of a new series of *Thunderbirds*, retitled *Thunderbirds Are Go*. The nature of animation production has changed considerably, and the new series is produced with a mixture of computer generated characters and craft and miniature sets and models. This gives the series a very interesting visual feel, in some ways in line with the original series. The writing for the series is supervised by Rob Hoegee in America, while the dialogue is recorded in London by a cast including Rosamund Pike as Lady Penelope and David Graham returning as Parker. Filming takes place in New Zealand, performed by the animation studio Pukeko Pictures and Weta Workshop, co-founded by *Lord of the Rings* director and noted Supermarionation fan Peter Jackson. CGI work on the series takes place in China, making *Thunderbirds Are Go* a truly international production.

With each episode lasting twenty-two minutes, this is a very different series than the original and aimed strictly at a younger audience. Nevertheless, the respect and love the makers have for the original series shines through.

It remains to be seen whether *Thunderbirds Are Go* will still be watched in fifty years' time, or go the way of other, now forgotten revivals of the original format, such as *Thunderbirds 2086* or *Turbocharged Thunderbirds* (the latter in particular heaping indignities on the *Thunderbirds* format). Either way, the high profile of the series will help to ensure that all of the original, classic Anderson series will continue to be seen for generations to come.

Now more than ever, Supermarionation is Go!

Bibliography

Books

Anderson, S., *My Fab Years!*, (Hermes Press, 2007)

Archer, S., & Hearn, M., *What Made Thunderbirds Go*, (London: BBC Worldwide, 2002)

Bentley, C., *The Complete Book of Captain Scarlet and the Mysterons*, (Carlton Books Ltd, 1999); *The Complete Book of Gerry Anderson's UFO*, (Reynolds & Hearn Ltd, 2003); *The Complete Book of Thunderbirds*, (Carlton Books Ltd, 2000); *The Complete Gerry Anderson: The Authorised Episode Guide*, (Reynolds & Hearn Ltd, 2005)

Canham, K., *The Hollywood Professionals Vol. 2*, (Tantivy Press, 1974)

Chibnall, S., and McFarlane, B., *The British 'B' Film*, (British Film Institute, 2009)

Dick, P. K., *The Golden Man* (New York: Berkeley Books, 1980)

Fletcher, W., *Powers of Persuasion: The Inside Story of British Advertising 1951–2000* (Oxford: Oxford University Press, 2008)

Henry, B., *British Television Advertising: The First 30 Years*, (Ebury Press, 1986)

Meddings, D., *21st Century Visions*, (Dragon's World Ltd, 1993)

Parsons, N., *My Life in Comedy: With Just Touch of Hesitation, Repetition and Deviation*, (BBC Audiobooks Ltd, 2011)

Perry, G., *The Great British Picture Show*, (HarperCollins, 1975)

Shubrook, P., and Shubrook, M., *Special Effects Superman: The Art and Effects of Derek Meddings*, (Shubrook Brothers, 2008)

Taylor, A., with Trim, M., *The Future was Fab: The Art of Mike Trim*, (Hermes Press, 2006)

Vaughn, R. A., *Fortunate Life*, (USA: St Martin's Griffin, 2009)

Walker, A., *Hollywood England: The British Film Industry in the Sixties*, (Orion, 2005)

Wenden, D. J., *The Birth of the Movies*, (New York: E. P. Dutton, 1974)

Articles

Anderson, G., 'Doppelgänger: The Anderson Tapes', *FAB*, issue 62, (United Kingdom: Fanderson: the Official Gerry Anderson Appreciation Society, March 2009)

Byrne, J., 'Johnny Byrne: The FAB Interview', *FAB*, issue 61, (United Kingdom: Fanderson: the Official Gerry Anderson Appreciation Society, November 2008)

Clark, M., & Cotter, B., 'An Interview with Fred Freiberger, Part 2', *Starlog*, issue 40, (USA: Starlog Group, November 1980)

Fryer, I., 'Nick Tate: Where Eagles Dare', *FAB*, issue 78, (United Kingdom: Fanderson: the Official Gerry Anderson Appreciation Society, July 2014); 'Tex Talks', *FAB*, issue 72, pp. 14-22 (United Kingdom: Fanderson: the Official Gerry Anderson Appreciation Society, 2012); 'The Making of Space: 1999, Part 1: The Void Ahead', *FAB*, issue 64, (United Kingdom: Fanderson: the Official Gerry Anderson Appreciation Society, November 2009)

Jones, M., & Fryer, I., 'Shane Rimmer Part 2', *FAB*, issue 66, (United Kingdom: Fanderson: the Official Gerry Anderson Appreciation Society, June 2010)

Other

Science Fantasy Film Classics, issue 4, (USA, October 1978)

Speech by Harold Wilson, Labour Party Conference, Scarborough, 1 October 1963.

Websites

catacombs.space1999.net/main/crguide/vcztd.html

www.launchingfilms.com/research-databank/uk-cinema-admissions